Paul Cleary grew up in Sydney's southwest and has worked as a journalist covering economic, social and tax policy for the *Sydney Morning Herald* and the *Financial Review* while based in Canberra Press Gallery for ten years. His revelations about secret Treasury analysis of the Howard government's 2000 Goods and Services Tax reform led to a Senate inquiry and, in turn, improvements for low income groups. In the mid-1990s he lived in Hanoi where he helped to establish the country's first English-language daily, while working as a correspondent and studying Vietnamese. In 2002 he was awarded a Chevening fellowship by the UK Foreign Office for a masters in the political economy of development. After first visiting East Timor in 1997 he was an adviser in the East Timor government's Timor Sea Office from 2003–05, while also travelling extensively around the country and learning Tetum, Portuguese and Brasilian *foho*.

To those who died and suffered as a result of the two invasions of East Timor of the twentieth century.

To Jeremiah Cleary who, among many other things, served on trans-Atlantic merchant ships from 1941–45.

SHAKEDOWN

Australia's grab for Timor oil

PAUL CLEARY

First published in 2007

Copyright © Paul Cleary 2007

All rights reserved. No part of this book may be reproduced or transmitted in any form or by any means, electronic or mechanical, including photocopying, recording or by any information storage and retrieval system, without prior permission in writing from the publisher. The *Australian Copyright Act 1968* (the Act) allows a maximum of one chapter or 10% of this book, whichever is the greater, to be photocopied by any educational institution for its educational purposes provided that the educational institution (or body that administers it) has given a remuneration notice to Copyright Agency Limited (CAL) under the Act.

Allen & Unwin
83 Alexander Street
Crows Nest NSW 2065
Australia
Phone: (61 2) 8425 0100
Fax: (61 2) 9906 2218
Email: info@allenandunwin.com
Web: www.allenandunwin.com

Cataloguing-in-Publication entry is available from the National Library of Australia.

ISBN 978 1 74114 926 5

The cartoons on pages 132 and 133 are copyright and have been reproduced with permission.

Maps by MapGraphics
Index by Russell Brooks
Typeset by Midland Typesetters, Australia
Printed and bound in Australia by Griffin Press

10 9 8 7 6 5 4 3 2 1

CONTENTS

Preface and acknowledgements	vii
Chronology	x
List of maps	xvii
Prologue	xxv

1.	The great divide	1
2.	The spoils of conquest	15
3.	The kelp in the coffin	34
4.	The get-out-of-gaol card	50
5.	Animal farm	67
6.	Tutorials in politics	79
7.	The creative solution	98
8.	The reluctant president	110
9.	The secret envoy	120
10.	The consummate diplomat	140
11.	People power	160
12.	The brainstorming trap	176
13.	The breakdown	187
14.	Calling in the commandos	200
15.	Independence day minus 1	221
16.	From ashes to ashes	243

Endnotes	268
Index	295

PREFACE AND ACKNOWLEDGEMENTS

There are at least a few good reasons for writing this book. The battle for the resources underneath the Timor Sea, spanning a period of more than three decades, is a compelling drama that deserves to be told. While some might like the details of the negotiations to never be revealed, there are strong public interest grounds for informing the people of all countries concerned about the Timor Sea dispute, which began more than 35 years ago and was concluded in February 2007.

During the more recent years, many people in East Timor and around the world went to great lengths to help bring about a degree of justice and fairness for East Timor. Many are acknowledged in these pages, though it is not possible to do so for everyone involved.

Perhaps most importantly of all, this story may be instructive for other developing countries and indigenous peoples in their struggle to secure rights to their natural resources. This is a story that goes beyond the issue of maritime boundaries and into the relations between rich and poor nations, and the practice by the powerful of a narrowly defined and sometimes abusive approach to foreign policy. During his time as president of the World Bank, James Wolfensohn emphasised the growing importance in the fight against world poverty of enabling poor countries to exercise their rights to their natural resources.

I am indebted to Lindsay Murdoch who first suggested that I write this book and then continued to remind me that I should do so. Rebecca Kaiser, managing editor of Allen & Unwin, strongly backed this project from the very beginning, and together with Alexandra Nahlous and Jane Bowring made many useful comments on the manuscript. Tom Dusevic gave helpful advice on how to approach this subject, and suggested taking 'Shakedown' from the strapline to the main title. I have benefited from research and insights into this subject by Frank Brennan SJ. During the writing of this book Brennan suggested I join him on a 20-hour return road trip to Bourke, New South Wales, for the blessing of a new headstone on the grave of Dr Fred Hollows. He provided comments on early drafts of several chapters as we journeyed through the Australian outback.

Many thanks also to Gabrielle Hooton for fabulous research support, and the former *Financial Review* subeditor who, upon learning that the Fairfax library's East Timor file was about to be thrown out, called me in Dili to tell me it was available and then delivered it personally to the East Timor Consulate in Sydney. This file included many useful articles and documents going back to the 1980s, and access to it was invaluable.

In East Timor it was a great privilege to work alongside colleagues in the Timor Sea Office: Manuel Mendonça, Manuel de Lemos and Marcos dos Santos. Former international advisers in this office—Jonathan Morrow, Catherine McKenna, Alisa Newman Hood and Kathryn Khamsi—put together an excellent set of files that proved to be a very valuable resource. Geir Ytreland, Nick Kyranis and Einar Risa shared with me more than I ever cared to know about the subject of petroleum. Max Stahl offered many rich insights into East Timor and especially the events of 2006, and over a long dinner one night at the height of the dispute held up one end of a very spirited and instructive debate on what it was all about (Frank Brennan held up the other end while also generously providing a few good bottles of red). Janelle Saffin provided sage advice on some of the more delicate elements of this work, and was supportive during some difficult moments in these negotiations.

Preface and acknowledgements

Back in Australia, Michael Kelly offered insightful comments about the direction of this book and a productive working environment for producing a manuscript in a fairly short space of time. Thanks also to Eleanor Hall, Hament Dhanji, Susan Bowman, Michael Brown, and Shauna Howe who also offered great support and helpful observations for this work. Thanks also to my agent Lyn Tranter who, in a similar vein to the Greater Sunrise negotiations, secured a deal that both sides could live with.

Finally, a note on referencing and the scope of this work. This book draws heavily on my own records of meetings, confidential briefings from those who attended other meetings, or from other confidential material which I was allowed to access. I have not referenced this material because it cannot be accessed by readers, but I have made every effort to do so with publicly available material. Although I was given permission to write this book by the East Timor government, the tragic events of 2006 prompted me to range more widely and be more forthcoming than would have otherwise been the case. Some in East Timor may find the commentary on the early years of independence too revealing and strident, but there are some important lessons to be learned from a full exposure of what went wrong. All of the views expressed here are mine, and do not reflect in any way on the East Timor government or any individual members of it.

Sydney,
March 2007

CHRONOLOGY

1701	Portugal begins to colonise the island of Timor.
1859	The Treaty of Demarcation between Portugal and Holland divides the island of Timor into East and West. This is formalised in a convention signed at The Hague in 1904.
1941, 17 December	Five hundred Australian and Dutch troops make a speculative landing in Dili. Japan now includes Timor in its war plan and lands a major force in February 1942.
1943, January–February	Australia withdraws from East Timor and drops leaflets titled, 'Your friends do not forget you', urging the Timorese to fight on alone. The invasion led to the deaths of at least 10 per cent of the population of around 400 000.
1952	An Australian defence white paper declares that Portuguese Timor is of immense strategic interest to Australia. Australia proposes defence cooperation, but this is rejected by Portugal.
1971	Portuguese Timor is considered completely irrelevant to Australian interests. The consulate in Dili is closed.
1972, 9 October	Australia and Indonesia sign a 'seabed boundary treaty' that puts the boundary line two-thirds of the way towards the island of Timor as Indonesia accepts Australia's assertion that the boundary should be based on Australia's natural prolongation to the edge of the Timor Trough. Portugal continues to insist on a median line after the treaty is signed.

Chronology

1974, 25 April	The Carnation Revolution in Portugal leads to rapid decolonisation after decades of colonial wars. In the same year Woodside Petroleum Ltd, then known as Burmah Oil, discovers the Sunrise and Troubadour oil and gas fields, known collectively as Greater Sunrise.
1974, 20 May	The revolution prompts the launch of the pro-independence party, *Associação Social Democráta de Timor* (ASDT), the Timorese Social Democratic Association, later to become *Frente Revolucionária do Timor-Leste Independente* (FRETILIN)—the Revolutionary Front for the Independence of East Timor.
1975, 11 August	The conservative *União Democrática de Timor* (UDT) party breaks from a coalition and launches a pre-emptive coup against FRETILIN. A two-month civil war ends with victory to FRETILIN.
1975, 16 October	Indonesian soldiers remove their insignia and cross the border under 'Operation Flamboyant'. Five Australian-based newsmen from the Nine and Seven television networks are killed in cold blood at Balibo by the Indonesians.
1975, 28 November	FRETILIN makes a unilateral declaration of independence with the knowledge that the Indonesian invasion will take place in a matter of days.
1975, 5–6 December	US president Gerald Ford and secretary of state Henry Kissinger visit President Soeharto and sanction the invasion of East Timor. They ask Indonesia not to use US weapons and equipment.
1975, 7 December	A full-scale military invasion is launched by Indonesia. Hundreds of innocent civilians, including Australian Roger East and Isobel Lobato, the wife of the first prime minister, are summarily executed on the Dili waterfront.

1975, 22 December	Adoption of UN Security Council Resolution 384 calling on all states to respect the territorial integrity of East Timor and on Indonesia to withdraw its forces from the territory.
1976	Indonesia annexes East Timor as its twenty-seventh province. A massive military operation leads to an official death toll of 183 000 over 24 years of occupation.
1978, 15 December	Foreign Minister Andrew Peacock announces Australia's de jure recognition of Indonesia's annexation of East Timor, and directly links this move to the start of negotiations with Indonesia over the Timor Gap.
1979, 14 February	Indonesia and Australia begin negotiations over the Timor Gap. Indonesia refuses to agree to close the Gap at the Timor Trough. It presses for a median line.
1989, 27 October	After a decade of negotiations Australia and Indonesia conclude the Timor Gap Treaty. This establishes a 61 000-square-kilometre Zone of Cooperation in which the revenue from Area A is shared fifty-fifty.
1991, 12 November	Indonesian forces open fire in the Santa Cruz cemetery killing up to 200 East Timorese. The killings are captured on film by Max Stahl.
1996, 1 October	Bishop Carlos Belo and exiled activist José Ramos-Horta receive the Nobel Peace Prize.
1998, 21 May	President Soeharto falls.
1998, December	Australian Prime Minister John Howard writes to his Indonesian counterpart, President B.J. Habibie, proposing an extended period of autonomy for East Timor followed by an act of self-determination. While Australia wants East Timor to remain part of Indonesia, Habibie opts for an immediate ballot on the territory's future.

Chronology

1999, 7 May	Adoption of UN Security Council Resolution 1236 welcoming the conclusion of an agreement between Indonesia and Portugal on a framework for consulting the people of East Timor.
1999, 30 August	A near 99 per cent voter turnout for the Popular Consultation.
1999, 4 September	UN Secretary General Kofi Annan announces 78.5 per cent of East Timorese vote for independence, unleashing widespread violence by Indonesian-backed militia groups that kills an estimated 1500 people.
1999, 15 September	Adoption of UN Security Council Resolution 1264 approving a multi-national peacekeeping force for East Timor.
1999, 20 September	Multinational force, InterFET, led by Australia lands in East Timor to restore order as Indonesia makes a hasty but complete withdrawal.
1999, 22 October	Adoption of UN Security Council Resolution 1272 establishing the United Nations Transitional Administration in East Timor (UNTAET).
2001, 30 August	First democratic elections for the Constituent Assembly. The FRETILIN party wins a majority of 55 seats in the 88-seat assembly.
2002, 14 April	Presidential election results in landslide victory to Xanana Gusmão.
2002, 20 May	Official handover of sovereignty from UNTAET to government of the República Democrática de Timor-Leste. East Timor Prime Minister Marí Alkatiri and his Australian counterpart John Howard sign the Timor Sea Treaty, giving East Timor 90 per cent ownership of the petroleum

resources in the new Joint Petroleum Development Area (JPDA), which transposes Area A of the Zone of Cooperation.

The new government tables in parliament its Maritime Zones Act in which it claims its 200-nautical-mile entitlement.

2002, 27 September	East Timor becomes the 191st member of the United Nations, and is officially known as Timor-Leste.
2003, 6 March	East Timor signs the International Unitisation Agreement (IUA) which allocates 20.1 per cent of the Greater Sunrise field to the JPDA, in turn giving it 18 per cent of the revenue. This field lies 144 kilometres off the southern coast of Timor, twice as close as it is to Australia.
2003, 2 April	The Timor Sea Treaty enters into force following belated ratification by Australia. The Australian government had refused to ratify the treaty until East Timor signed the International Unitisation (IUA) Agreement.
2003, 12 November	The first meeting on permanent boundaries is held in Darwin. East Timor presses for sustained, monthly meetings to resolve the dispute. Australia claims it only has resources to meet twice a year.
2004, 29 March	On the same day that the IUA bills are approved by the Australian Parliament the Australian government advertises more exploration blocks in the disputed areas.
2004, 19 April	The first formal maritime boundary meeting results in a stalemate. Prime Minister Alkatiri accuses Australia of benefiting from 'a crime' and of unlawfully collecting US$1 million a day in disputed oil revenue from the Buffalo,

	Laminaria and Corallina fields. Buffalo is located on the western border of the JPDA and Laminaria just 2 nautical miles to the west. (One nautical mile is 1.852 kilometres.)
2004, 11 August	Foreign Ministers Downer and Ramos-Horta meet in Canberra to discuss the dispute. Downer tacitly recognises East Timor's claim outside the JPDA and they settle on a framework to resolve the dispute by the end of the year.
2004, 20 September	The first of an intensive series of meetings begins.
2004, 27 October	Negotiations break down when East Timor refuses to accept Australia's offer of a US$3 billion settlement for Greater Sunrise.
2005, January	Alkatiri writes to Howard proposing that the two countries restart talks. Ramos-Horta also meets Howard in Jakarta.
2005, 7–11 March	Productive talks take place in Canberra. A framework for resolving the dispute emerges. Further talks are held in April and May, leaving final 'details' to be resolved.
2005, 25 April	Anzac Day is celebrated in Australia. Veterans who fought in East Timor during the Second World War appear on national television and declare that they owe their lives to the bravery and support of the Timorese who volunteered to come to their aid, and they call on Prime Minister John Howard to negotiate fairly.
2005, July	President Xanana Gusmão visits Australia on a state visit. Only a year earlier he had accused Australia of trying to make East Timor a permanent beggar state, and he likened its 'occupation' of the Timor Sea to the Indonesian occupation.

2005, 27 November	After waiting six months for a resolution Australia threatens to dump the agreement and proposes one final meeting to reach a resolution.
2006, 12 January	In Sydney the foreign ministers sign a new Treaty on Certain Maritime Arrangements in the Timor Sea (CMATS) that divides revenue fifty-fifty from the Greater Sunrise field, and defers maritime boundary claims for 50 years.
2006, 25 May	Australian soldiers land again in Dili as gun battles rage amongst rival armed forces factions. The violence follows the sacking of almost half the East Timor army.
2006, 26 June	Prime Minister Alkatiri resigns amid allegations that he helped to arm civilian hit squads to assassinate political opponents. He denies the allegations and claims the Australian government was determined to undermine him after the strong stand he took in the Timor Sea negotiations.
2007, 23 February	The new CMATS treaty enters into force with an 'exchange of notes' between the two governments in Dili. This followed the passing by the East Timor parliament on 20 February of both the new Treaty and the 2003 IUA. Days later Australians were evacuated as more violence flared after Australian soldiers shot dead youths in Dili and rebel soldiers in the town of Samé.

LIST OF MAPS

Map 1: Australia's Expanding Maritime Empire
The area of high seas acquired by Australia as a result of the United Nations Law of the Sea Convention, and new areas claimed in 2004 under the Commission on the Limits of the Commonwealth Shelf.

Map 2: Mine the Gap
The 1972 Australia–Indonesia seabed boundary, showing the end points A16 and A17 and the 'gap' left in the middle, which became known as 'the Timor Gap'. The map also shows the boundary and gap relative to the median line between Australia and East Timor, and their respective 200 nautical mile claims.

Map 3: The End-point Game
The simplified equidistance lines used to derive the end points of the 1972 boundary. The lines were drawn from East Timor's territory even though it was not a party to the negotiation. East Timor claimed that the boundary 'encroached' into its maritime area and there was a valid case for finishing the 1972 boundary at A18 and east of the Sunrise field. The lateral equidistance lines are indicative only of how the end points were derived in the 1972 negotiations.

Map 4: The Coffin-shaped Compromise
The three areas in the Zone of Co-operation under the Australia–Indonesia Timor Gap Treaty 1989. The area covered by

the 2002 Timor Sea Treaty between Australia and East Timor was identical to Area A, and became known as the Joint Petroleum Development Area (JPDA). As the Greater Sunrise field straddles the eastern border of the treaty area, 20.1 per cent was allocated to the JPDA, and 79.1 allocated to Australia.

Map 5: The No-Go Zones
The areas in which East Timor argued that Australia had an obligation under the law of the sea convention to exercise 'restraint' by not licensing petroleum exploration or development. Also showing East Timor's 'optimistic' eastern and western lateral boundaries, and the horizontal median line.

Map 6: Stakeout
Permits issued or advertised in the disputed areas by the Australian government for exploration and production before and during the Timor Sea dispute, excluding the area covered by the Timor Sea Treaty.

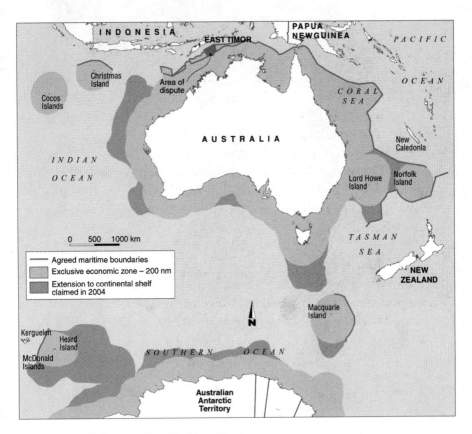

Map 1: Australia's Expanding Maritime Empire

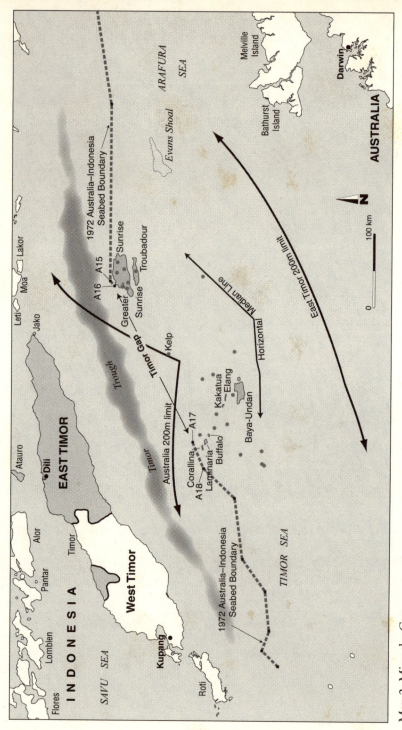

Map 2: Mine the Gap

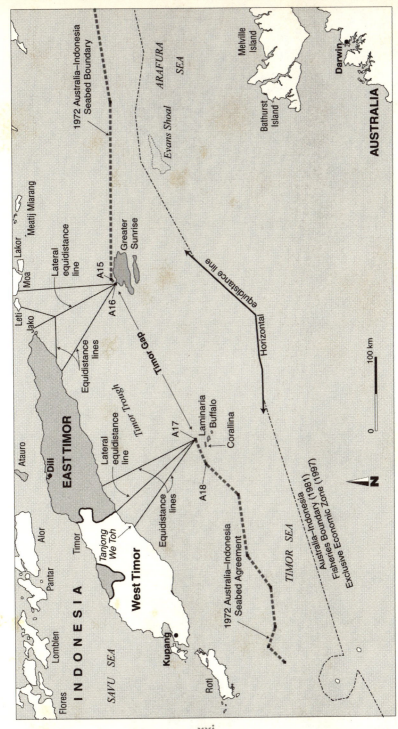

Map 3: The End-point Game

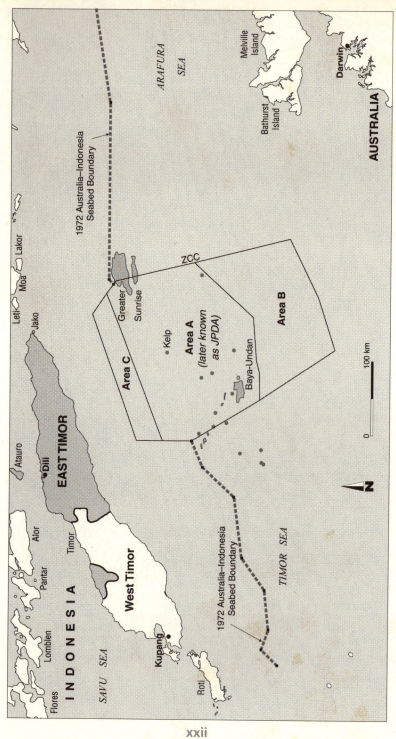

Map 4: The Coffin-shaped Compromise

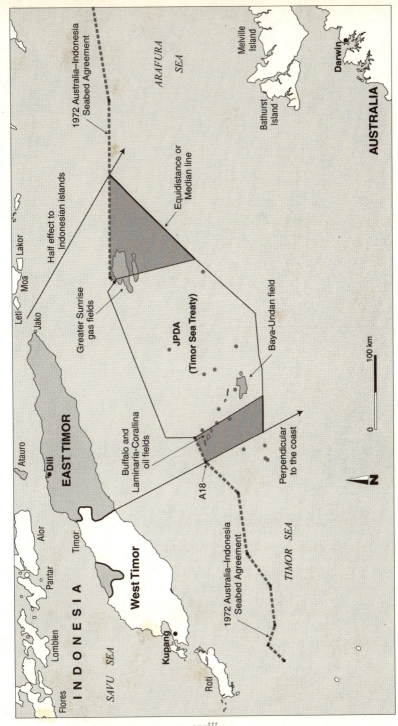

Map 5: The No-Go Zones

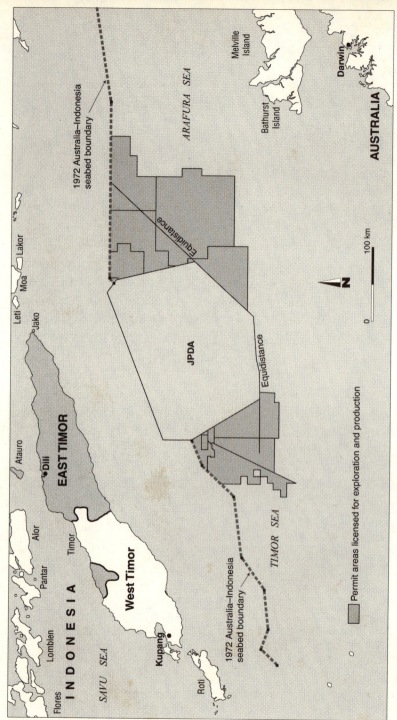

Map 6: Stakeout

PROLOGUE

Dili, 19 April 2004

On a sweltering afternoon in the dusty capital of one of the world's poorest nations, a delegation from the government of a wealthy western neighbour waits uneasily in the spacious lobby of a hotel. The city's diesel generators are holding up today and a battery of air conditioners keeps the temperature inside at a chilly 17C, but the visiting officials appear to be recovering from their exposure to the intense heat outside. These officials are not ordinary public servants—they are from the elite of their country's civil service and they are dressed for the part. It is a good-looking group on the whole—five men, one woman—and one of them, a Queen's Counsel, has donned a signature bow tie. They appear to be reluctant visitors, as though they belong in a completely different place—in the lobby of a fashionable European hotel, perhaps.

Outside the hotel it could be the capital of any one of those broken-down African countries that those living 'uninterrupted lives in placid places'[1] would rather not contemplate. The nameless streets are strewn with the burnt out shells of buildings—a legacy of the scorched-earth departure of the country's other big neighbour. The president occupies one such building and he named it *Palácio das Cinzas* (Palace of Ashes). The city is more a dilapidated, semi-rural provincial town than a capital; goats roam the streets and pigs root around in rubbish drops. Natural features are its saving grace—a sweeping waterfront with palm trees and beaches, soaring mountains behind, all enveloped by sparkling turquoise water and an impossibly blue sky. But the town itself is a flat, hot, languid place where the sun beats down relentlessly. There's barely any shade, as though no-one was able to plant trees during long decades of oppression. The people are open, engaging and curious, and they smile all day, but as they amble about in tiny, undernourished frames a haunting grief lingers about this place where an orchestrated campaign of the most abominable terror has run amok. And not for a year or two—it went on for an entire generation. It is heaven and hell, all in one place.

The visitors have come for one thing, the only thing that this dirt-poor speck of a country has of value to an affluent western nation—increasingly scarce oil and gas, resources of intense interest to Australia which has the highest greenhouse gas emissions per capita in the world. The fields lie under the seabed between the two countries, although all of them are much closer to the newly independent East Timor, which on this day is a fragile, traumatised country one month short of its second birthday. Under international law most, if not all, of the known resources would belong to East Timor. The Australian government knows this full well and has refused to agree to a maritime boundary to divide up the potential bonanza. Australia licensed development of oil fields worth US$6 billion during East Timor's occupation, which went into production in 1999 just as the country was being torched. By dragging out the negotiations, Australia's advisers think they can secure 80 per cent of the biggest field in the disputed area, worth more than US$50 billion at conservative oil prices.

The officials are here under an obligation. International law requires Australia to demonstrate that it is willing to negotiate over the disputed resources, even though it has no interest whatsoever in agreeing to a boundary set according to established international legal principles. Just two months before the independence of East Timor, Australia withdrew from international arbitration for maritime disputes, thereby deliberately denying justice to this new country. This pre-emptive strike in defence of national interest no doubt followed from the legal advice provided by the man in the bow tie.

It is 2 p.m.—the appointed time—and the Australians make their way down a long corridor to a conference room at the back of the hotel, but their passage stops at a set of closed double-glass doors with a curtain behind it. Suddenly, the curtain is drawn, and the show begins with an explosion of colour and sound. Waiting behind the curtain is a group of angelic teenage girls wearing traditional dress of deep pink, purple and black. A rhythmic, ancient beat is sounded from small drums tucked under their arms, and they dance in a circular pattern as they perform a traditional welcome. The Australian officials quickly make their way past the girls to their seats as the show continues.

Next, on cue, a shiny new 4WD ascends a ramp and stops at the main entrance of the hotel. A man of slight build jumps out and strides into the foyer. He is East Timor's first independence prime minister. He has an intense, severe gaze and looks absolutely driven, like a Cold War icon. He has a short goatie beard similar to the one favoured by Ho Chi Minh, and wears a loose fitting, deep blue silk shirt with a Mao collar. Without missing a beat, and flanked by advisers and security guards, he proceeds through the foyer and down the long corridor. He is trailed by a flotilla of cameramen and journalists, tape recorders held in outstretched arms. He reaches the conference room now crowded with cameras, including those from two of Australia's leading current affairs programs.

The officials from both countries stand behind two rows of long tables facing each other, like two First World War trenches with no-man's-land in between. The Australians are treated to more ritual as the young girls place hand-woven scarves, called *tais*, around each of their necks. Their level of discomfort in being part of this spectacle is painfully apparent. This was meant to be a non-event—a tedious meeting of officials that would go nowhere. Prior to the meeting, Australian officials had told the media that it would be the start of a dull and drawn-out process that might take 30 years—long after the oil had been extracted by Australia's unilateral issuance of production licences. In an instant, it has become a spectacle and the world is watching.

Both delegations sit, the room goes strangely silent, and the prime minister begins to speak. When the head of the Australian delegation had enquired before the meeting about the presence of so many cameras, he had been told they were there just to film the formal welcoming remarks by the prime minister. The prime minister, however, is about to turn this 'welcoming' address into a manifesto.

Reading a speech written entirely by foreign advisers and handed to him just an hour earlier, he tells the officials that dividing up the oil and gas resources under the seabed is much more than an academic exercise for a country with one of the highest rates of child and infant mortality in the world (12 per cent die by the age of five). For a country where children die routinely of curable diseases, where TB is common, where people still contract leprosy, and where 40 per cent of all children show the physical effects—stunting and wasting—of undernourishment, the prime minister says that resolving the dispute is a matter of life and death.

He insists that his country, though it is most certainly very poor, is not asking for charity. It simply wants to exercise its right to a fair and equitable settlement under international law. He subtly reminds the officials that Australia was the only western nation to recognise the illegal occupation of East Timor by Indonesia. He also reminds them that this occupation led to, among other things, the appropriation of his country's resources by its two big neighbours. And one of the legacies of that appropriation is a set of invisible lines drawn in the seabed to divide the oil and gas resources. These lines, which his country is now being pressed to accept, give a less favourable share to East Timor than it is entitled to under international law; such was the price paid by Indonesia for Australia's de jure recognition of its murderous occupation of East Timor.

The prime minister's blunt message to Australia, which holds itself up as a beacon of western democratic values, is that it cannot continue to benefit from 'a crime'. That's what he says. He accuses this country of profiting from an illegal invasion and occupation.

The subsequent death toll is on par with the nuclear bombings of Hiroshima and Nagasaki, except that in East Timor most of the killings were kept hidden as the country was hermetically sealed off from the outside world. In proportional terms, the estimate of 183 000 deaths by a UN-sponsored, 2500-page report[2] is about one-third of East Timor's population at the time of the invasion, making it one of the worst cases of genocide of the twentieth century. The true dimension of the Indonesian occupation's impact on the Timorese is perhaps best revealed by this fact: East Timor's population remained completely unchanged at around 700 000 between 1975 and 2002.[3] Since independence, it has increased by more than 200 000 and at current growth rates should double over the next 20–25 years.

The speech is no more than two pages long. It need not be any longer. Three members of the Australian delegation remove their *tais*, including the Australian ambassador. The head of the delegation angrily removes his as the speech is finished. The prime minister jumps to his feet, strides across no-man's-land to the Australians and offers a handshake to each of them. The officials are floored—they can barely extend their arms.

After the prime minister departs and the media are ushered out of the room, the delegation head manages to utter a dismissive riposte that echoes Australia's nationalistic sporting ethos: 'I guess you'd call that a home ground advantage.'

Since the start of the negotiations in October 2000, East Timor had been appealing to the international community to support its rights over the vast oil and gas resources off its southern coastline. The prime minister's speech, and the huge amount of media attention that followed, marked East Timor's loudest and clearest appeal for justice and fairness in its 'David and Goliath' struggle with Australia over the disputed resources in the Timor Sea. Australia's withdrawal from international courts and tribunals meant that East Timor had only one avenue to secure justice: the court of public opinion. Its simple and tenacious appeal to foreign governments, international institutions and the media was the only recourse that this tiny nation of less than one million people had. Very little, if anything, would be achieved through negotiation in the formal manner; that is, with officials from both countries holding quiet meetings behind closed doors (as East Timor did with Indonesia to secure its land boundary). The Australian government believed it could grind down its opponent by dragging out the negotiations for decades. Over the course of these negotiations, which spanned six years, the Australian government's tactics even involved threatening to block development that would provide vital revenue for the mammoth task of post-war reconstruction.

After the prime minister left the room the Australians said they did not recognise East Timor's claim to the disputed resources that lay twice as close to East Timor's coastline. There was nothing to be negotiated, they said defiantly. Incredibly, the Australian government also claimed at an earlier meeting that it did not have the resources to negotiate expeditiously to settle the dispute.

This is a story about what happens when a bountiful natural resource lies beneath the seabed between one of the poorest countries in the world and one of the most advanced. It is about the practice of diplomacy and the aggressive pursuit of national interest by the powerful in these circumstances. East Timor's campaign to have its rights recognised, its defiant stand against bullying, blackmail and dirt cheap buyouts echoes the refrain of its independence struggle: *Resistir é Vencer* (To resist is to win). But this new country's bid for economic independence, which involved mounting a vociferous attack on the unlawful appropriation of disputed resources, would come at an enormous cost—it would be a Pyrrhic victory.

1 THE GREAT DIVIDE

'There is . . . no scope for negotiating a boundary since nature has already done this for us.' Keith Brennan, Australian Department of External Affairs official, to Portugal's ambassador to Australia, Carlos Empis Wemans, 25 May 1971

In a remote corner of the Indian Ocean there is a turbulent body of water known to the local island people as *Tasi Mane* (Male Sea). On the other side of the island the more placid *Tasi Feto* (Female Sea) gently laps against the northern coastline. Anyone who makes the six- to seven-hour drive from the capital over the rugged spine of the island to *Tasi Mane* will appreciate the strength and ferocity of the Timor Sea, as it is known to Anglophone cartographers. Lashed by cyclones, the Timor Sea swirls in different directions and intimidates the local people, who rarely venture far from the shoreline. Its natural attributes are a reflection of the fierce, treacherous and tragic contest over this tiny patch of sea that has spanned more than three decades.

The Timor Sea separates two of the most disparate neighbouring countries in the world. A short, 90-minute flight from Darwin, capital of Australia's Northern Territory, to Dili, the capital of East Timor, is a journey from a first world country ranked by the United

Nations Human Development Index (HDI)—a socioeconomic scorecard—as the third most agreeable country in which to live, to one ranked 142nd. Under the seabed dividing these two countries is a treasure trove of more than US$100 billion in known oil and gas resources in a region that is still largely unexplored.

In early 2005 the crew of a former Soviet navy minesweeper gained a rare insight into life on the Timor Sea and along the coastline of East Timor. Commissioned to undertake the first complete seismic survey of the seabed off the southern coast, the RV *Zephyr-1* sailed in straight lines parallel and perpendicular to the coastline over a total distance of 6600 kilometres, forming a grid pattern along a narrow strip stretching about 100 kilometres from the coast. Originally contracted by the East Timor government for a period of three months, the crew completed their work in just seven weeks. This was not because of the efficiency of the crew or the *Zephyr-1*—a vessel which still had nuclear and chemical attack warning lamps in the gangways—but because they encountered a sea completely devoid of any human activity. There were no fishing vessels or freighters crossing the ship's path to become entangled in the trailing 10-kilometre censor lines, as was invariably the case in other surveys. A crew member spoke upon his return of witnessing a completely basic human existence. The locals' only vessels were small outrigger canoes that went a short distance from the shore. Most people lived in huts with mud floors and thatched roofs. The Englishman mused that this was just like what Captain Cook would have seen.

East Timor is unquestionably one of the poorest and most underdeveloped countries in the world. About half the population is illiterate, and even fewer have access to electricity and safe drinking water. The 2004 census for East Timor identified a population of 924 000 that was growing at 4 per cent per annum—the fastest rate in the world. The predominantly Catholic country is experiencing a post-war baby boom; on average each woman has eight live births, the highest fertility rate in the world. With a land area of just 15 000 square kilometres, East Timor is less than one-quarter the size of

Tasmania, three-quarters the size of Wales and slightly larger than Connecticut, the third smallest state in the United States. Much of the land surface is rugged mountainous terrain upon which the vast bulk of the expanding population eke out a semi-subsistence, marginal existence. There is remarkably little flat land for intensive agriculture, and even in these areas the yields for rice are a miserable one tonne per hectare, about a quarter the regional average.

For most of those who live in the remote areas of East Timor, the cash economy is barely existent. The United Nations' 2006 Human Development Report did not produce a per capita income estimate for East Timor, making it one of the few countries in the report to miss out. World Bank statistics indicate that annual per capita income is around US$380, or about US$1 a day, ranking East Timor in terms of income among the 20 poorest countries in the world. Forty per cent of the people are considerably poorer, falling below an arbitrary poverty line of US$0.55 a day.[1] However, income figures in a country where barter remains a form of exchange can be meaningless. Many of the small towns and village centres do not have shops or kiosks because the people have no money. Most people living outside district centres have no electricity or running water or access to telephones, and those in district centres only have power for a few hours each evening.

A revealing socioeconomic indicator can be found in the cemeteries that look out to the Timor Sea, in the remotest and poorest part of the country, where loose stones and wooden crosses mark many of the graves. This is a departure from the elaborate, ornamental headstones that populate the cemeteries in the towns and on the mountain ranges, reflecting the influence of animist and Roman Catholic devotion to forebears.

This poverty seems all the more incongruous given the existence of tens of billions of dollars worth of oil and gas close to the coast and, indeed, under the feet of the people. Oil literally oozes out of the ground in East Timor, and leaking methane is ignited to produce 'eternal flames'. There are more than 30 places in East Timor, mainly in the southern part of the island, where oil and gas seeps are found.[2] Remarkably, given that Dutch and Portuguese colonists divided Timor arbitrarily into east and west in 1859, followed by a formal demarcation in 1904, there are only a handful of seeps on the western side of the island, now controlled by Indonesia, and very little oil and gas has been found under the seabed off West Timor.

Such an abundance of natural resources, however, has not proved to be a passport to prosperity for many countries around the world, especially those in the developing world. For most of them, significant resource wealth has led to the paradox of plenty, or the resource curse: an abundance of natural resources can drive uneven, unbalanced and unequal economic development, often leading to rampant corruption and deadly conflict. The people of East Timor have had their own unique experience of this paradox.

* * *

From the southern coast, the seabed drops sharply and then about 100 kilometres from shore the water depth plunges to more than 2000 metres, and in some places to more than 3000 metres. The exact depth remains a mystery because a comprehensive seabed study is yet to be conducted. This deep trench, or trough, runs roughly parallel to the island for more than 1000 kilometres. It has been called variously the Timor Trough or the Timor Trench, but whatever the name this natural feature has played an absolutely pivotal role in the contest over the Timor Sea's resources.

The origins of this contest go back to the time when Portugal still ruled East Timor, and when Australia was seeking to stake out its maritime empire. As the Timor Sea became a focus of petroleum exploration from the 1960s onwards, the Australian government unilaterally claimed more than two-thirds of the area. It did so by declaring that the Timor Trough represented a definitive break in the continental shelf between Australia, Indonesia and East Timor. It said there were two distinct shelves. A continental shelf is the extension, or natural prolongation, of a landmass under the sea, as distinct from a deep seabed that does not extend from the landmass. The concept originated with the proclamation by President Truman in September 1945 that the United States had jurisdiction and control over 'the natural resources of the subsoil and seabed of the continental shelf beneath the high seas but contiguous to the United States'. This marked the beginning of a race by coastal states to stake out their adjacent seas, oceans and seabed. Australia, as an island nation, stood to gain an area bigger than its landmass.

Australia followed the Truman Proclamation in 1953 when it claimed control of the continental shelf to a depth of 100 fathoms (about 200 metres),[3] a unilateral action that soon gained the backing of the United Nations. In 1958 the UN released for signing the first Law of the Sea Convention which allowed coastal states to exercise sovereign rights over their continental shelf to a depth of 200 metres. Article 2 states:

1. The coastal State exercises over the continental shelf sovereign rights for the purpose of exploring it and exploiting its natural resources.
2. The rights referred to in paragraph 1 of this article are exclusive in the sense that if the coastal State does not explore the continental shelf or exploit its natural resources, no one may undertake these activities, or make a claim to the continental shelf, without the express consent of the coastal State.[4]

The 1958 Convention had the effect of defining ownership of what had previously been thought of as the 'high seas', and this in turn gave Australia one of the largest maritime areas in the world, measuring 15 million square kilometres, almost double the size of the Australian landmass, as shown in Map 1.[5]

The right to claim a continental shelf, however, could not be absolute when there was an opposite or adjacent country with an overlapping claim to the same area. The 1958 Convention addressed this situation by establishing the principle of the median line; this was the default that should apply to resolve overlapping claims of neighbouring states. Article 6 states:

> Where the same continental shelf is adjacent to the territories of two or more States whose coasts are opposite each other, the boundary of the continental shelf appertaining to such States shall be determined by agreement between them. In the absence of agreement, and unless another boundary line is justified by special circumstances, the boundary is the median line.[6]

The Australian government, having signed and then ratified the 1958 Convention in 1963, was bound by it in its entirety,[7] but it argued that this article could not be applied in the Timor Sea because the neighbouring countries did not share the 'same' continental shelf. In the Timor Sea, Australia's continental shelf extends from the Australian continent at a shallow depth of no more than 150 metres until it reaches the Timor Trough, about 300 kilometres from the Australian coastline. This deep trough, the Australian government claimed, marked the division between two continental shelves.

In 1967 the Australian parliament passed the *Petroleum (Submerged Lands) Act* which gave the federal government the right to coordinate the licensing of all offshore exploration and development activities. Woodside Petroleum, then known as Burmah Oil, had held permits issued by Australian state and territory governments since 1965. In 1968 the US-based company Oceanic Exploration applied to the Portuguese administration in Dili for exploration rights offshore from East Timor for a period of five years. Oceanic was a small, speculative venture following the practice of acquiring leases that could later be on-sold to major companies. The Australian government, through its embassy in Lisbon, provided the Portuguese government with a copy of its new act and a map showing the permits issued by Australia on the south side of the Timor Trough.[8] Since the Oceanic application would overlap in areas where Australia had granted concessions, in 1970 Portugal proposed to Australia the opening of formal negotiations to determine a maritime boundary.[9]

The Australian government responded by moving, unilaterally, to claim the entire seabed south of the Timor Trough, proclaiming in October 1970 the existence of 'two shelves' in the Timor Sea divided by the Timor Trough. William McMahon, then minister for external affairs, later prime minister, told parliament:

> An article in a financial newspaper recently criticized the principles on which Australia had acted in granting petroleum permits between the northern coast of Australia and Indonesian Timor, and questioned the international validity of Australia's actions.
>
> The rights claimed by Australia in the Timor Sea area are based unmistakably on the morphological structure of the sea-bed. The essential feature of the sea-bed beneath the Timor Sea is a huge steep cleft or declivity called the Timor Trough, extending in an east-western direction, considerably nearer to the coast of Timor than to the northern coast of Australia. It is more than 550 nautical miles long and on the average 40 miles wide, and the sea-bed slopes down on opposite sides to a depth of over 10 000 feet. The Timor Trough thus breaks the continental shelf between Australia and Timor, so that there are two distinct shelves, and not one and the same shelf, separating the two opposite coasts. The fall-back median line between the two coasts, provided for in the Convention in the absence of agreement, would not apply for there is no common area to delimit.[10]

While Australia was a huge beneficiary of the 1958 Convention, it chose to ignore one article that challenged its claim to the resources of the Timor Sea; Article 6 did not apply because it conflicted with the government's ambitions in the Timor Sea. Three days later Portugal made clear that it did not accept the minister's statement and said it would continue to grant concessions on its side of the horizontal median line.[11]

The Australian government moved quickly to enter into negotiations with Indonesia to secure a permanent maritime boundary between the two countries that followed the Timor Trough. Negotiations of this nature have generally taken a number of years because such agreements are permanent; once signed and ratified, they cannot be undone. The seabed boundary negotiated with Indonesia was finalised in just 17 months. After securing an agreement for the seabed in the Arafura Sea off the coast of northern Australia in May 1971, they then entered into negotiations over the Timor Sea. The two parties signed off on an agreement for 'Certain Seabed Boundaries in the Area of the Timor and Arafura Seas' in October 1972.[12]

A week after the Arafura Sea agreement with Indonesia was reached in May 1971, the Portuguese ambassador, Dr Carlos Empis Wemans, was summoned to the Department of External Affairs in Canberra and told that the two countries should agree to a boundary at the Timor Trough since 'nature has already done this for us'.[13] The Australian government told its consul general in San Francisco to deal directly with Oceanic Exploration. A cablegram said that 'Oceanic should be informed that their application, in part, relates to areas within the scope of the Australian offshore petroleum legislation'. Following the signing of the seabed agreement with Indonesia, the Australian government proposed to Portugal that the two countries commence their own negotiations in March 1973. In a preliminary communication in July 1972, Australia said that it would not accept a boundary lying more than 50 nautical miles (92.6 kilometres) off the coast of East Timor.[14] Portugal remained defiant and on 31 January 1974 proceeded to issue a concession to Petrotimor Companhia de Petroleos, S.A.R.L., a subsidiary of Oceanic Exploration. The concession covered an area of 60 000 square kilometres—extending from the southern coastline to the median line—with production rights for 30 years. The Province of Timor would hold a 20 per cent interest in the company.[15]

* * *

Australia's reliance on the shape of the seabed to avoid having a median line in the Timor Sea was questionable at the time. Geological opinion suggested that both Australia and East Timor sat on the same continental shelf, and that the Timor Trough represented what some have called a geological 'wrinkle'. In the mid-1960s geologist Michael Audley-Charles made a remarkable discovery during 28 months of fieldwork in East Timor and three years of laboratory work. He found that many of the fossils in the rocks were comparable to those in the Carnarvon basin in Western Australia.[16] The island of Timor was joined to the Australian continent; there was no break in the continental shelf. A review of the geological evolution of Southeast Asia by Charles Hutchison puts it succinctly: 'The continental shelf unit extends from the Australia Sahul shelf, beneath the axis of the Timor Trough, to reappear uplifted and folded on the island, where it is widely exposed.'[17]

Additional geological information has been gathered through seismic surveys since the Audley-Charles study, culminating in the *Zephyr-1*'s 2005 survey of the entire area from the coastline to the Timor Trough in 2005. These studies have proved conclusively that the Timor Trough does not mark a break in the shelf between Australia and Timor. The trench was formed by the collision between the Australian plate and the Indonesian islands north of Timor, known as the Banda Arc, many millions of years ago. It is like a 'crumple zone' resulting from the impact. Geir Ytreland, a Norwegian geologist with more than 30 years' experience, spent two years analysing geological and seismic data in East Timor from early 2004. He says:

> There is no doubt today in the scientific community that Timor is geologically a part of the Australian plate, which the Australian continental shelf is also a part of. Seismic data from the 1990s, and particularly a large survey acquired in 2005, confirms this.
>
> The geology of the Timor island is quite closely related to the geology seen on the Northern Australian Shelf. However, the nature of the collision has deformed the geology on the island much more than on the Australian shelf to the south.[18]

These facts explain why gum trees are found all over Timor, and why the landscape at times bears a striking similarity to Australia's north-west Kimberley region. East Timor is covered with luminous green foliage for about six months of the year when the wet-season rains beat down, but during the dry season in the middle of the year the rocky landscape reveals those ochre colours that are a trademark of the Australian outback. An abundance of Australian wildlife is also found on Timor. There are two Australian mammals, the cuscus, and the fruit bat, as well as cockatoos, honeyeaters and multi-coloured lorikeets. Many of the dogs have the familiar rusty colour and menacing look of the Australian dingo.

The Australian commandos who fought in the hills and mountains of East Timor during a twelve-month guerilla campaign in the Second World War also discovered a remarkable similarity with the Australian outback. The novelist Nevil Shute wrote that more than 90 per cent of the 2/2 Independent Company were Western Australians, and those from the country districts encountered a very familiar landscape.

> Parts of Timor are covered in tropical jungle but the greater part of the country consists of stony hills covered in thin forest scrub, not unlike many of the outback districts in Australia. In their campaign in Timor the 2/2 Independent Company were fighting in a type of country that they understood and were accustomed to.[19]

* * *

By the early 1970s, Indonesia was still emerging from a bloody campaign to wipe out the Indonesian Communist Party, a campaign which is believed to have led to at least 500 000 deaths. The Soeharto regime was eager to gain legitimacy by doing deals with the west and, despite being a powerful and populous country, it accepted Australia's arguments about the geology of the Timor Sea, and how this meant that a default median line required by Article 6 of the 1958 Convention in an area of overlap did not apply.

Indonesia signed off at the time when the principal of equidistance had become clouded by the International Court of Justice's (ICJ) 1969 decision on the *North Sea Continental Shelf cases (Germany/Denmark, Germany/Netherlands)*. In this ruling the ICJ had given great emphasis to the concept of natural prolongation in determining maritime boundaries.[20]

In a *Four Corners* interview in 2004 Dr Hasjim Djalal, the former Indonesian ambassador for maritime affairs, said the agreement with Australia reflected the state of maritime law at the time. 'But that was the law then, you know. That was the existing Indonesian legislation and that was also the normal international legislation at that moment, so considering that one, I think it's somewhat fair at that time.'[21]

It might have been fair at the time, but it was the worst possible time for Indonesia to settle its maritime boundaries. The North Sea cases had created a misconception. While the ICJ said that natural prolongation was important, the result of any maritime boundary agreement must also take into account considerations of equity and fairness between opposite states. Victor Prescott, a professorial fellow at Melbourne University, who has had a lifelong interest in maritime boundaries, says the agreement was concluded at a time when, in the wake of the 1969 judgement in favour of West Germany, the 'concept of natural prolongation had a novel force which Australia tried to exploit'. Subsequent negotiations in the 1980s between Australia and Indonesia—which focused on equidistance—'reflect the decline in importance of the concept of natural prolongation in seas narrower than 400 nm'.[22]

The 1972 boundary followed the southern edge of the Timor Trough. In deference to the existence of East Timor, a 'gap' was left between points A16 and A17, as shown in Map 2. This became known famously as the 'Timor Gap'. But the Gap should have been wider—the boundary encroached into areas which might be part of East Timor's maritime jurisdiction.

The end points are known as trijunction points, meaning that they involve the claims of three countries, but they were only negotiated by two states. The notion that the boundary had gone too far—that the A15, A16 and A17 end points of the boundary had extended into East Timor's area—is explicitly acknowledged in Article 3 of the agreement:

> In the event of any further delimitation agreement or agreements being concluded between governments exercising sovereign rights with respect to the exploration of the seabed and the exploitation of its natural resources in the area of the Timor Sea, the Government of the Commonwealth of Australia and the Government of the Republic of Indonesia shall consult each other with a view to agreeing on such adjustment or adjustments, if any, as may be necessary in those portions of the boundary lines between Points A15 and A16 and between Points A17 and A18.[23]

The only governments that could exercise rights in this area would be Portugal as the colonial authority or East Timor as a newly independent country.

The end points of the 1972 agreement reflect vertical (or lateral) median lines to divide up the Timor Sea to the east and west. In the world of maritime law, they are known as simplified lines of equidistance, meaning that they take no account of any special circumstances, such as islands or capes which unfairly influence the line. These equidistance lines are drawn so that each point is equidistant from the coast (or baselines) of each respective state. In the 1972 agreement these lines were drawn by making reference to the distance from the coastline of Indonesia and East Timor, even though East Timor was not a party to these negotiations. In drawing the eastern arm of the boundary the negotiators did not include East Timor's island of Jaco, and this omission alone caused the eastern arm of the boundary to encroach by 2 nautical miles.[24]

As shown in Map 3, the vertical equidistance lines used to determine the 1972 boundary end points are influenced by prominent points and islands in Indonesia. In the west it is the cape of Tanjong We Toh, and in the east the islands of Leti, Moa and Lakor, and the atoll of Meatij Miarang. These points cause the equidistance line to swing inwards towards East Timor and, incredibly, this happens exactly where significant resources are located. In the east the line swings in where the giant Sunrise and Troubadour fields are located, known collectively as Greater Sunrise, and in the west over the Buffalo, Laminaria and Corallina fields (the BCL fields). Adjusting for these circumstances, as courts have done in numerous cases since the signing of this agreement, might have delivered a much bigger share of the Timor Sea to East Timor.

Six years after the seabed agreement was signed the new Indonesian foreign minister, Professor Mochtar Kusumaatmadja, a law of the sea expert who had been a prominent member of Indonesia's negotiating team, said Australia had taken Indonesia 'to the cleaners'.[25] The 1972 Australia–Indonesia agreement is absolutely unique. It is the only example in more than 60 such agreements where overlapping claims have been settled exclusively on the basis of the natural features of the seabed. There was nothing Indonesia could do about this unhappy settlement—it had signed for eternity.

The 1972 agreement had a profound effect on Australia's posturing in advance of the invasion of East Timor in 1975. Portugal proceeded to act in accordance with its right to license activity up to the median line. Gough Whitlam challenged the Portuguese government on national television after it granted the Petrotimor concession, but time was running out for the people of East Timor. When Portugal set in motion a program of rapid decolonisation in East Timor in 1974–75, and Indonesia revealed its interest in the territory, the Australian government believed that its national interest would be greatly advanced by having an Indonesian-controlled East Timor, rather than an independent nation or a nation under continued Portuguese control. Western countries, led by the United

States, did not want a 'Little Cuba' in Southeast Asia. The prize of securing Timor Sea oil by closing the Timor Gap emerged as an additional and compelling element in Australia's strategic thinking at this critical juncture. Portugal's defiant stance against Australia's ambitions in the Timor Sea and its botched exit from its most far-flung dominion doomed the people of East Timor to invasion and 24 years of occupation.

2 THE SPOILS OF CONQUEST

> *'It would seem to me that this Department might well have an interest in closing the present gap in the agreed seabed border and that this could be much more readily negotiated with Indonesia by closing the present gap than with Portugal or an independent Portuguese Timor.'* Richard Woolcott, Australia's ambassador to Jakarta. Cablegram to Canberra, 17 August 1975

Portugal's hasty exit from East Timor in 1975 and Indonesia's subsequent invasion provided foreign policy advisers in Australia with one of those once-in-a-career moments in the practice of diplomacy. It sparked a vexed debate, involving a stark choice between taking a principled stand in support of the right to self-determination, as Australia had done with Portugal's African colonies, versus a national-interest decision that could eliminate a potential nuisance while possibly enriching Australia. It was the very stuff of modern diplomacy.

This episode became a defining moment in the rise of a new generation of Asia-minded foreign affairs officials whose influence continues to this day. They saw it as an opportunity to forge a much closer relationship with Indonesia, Australia's near and populous neighbour, and the only country that posed an immediate security threat to Australia. From the very beginning of the debate within the then Department of Foreign Affairs (DFA), the desire to control oil and gas in the Timor Sea influenced thinking in favour of East Timor's integration with Indonesia. In the bigger picture, Australia did not want a left-leaning, aid-dependent micro-state on its doorstep. In the context of the Cold War, East Timor had the potential to become more than a nuisance as it could forge alliances with China or the Soviet Union. Australia, the United States and, most importantly of all, the Soeharto regime saw only trouble when the prospect of an independent East Timor came onto the horizon. The neatest, simplest solution was integration into Indonesia. But on top of this geo-political agenda, there was the added bonus for Australia of closing 'the Gap' at the edge of the Timor Trough and securing a potential bonanza in petroleum wealth.

Policy development in Canberra swung into gear when on 25 April 1974 a young generation of Portuguese military officers staged a coup in Lisbon. Telling their troops to put carnations in their rifles rather than bullets, they swept aside a regime that had pursued futile and costly colonial wars in Africa since the early 1960s. The immediate agenda of the Carnation Revolution was to launch a process of decolonisation.

Eight days after the coup, officials in Canberra discussed a policy paper that firmly established the mistaken notion that Australia would get a more favourable seabed agreement with an Indonesian-controlled East Timor. The *Policy Planning Paper* of 3 May 1974 makes clear that a favourable seabed boundary that would deliver the Timor Sea's oil resources to Australia was part of the department's thinking as it began framing its policy response to the regime change in Portugal. In a concluding section on 'Australian attitudes' the paper says:

> We should press ahead with negotiations with Portugal on the Portuguese Timor seabed boundary, but bear in mind that the Indonesians

would probably be prepared to accept the same compromise as they did in the negotiations already completed on the seabed boundary between our two countries.

Such a compromise would be more acceptable to us than the present Portuguese position. For precisely this reason, however, we should be careful not to be seen as pushing for self-government or independence for Portuguese Timor or for it to become part of Indonesia, as this would probably be interpreted as evidence of our self-interest in the seabed boundary dispute rather than a genuine concern for the future of Portuguese Timor.[1]

A cable from John McCredie, the deputy ambassador in the Australian embassy in Jakarta, a few weeks later reinforced this conventional wisdom and left no doubt as to the embassy's view:

We are at the beginning of an eternity of relations with the Indonesians in the Indian Ocean. They have been very cooperative in getting the Seabed Agreement and in the various PNG areas … Indonesian absorption of Timor makes geopolitical sense. Any other long-term solution would be potentially disruptive of both Indonesia and the region. It would help confirm our seabed agreement with Indonesia. It should induce a greater readiness on Indonesia's part to discuss Indonesia's ocean strategy.[2]

As events unfolded over the next 18 months, culminating in Indonesia's invasion of East Timor, a favourable seabed boundary and Timor Sea oil were recurring themes in cables.

Australia's foreign minister, Alexander Downer, has dismissed the link between Timor Sea oil and Australia's policy of backing the Indonesian invasion. In 2004 he said that this conclusion relies on 'selectively quoting one document', and added, 'If that were true, then that would be a theme that ran through many documents and many public statements at the time. I don't think that that was something which would have been significantly in their contemplation.

I'd be certain of that.'³ In 2000 Downer released documents on East Timor from 1974–76, and some from 1978–79 relating to Australia's granting of de jure recognition. Discussion of the prospect of securing a more favourable seabed boundary under an Indonesian-controlled East Timor appears in at least four documents, including ministerial submissions and policy papers, from April 1974 to December 1975. A 1978 ministerial submission links recognition of Indonesian sovereignty in East Timor with the favourable boundary.

There was a genuine debate in DFA about the principle of self-determination, but the pro-Soeharto lobby never looked like losing the contest. Richard Woolcott, an ever-beaming, slick high-flyer who became ambassador to Jakarta on 3 March 1975, emerged as the most influential player in promoting East Timor's integration with Indonesia. Woolcott came from the elite background that typified the Australian foreign service at that time, and to some extent to this day. He studied at Geelong Grammar, the school later attended by Prince Charles, and then Melbourne University. Later he went to London University's School of Slavonic and Eastern European Studies in the bohemian Bloomsbury area of central London. In the 1950s he was posted to Moscow, then South Africa, but by the late 1950s Asia had become his special interest. He became head of the Southeast Asia section and postings to Singapore and Malaysia in the early 1960s followed. Considered capable of shaping policy direction, he was elevated to head of research in the early 1970s, then first assistant secretary of the Asia division, before becoming deputy secretary in 1974. Woolcott's career as a diplomat culminated in his appointment as secretary of the department in 1988, a position he held until his retirement at the age of 65 in 1992. The Indonesian government acknowledged his endeavours in developing Australian–Indonesian relations in 2000 when it awarded him the Star of the First Great Prince. The Keating government bestowed Australia's highest honour on Woolcott on the Queen's Birthday in June 1993. He was made a Companion in the Order of Australia

(AC) for his services to 'international relations and to Asia-Pacific Economic Co-operation'.[4]

Woolcott remains actively engaged in Asian affairs, particularly in relations with Indonesia. In 2004 he travelled to Indonesia to take part in a conference on the presidential elections. Typical of some senior officers, Woolcott's son, Peter, joined DFA after first becoming a barrister and working for the failed tycoon Alan Bond. In his early years, he befriended another young diplomat from an elite background—Alexander Downer. Peter Woolcott joined DFA in 1981 but took leave to work for the conservative opposition leader, Andrew Peacock, from 1984–86. He served as director of the Law of the Sea Branch within DFA at the time when the Timor Gap Treaty came into being, and also served as a deputy head of the Australian embassy in Jakarta. He returned to politics when he worked as chief of staff for Downer from 2002–04, exactly the time when Australia was taking a very tough stand in the Timor Sea negotiations with the newly independent East Timor.

Australia's fateful policy on East Timor in the 1970s was the result of a meeting of minds between Prime Minister Gough Whitlam and the Woolcott-led, pro-Indonesia clique. A key moment came in September 1974 when Whitlam met with President Soeharto in Yogyakarta, the royal capital of central Java. DFA advised in a brief written for Whitlam that Indonesia 'would rather absorb Portuguese Timor than see it emerge into independence', and that Soeharto found this policy 'persuasive'. The brief, however, remained consistent with DFA's support of the principle of self-determination—the right to vote. It asserted DFA's policy that an 'act of self-determination should be accepted as a genuine test of Timorese opinion'.[5] Over in Jakarta, the Australian ambassador Robert Furlonger tried to sway Whitlam's view by sending him a cable on the eve of the meeting that raised the frightening prospect of a Chinese satellite on Australia's doorstep. Furlonger said Indonesia did not want a 'weak and impoverished state which would be a tempting client for other major powers, particularly but not exclusively China'.[6]

The record of the meeting shows that Whitlam signalled strongly that he favoured incorporation of Portuguese Timor into Indonesia. He cautioned Soeharto on the reaction of the Australian public to armed intervention, not the reaction of the government, as the following section of an edited record shows:

> Portuguese Timor should become part of Indonesia. Second, this should happen in accordance with the properly expressed wishes of the people of Portuguese Timor. The Prime Minister emphasized that this was not yet Government policy but was likely to become that.
>
> He believed that Portuguese Timor was too small to be independent. It was economically unviable. An independent East Timor would inevitably become the focus for others outside the region. Indonesia should be aware, however, of the effects on public opinion in Australia of incorporation of the province into Indonesia against the wishes of the people.[7]

Departmental secretary Alan Renouf had upheld the view that the principle of self-determination should be respected. He wrote later: 'I directed that Australia's policy should be self-determination. Foreign Minister Don Willesee approved this. In his talks with Soeharto, Whitlam changed the policy'.[8] Whitlam sidelined Renouf and made Woolcott part of his 'inner loop' on the Timor question.

In April 1975, a month after becoming Indonesian ambassador, Woolcott warned in a letter to Whitlam, ahead of another meeting with President Soeharto, of the danger of a principled stand on East Timor. In his contribution to this debate Woolcott excelled in the use of dramatic metaphor in a way that Whitlam would have appreciated:

> While we are committed to such principles as human rights and self-determination, I do not think we should, from the relative comfort of our Continental pulpit, lecture the Indonesians on how to conduct their domestic affairs. Despite our proper concern for

these issues I believe we should seek to avoid a meddlesome attitude, or, as I have said before, seek to become the conscience of Asia.

I remain somewhat worried about Timor. We could be working ourselves into a position where we are impaling ourselves on the hook of self-determination. Do we want actually to encourage an independent East Timor? I would doubt it. It is not wanted by Indonesia; nor, I believe, by any of the other countries in the region.[9]

Woolcott never took a backward step in the vigorous debate within the department that ensued throughout 1975, even when trading cables with Renouf. Woolcott's cables show that he was fully aware that he was dispensing with principles in the pursuit of the 'national interest'.

Portugal remained the governing authority in Timor at this time, but it had allowed political parties to form as part of its decolonisation process.

Civil war broke out on 11 August 1975 after the Indonesian government told the conservative UDT party (*União Democrática de Timor*) that FRETILIN (*Frente Revolucionária do Timor-Leste Independente*, or the Revolutionary Front for the Independence of East Timor) was about to launch a coup. The Indonesian government feared that FRETILIN could forge alliances with China and other communist countries after overturning in September 1974 a policy of aligning its foreign relations to those of Indonesia and adopting one of non-alignment. UDT then made a unilateral grab for power, although FRETILIN supporters had already been well armed and quickly gained the upper hand. A week later Woolcott sent a cable to Canberra in which he linked support for Indonesia's intervention in East Timor with closing the Timor Gap and securing Timor Sea oil. He introduced oil into the debate by noting:

> I wonder whether the Department has ascertained the interest of the Minister or the Department of Minerals and Energy in the Timor Situation. It would seem to me that this Department might

well have an interest in closing the present gap in the agreed seabed border and that this could be much more readily negotiated with Indonesia by closing the present gap than with Portugal or an independent Portuguese Timor.

I know I am recommending a pragmatic rather than a principled stand but this is what national interest and foreign policy is all about.[10]

In this cable Woolcott set out a strategy for Canberra to publicly presage the need for armed intervention in East Timor. He said the Minister could answer a question in Parliament or at a press conference in which he stated that Australia 'cannot condone the use of force in Timor' while then explaining the need for such action from Indonesia's standpoint. This was a brazen move on his part and very shrewd in its execution. He set out the strategy in detail, but he covered himself by recommending that it not be used.

Other alternatives to a message—although I would not recommend them—would be an answer to a question in the House or a statement, possibly at a press conference. These could assert that Australia cannot condone the use of force in Timor, nor could we accept the principle that a country can intervene in a neighbouring territory because of concern, however well-based that concern might be, over the situation there. At the same time such an answer to a question in Parliament or from the press could concede that Indonesia has had a prolonged struggle for national unity and could not be expected to take lightly a breakdown in law and order in Portuguese Timor, especially when the colony is surrounded by and geographically very much part of the Indonesian Archipelago.[11]

At this time, the Jakarta embassy became aware of Indonesia's plans for a full-scale invasion, which began with a series of border raids in October 1975. The embassy's deputy ambassador, Malcolm Dan,[12] and political counsellor Allan Taylor[13] began receiving detailed briefings from the mercurial Harry Tjan of the Centre for Strategic and International Studies (CSIS) in Jakarta on 'Operation Flamboyant'—Indonesia's strategy of destabilisation as a precursor to the invasion of East Timor. Ostensibly an independent think tank, CSIS was chaired by the very influential Lieutenant General Ali Murtopo, a close confidant of President Soeharto who served as information minister and head of the Special Operation Service (OPSUS). In October 1974 Murtopo gained control of the Timor 'project'.[14]

Dan and Taylor were the second and third ranking officials in the embassy and through their frequent visits to CSIS the Australian government was being made a confidant of the Indonesian government. There were concerns at the senior levels of DFA that this access could compromise the Australian government. Desmond Ball and Hamish McDonald concluded in their book *Death in Balibo, Lies in Canberra—Blood on Whose Hands?* that the 'astonishing insights' into Indonesia's plans risked making the Australian government 'deeply complicit in the Indonesian campaign'. With the benefit of this explosive information, neither the embassy nor the Australian government pressed Indonesia to adopt a different strategy and allow a proper act of self-determination. The embassy officials remained passive information gatherers. Nor did the Australian government warn those of its citizens who were walking into the firing line.

On the evening of 14 October 1975, the Seven television network broadcast a report from a news team in East Timor that was en route to Balibo on the Indonesian border. That day a cable from Woolcott had been sent to ministers, senior officials in DFA and intelligence agencies outlining in detail Indonesia's plans to attack East Timor's border towns, including Balibo. The relevant desks in DFA received transcripts of the Seven report, yet no-one in the government contacted the networks to warn them of the imminent danger. In the early hours of 16 October Indonesian soldiers, after removing the insignia from their uniforms, attacked Balibo. Newsmen Gary Cunningham 27, Brian Peters 26, Malcolm Rennie

29, Greg Shackleton 29 and Tony Stewart 21 were rounded up and executed soon after the Indonesians entered the town. After an exhaustive study Ball and McDonald concluded, 'This is a rare case where officials decided, in peacetime, to sacrifice some of their fellow citizens to protect security and intelligence interests.'[15] Subsequently, conflicting reports have emerged about the possible launch of an SAS rescue mission prior to the Indonesian attack on Balibo. In 2001 an anonymous source claimed he had led a twelve-member SAS unit sent to Timor to rescue the newsmen, but was unable to locate them. Another report in 2006 quoted claims from an unnamed source that an SAS mission poised to mount the rescue operation from a Darwin airbase was ordered to stand down.[16]

Taylor's intelligence gathering prowess put his career on an upward trajectory. He became ambassador to Indonesia and his rise culminated in his appointment as Director-General of the Australian Secret Intelligence Service (ASIS) in 1998, Australia's equivalent to the CIA and MI6. Dan, after serving as deputy to two ambassadors in Jakarta, became ambassador to Argentina and Chile.

The full-scale invasion of East Timor on 7 December 1975 coincided with a constitutional crisis in Australia, which proved to be a significant distraction at a critical juncture. On 11 November 1975 the Labor government led by Gough Whitlam was dismissed by the governor-general after the Opposition had blocked the budget in the Senate. An election was called for 2 December and the conservative Coalition won in a landslide victory.

The oil factor loomed again when the DFA put its policy agenda to a newly minted foreign minister, Andrew Peacock, the Liberal MP for Kooyong. Now that the invasion was a fact, Woolcott's pragmatism prevailed. Peacock, seen as a liberal in the true sense of the word, had shown some support for self-determination in East Timor while in opposition, but that was all about to change now that he came under the direct influence of his department.

A formal submission landed on the minister's desk three days before Christmas 1975. The department wrote:

> We think that Australian interests in Portuguese Timor, deriving from the territory's proximity, its straddling of important shipping routes, its nearness to our seabed resource zone and some small residual Australian commercial interests would all be well served by its incorporation into Indonesia.[17]

As well as confirming that the seabed was part of the real agenda, the department's reference to East Timor's 'nearness' to the Timor Sea resources was either a tacit or, indeed, unwitting acknowledgement that an independent East Timor might have a claim under international law to resources that Australia was claiming as its own.

In early January 1976 Woolcott wrote a lengthy cable of more than 3000 words in which he set out the case for fully supporting Indonesia's actions. His new minister and most of his colleagues would have been on holiday at the beach at this time, but this cable would be ready for them upon their return to work. Woolcott challenged the Australian government's support for the UN General Assembly's resolution that condemned the invasion and called for an immediate withdrawal.[18] He argued that incorporation by Indonesia was a *fait accompli* as Indonesia mopped up a fragmented resistance. At this time the new prime minister, Malcolm Fraser, had privately advocated Australian military intervention in East Timor and the withdrawal of Indonesian forces, and after being dissuaded by public servants remained in favour of UN intervention and a genuine act of self-determination.[19] A month after the invasion Woolcott set out the case for a pragmatic approach:

> The reality on which Australia needs now to base its policy assumptions is that, whatever the difficulties Portuguese Timor will be incorporated into Indonesia.
>
> It is on the Timor issue that we face one of those broad foreign policy decisions which face most countries at one time or another. The government is confronted by a choice between a moral stance,

based on condemnation of Indonesia for the invasion of East Timor and on the assertion of the inalienable right of the people of East Timor to self-determination, on the one hand, and a pragmatic and realistic acceptance of the longer term inevitabilities of the situation, on the other hand. It is a choice between what might be described as Wilsonian idealism and Kissingerian realism.[20]

Within two months of the invasion the Fraser government had accepted and was running the official line from the bureaucrats: while Australia remained critical of the means by which Indonesia had intervened, East Timor's integration into Indonesia was now a *fait accompli*. In February 1976 the new cabinet decided not only to continue defence cooperation with Indonesia but to increase it by 25 per cent.

Moral issues aside, the Woolcott-inspired policy overlooked the strong sense of national identity in East Timor and its ability to wage an effective guerilla war. This assessment was made despite Woolcott having attended a key policy discussion meeting on 11 December 1974 in which Gordon Jockel, a former ambassador in Jakarta and then head of the Joint Intelligence Organisation, argued that Indonesia would have great difficulty moving into East Timor. Jockel noted that there were 15 000 men in East Timor with military experience, including 1000 regular soldiers and a further 3000 reservists who received regular training, and that the rugged terrain would aid their resistance. He warned prophetically that East Timor might become a 'running sore' for Indonesia.[21] Jockel could have added that this sizeable army had thousands of NATO-issue, semi-automatic G3 rifles, massive ammunition reserves and hundreds of battle-hardened veterans from Portugal's colonial wars.

The disposal of any moral stance in support of the 'inalienable right of the people of East Timor to self-determination' fits squarely within the conventional framework of foreign policy formulation. After all, the ultimate objective of foreign policy is survival—not political survival from one election to the next, but the advancement of a nation state for the very long term, for decades and centuries. For the Woolcott clique, the rights of just over half a million people in a tiny half island nation to Australia's near north were not going to stand in the way of building good relations with Indonesia. The Republic of Indonesia at that time had a population of around 130 million, 10 times the size of Australia's population, spread over a vast archipelago of more than 7000 islands (with almost another 7000 uninhabited islands). Indonesia, after having killed an estimated 500 000 or more of its own people in an attempt to eradicate the Indonesian Communist Party just a decade before, did not want what it perceived as a communist outpost within its archipelago. In the context of the Cold War and the fall of Saigon, Australia, and its ally the United States, did not want this either.

Nine months before the invasion Secretary of State Henry Kissinger had received a State department cable urging him to take a pragmatic approach to Indonesia's plans. The cable said the United States had 'considerable interests' in Indonesia and none in Timor. In December 1975 President Gerald Ford and Kissinger visited Jakarta as part of a sweep through Asia that also took in China and the Philippines. President Soeharto advised them of the imminent plans for invasion. Soeharto said Indonesia had no territorial ambitions but it was concerned about 'security, tranquillity and peace'. Ford wrote later that Soeharto's efforts to 'uphold the cause of anti-communism there' impressed him. In response to the proposed invasion, Ford said 'we understand and we will not press you on the issue'. Kissinger said it would be better if it were done after they had returned, and that using US equipment 'could create problems'.[22]

Should foreign policy makers at the time have looked at the situation any differently? Was East Timor just like any one of a number of underdeveloped islands in Australia's orbit whose interests could so easily be dispensed with? DFA might have thought so at the time given Australia's new strategic interests, but this was not the case with the Australian public who had a deeper, longer term perspective on a rather unique relationship that went back to the dark days of the

Second World War when the Japanese came within striking distance of Australia. During this campaign the Timorese, together with their Portuguese administrators, gave unstinting support to the Australian commandos who were able to tie down a Japanese force of 20 000 troops. Despite having been dragged into the global conflict as a neutral territory, the Timorese made great sacrifices in support of the Australians. A foreign policy that had a broader framework might have taken these elements on board.

Immediately after the Second World War East Timor emerged as a place of significant strategic interest to Australia. A 1952 defence paper said the 'island of Timor . . . lies like an unsinkable aircraft carrier [300–400] miles off Australia's north-western coast, covering the approaches to the Le[e]uwin, the Kimberlys, to Darwin and to the Torres Straits. It is a menace, actual and potential: but if action is taken now it can be turned into a protective shield.'[23]

Australia made overtures to Portugal about establishing defence cooperation in Timor but Portugal showed no interest at all. Had it accepted the proposal history may have taken a very different course. For the next two decades Portugal continued to administer East Timor with benign neglect. Sealed roads and electricity did not exist outside the capital. Secondary education was limited to a handful of places for the elite, and there was no university. Portugal's most far flung dominion was left as a sleepy backwater, and Australia soon forgot about a place that two decades earlier had been of immense strategic importance. By the early 1970s East Timor was considered irrelevant to Australia's interests, even though Australian oil companies were active in the Timor Sea, and in 1971 the government closed its consulate in Dili in the name of cost saving. It had employed just one Australian.

For Australian policy makers it was time to build a relationship with a neighbour that really mattered. Strategic interests were the driving force of this grand betrayal, but oil moved to centre stage in the aftermath of the invasion. Foreign affairs officials were quick to advise their political masters that Australia stood to benefit considerably from this geo-political shift and that it should move to recognise Indonesia's sovereignty in East Timor.

Just two years after the invasion, in January 1978 when Indonesia's occupation was being vigorously contested by the resistance army, *Forças Armadas de Liberação Nacional de Timor-Leste* (FALINTIL), Foreign Minister Andrew Peacock declared that Australia would now grant de facto recognition of Indonesian control of East Timor. His statement gave no justification for this move.

> The Minister for Foreign Affairs, Mr Andrew Peacock, announced today that the Government had decided to accept East Timor as part of Indonesia. Accordingly, the government has decided that although it remains critical of the means by which integration was brought about it would be unrealistic to continue to refuse to recognize de facto that East Timor is part of Indonesia.[24]

This statement paved the way for the formal de jure recognition of Indonesia's occupation, and the *only* reason for this speedy decision was the seabed boundary, which of course meant oil. In a submission from the department dated 26 April 1978 Peacock was told that Australia's commencement of negotiations over the seabed boundary meant effective recognition of Indonesian sovereignty in East Timor. The department's submission recommended that the government need not make any new announcement on such a monumental policy shift—it could simply '"slip" into de jure recognition of Indonesia's incorporation of East Timor. This would not require any new announcement.'[25]

DFA advised Peacock on how he could deflect any criticism by emphasising the potential benefit to Australia of the seabed agreement in the Timor Gap:

> If questions are asked about these changes the Government could explain its position by arguing that it was necessary to acknowledge Indonesia's claim to East Timor for the purpose of negotiating an

international agreement which is very much in Australia's interest, but that the Government remains critical of the means by which integration was brought about.[26]

As instructed, the government did not issue a formal statement on this decision. As advised, Peacock let it slip on 15 December 1978 when he met with the Indonesian foreign minister, Professor Mochtar: 'After meeting with Indonesian Minister Mochtar, Peacock announced to a press conference that as a result of seabed negotiations Australia would give de jure recognition to Indonesia's incorporation of East Timor.'[27]

Making this statement at a time of continuing strong public opposition to Indonesia's occupation was a political gamble on the part of the Australian government. It calculated that another betrayal of East Timor was a fair price to pay for Australia's objective of closing the Timor Gap and securing a potential bonanza in oil and gas resources on the southern side of the Timor Trough. These two critically important decisions were made during the bloodiest year of Indonesia's military campaign in East Timor, when the country was completely sealed off from the outside world and virtually turned into a huge concentration camp.

Xanana Gusmão, who led the resistance army FALINTIL after its leaders were wiped out in 1978, wrote that in late 1977 Indonesia brought in an additional 15 000 fresh troops to begin a new offensive. In a letter to Gusmão in November that year a local priest reported:

> [The war] continues with the same fury as it started. The bombers do not stop all day. Hundreds of human beings die every day. The bodies of the victims become food for carnivorous birds (if we don't die of the war we will die of the plague), villages have been completely destroyed, some tribes decimated. The barbarities, the cruelties, the pillaging, the unqualified destruction of Timor, the executions without reason, in a word all the 'organised' evil, have spread deep roots in Timor.[28]

The spoils of conquest

At the start of the dry season in May 1978, Indonesia commenced a new campaign in preparation for the visit of President Soeharto. Aided by US Bronco OV 10 aircraft, the Skylight Offensive, as the campaign was known, overcame the advantage afforded to FALINTIL by the rugged terrain.[29] Unlike other successful guerilla forces, FALINTIL did not have a neutral territory that it could use as a safe haven. Its only respite came from the mountains, but the offensive's 'campaign of encirclement' was designed to nullify that advantage.

Given that Australian intelligence had a long-established practice of intercepting the Indonesian military's communications in East Timor, it beggars belief that DFA and Peacock would not have known of this wanton slaughter at the time Indonesian sovereignty was recognised. The interception began in late 1975 and continued throughout the occupation.[30]

During a 22-year career in the Department of Foreign Affairs and Trade (DFAT), as DFA was renamed in 1987, Bruce Haigh[31] headed the Indonesia desk from 1984 to 1986 where he began receiving intercepted monthly reports of casualties from the conflict in East Timor. The reports contained signals intelligence relating to military and civilian deaths and injuries, and 'references to areas or villages having been secured'. Haigh began a practice of sending these reports to the minister's office, but he was later instructed to send a six-monthly summary. Haigh refused to stop sending the monthly reports, but doubts whether they were seen by the minister.

Haigh resigned from DFAT in 1994 over the failure of Australian diplomacy in a number of key areas. He and his wife now run a vineyard in Mudgee, New South Wales. While working on the Refugee Review Tribunal from 1995–2000, Haigh thought hard about the Australian government's blind approach to the atrocities in East Timor. 'What do you do when you know the extent of human suffering in a neighbouring country, including the deaths of young children?'[32] He says there was a cover-up in the department from the time of the invasion in 1975, at the time of de jure recognition, right through to the militia rampage of 1999.

This big lie that nothing untoward was happening in East Timor. Woolcott lied about it. Then his successors had to lie. For senior ranks, in DFAT, Defence and ONA [the Office of National Assessments], it was a precondition for advancement. It's had an effect on the ethics of this country. You see it being played out in the daily deniability games of Howard and the federal public service, particularly the department of immigration and the AFP [the Australian Federal Police].[33]

Successive Australian governments were complicit in Indonesia's campaign of systematic violence in East Timor. It was a policy approach rooted in the desire for oil.[34]

* * *

Early one evening in the spring of 2004, Richard Woolcott skirted the edge of Sydney's Kings Cross red light district, past the vagrants and drug addicts, to reach the basement of the sandstone church of St Canice. He had retained the slim, agile build seen in photographs taken three decades ago in meetings with President Soeharto and Prime Minister Whitlam, but on this occasion his beaming smile was missing. Woolcott had agreed to launch a discussion paper[35] on the Timor Sea dispute by Professor Frank Brennan SJ, the acclaimed Jesuit lawyer and civil rights activist designated a 'National Living Treasure' by the National Trust of Australia.

Woolcott knew some in the audience would be hostile towards him, and he had agreed to launch the paper against the advice of his son, Peter, who had recently finished working as chief of staff for Downer. That week Woolcott had joined 42 other former diplomats, service chiefs and intelligence officers who had signed a letter accusing the Australian government of misleading the public in entering the Iraq war. Woolcott said that some may think of him as 'complicit' in Indonesian policy on East Timor, but he hoped after reading his biography[36] they would have a different view. On the dispute, Woolcott said East Timor was a fragile country deserving of Australia's support, and deserving of fairness:

> I believe that it is very important to avoid a fifth tragedy befalling the East Timorese people in the form of a breakdown in governance which would lead to East Timor becoming a failing, or a failed, state within its first decade of independence. Independence in a small state with limited resources is usually fragile and can be threatened, as we have seen in some African countries and in the South West Pacific, most recently in the Solomon Islands.
>
> We must cooperate therefore with East Timor and Indonesia to consolidate Timor-Leste's independence and nurture its fragile institutions.[37]

After the speech an adviser from the East Timor government approached Woolcott and presented him with a one-kilo bag of Arabica coffee beans which had been roasted by hand at a rudimentary, Portuguese-era processing facility in Dili. The adviser explained that while coffee was the country's biggest non-oil export, the bag of beans had sold for just US$2, and that most of Timor's coffee was sold unprocessed and for much less. Without a fair settlement in the Timor Sea, East Timor did not have a future, the adviser explained. Woolcott accepted the gift and nodded in agreement.

Brennan, a towering figure in both reputation and stature, acknowledged in his remarks that the choice of Woolcott to launch the paper was surprising for many. He joked that he had chosen him because the Jesuits 'specialise in redemption'.

3 THE KELP IN THE COFFIN

'The agreement that has been reached on a joint development or area of cooperation approach represents, I think, a triumph for creative solutions to diplomatic impasses.' Foreign Minister Gareth Evans, speaking at the conclusion of 10 years of negotiations on the Timor Gap, 27 October 1989

When delegations from Australia and Indonesia met on Valentine's Day 1979 to commence maritime boundary negotiations, the Australian side came in for a rude awakening. The premise underpinning Australia's Timor policy since 1974—that a compliant Indonesia would agree to close the existing seabed border at the Timor Trough—proved to be entirely false.

But Indonesia's new resolve may not have come as a complete surprise on the day as Australian intelligence agents succeeded in obtaining confidential papers outlining Indonesia's negotiating position throughout these decade-long negotiations, according to the journalist Brian Toohey. He also noted that Foreign Minister Bill Hayden, who gained this post as a consolation prize after losing the Labor leadership to Bob Hawke, put 'great emphasis' on acquiring documents outlining the 'negotiating position' of trade partners. When pressed for tangible evidence of what the Australian Secret

Intelligence Service (ASIS) had achieved with the considerable resources bestowed upon it, the obtaining of Indonesia's highly valuable papers was one of the few successes that senior intelligence officers could cite.[1]

The Indonesian government had realised the full extent of its blunder in signing the 1972 Treaty, and in these negotiations it pursued a very different approach. Indonesia claimed a 200-nautical-mile entitlement that stretched nearly two-thirds of the way towards the Australian coastline, overlapping Australia's claim. Australia's delegation, comprised of officials from the attorney-general's and foreign affairs departments, insisted on Australia's claim to the edge of the Timor Trough. The respective agendas were irreconcilable and the negotiations failed to make headway.

Four years later, in March 1983, the election of a new federal government in Australia raised another obstacle. The Labor government, led by Prime Minister Bob Hawke, had a party platform that expressed support for an act of self-determination in East Timor. This was inconsistent with the Fraser government's recognition of Indonesian sovereignty. In order to restart negotiations Labor had to change the platform at the 1984 National Conference in Canberra.

A resolution proposing a continuation of the Labor Party's support for self-determination went to the conference, but this was substituted with another. The new platform said the 'ALP expresses its continuing concern' at the situation in East Timor, and its objection to incorporation without an internationally supervised act of self-determination. It expressed 'grave concern' at reports of renewed fighting and called on the UN secretary-general to bring about a resolution. These points were covered in the first three paragraphs, while the final three paragraphs dealt with the 'vital importance' of building a good relationship with Indonesia in order to advance its overall social and economic development.

Still, the negotiations went nowhere. The two sides remained an ocean apart and they stayed that way for another four years. In such circumstances, one or both parties could have gone to international arbitration, but both declined to do so. One member of the Australian negotiating team, Ernst Willheim, noted in an article at the time: 'At this stage, neither side has shown any disposition to have the matter resolved other than by bilateral negotiations.'[2] Some have argued that taking this dispute to an international arbiter would have drawn attention to the illegality of Indonesia's occupation. Peter Galbraith, a former US diplomat who advised East Timor in later negotiations, argued in a speech in 2001:

> If the Courts and the Law of the Sea favour a midpoint, why didn't Indonesia just ask the International Court of Justice to define a maritime boundary between Australia and Indonesia? Indonesia could not go to court because the first issue that would be raised (not by Australia but by Portugal) would be the illegality of Indonesia's occupation of East Timor.[3]

Willheim contends that a court would not have raised this issue of its own accord as both parties in the negotiation accepted Indonesian sovereignty as a fact.[4]

Illegality of occupation aside, developments in international law during the course of the negotiations further strengthened Indonesia's claim to a much bigger area of the Timor Sea than Australia had been willing to acknowledge. The United Nations' Convention on the Law of the Sea 1982 went further than the 1958 convention by codifying for the first time the right of all states to claim an Exclusive Economic Zone (EEZ) stretching out for 200 nautical miles, and it strongly reaffirmed the concept of applying an equidistance line to resolving overlapping claims. The right to claim a continental shelf was not absolute when there was an opposite or adjacent state that also had a claim in that area. This occurred when two countries were less than 400 nautical miles apart. The aim of these agreements was to achieve an 'equitable solution' to competing claims, as outlined in Article 74(1).[5]

The Australian government signed this agreement on 10 December 1982, but it did not ratify it until twelve years later, well after the Timor Gap negotiations with Indonesia were bedded down. Ratifying it during the course of the negotiations would most likely have weakened Australia's position. But Indonesia, since its claim was buttressed by the convention, ratified it in 1986. Australia continued to assert that it was entitled to claim the seabed to the deepest point of the Timor Trough even though international law had swung decisively in favour of a median line. Australia's negotiating team knew that their claim to a continental shelf was being eroded during the course of the negotiations. 'We knew all along that the legal argument was shifting away from continental shelf to equidistance. Our legal approach was the sooner we get this sown up the better,' says Willheim,[6] who at the time was a general counsel—a specialist legal adviser—for international law in the Attorney-General's Department.

The irreconcilable positions of the two countries were outlined in a 19 June 1984 submission[7] from DFA to Foreign Minister Bill Hayden: 'The preferred Indonesian position is to have a median-line closure of the Gap which would result in a "bite" in the boundary south of East Timor. The preferred Australian position to date has been straight-line closure.' DFA's concern was not that the 'bite' would create an inelegant, tooth-shaped boundary, but would mean the loss of a potentially enormous resource known as the Kelp Prospect. The department said this prospect could have between 1 and 6 billion barrels of oil, and 3 to 17 trillion cubic feet of natural gas, potentially making it Australia's biggest petroleum resource zone. 'Our room to manoeuvre is limited by the fact that a boundary much south of a straight-line closure could lose us the Kelp Prospect,' DFA said.

In negotiations in 1984 DFA for the first time proposed a small joint development zone (JDZ) in the Timor Gap, but Indonesia rejected this proposal because it was denied a slice of the Kelp Prospect. DFA said: 'The Indonesian delegation reacted adversely to the Australian suggestion on where the JDZ might go—i.e., [a] small area straddling the gap between the existing lines.'

The estimates in the DFA submission are similar to a 1977 study by the French company Elf Aquitaine which said that the Kelp Prospect might contain a mammoth 7 billion barrels of crude oil, 1.1 billion barrels of light oil and 5.5 trillion cubic feet of gas.[8] This meant that Kelp could hold more than twice the total reserves of Bass Strait, which at the time was Australia's biggest oil province.

In 1985 a landmark decision by the International Court of Justice in the case between Libya and Malta strengthened even further Indonesia's position in the negotiations. The facts were very similar to those of the Timor Sea—an overlap between the claims of an island and a mainland. In the judgment, the ICJ ignored the shape of the seabed. It said 'there is no reason to ascribe any role to geological or geophysical factors' when such an overlap occurred. This decision confirmed that the median line was the default boundary for resolving overlapping claims; it dismissed the significance of natural features in maritime boundary agreements. The judgment rejected the notion that Libya's far greater landmass was a relevant consideration in determining the outcome. The entitlement to a continental shelf was the same for an island as for a mainland. The Libya–Malta case established the primacy of 'the distance criterion', making the shape of the seabed all but irrelevant.[9]

In the same year, the Indonesian foreign minister, Professor Mochtar, visited Australia and began discussions concerning a massive resource sharing area that fully reflected Indonesia's and Australia's 200-nautical-mile entitlements, thereby encompassing the Kelp Prospect. Negotiations inched forward. Three years later, the Australian foreign minister, Bill Hayden, visited Jakarta to meet Professor Mochtar, just before the indefatigable Ali Alatas became the new foreign minister. At this meeting Hayden put forward DFA's detailed proposal for a large joint development area that would give Indonesia a share in the Kelp Prospect. This provided the impetus to secure a deal.

In negotiations in Jakarta in late 1988, the two sides agreed to create a Zone of Cooperation that had a southern boundary defined by Indonesia's 200-nautical-mile claim, while the northern boundary went beyond Australia's 200-nautical-mile claim and was defined by the Timor Trough. The lateral (vertical) boundaries lines were defined by the unmovable end points of the 1972 treaty.

The treaty created three areas as shown by Map 4. In the largest area, Area A, the government revenue would be shared fifty-fifty between the two countries. The southern edge of Area A was the median line. Area B extended from the median line to approximately the end of Indonesia's 200-nautical-mile claim, with revenue to be shared 90 per cent to Australia and 10 per cent to Indonesia. The northern zone, Area C, stretched to the 1500-metre depth of the Timor Trough, with 90 per cent of the revenue to go to Indonesia and 10 per cent to Australia. The negotiators had created a mammoth 61 000-square-kilometre diplomatic compromise. Under international law, Indonesia had a strong claim to 100 per cent of Area A, the largest and most prospective part of the Treaty area, but this was a 'package deal'. Indonesia had to compensate Australia for recognising its occupation of East Timor.

In a macabre twist, the Zone of Cooperation closely resembled the shape of a coffin. Given the bloodshed in East Timor before and during the negotiations, the negotiators had created possibly the worst imaginable symbol for any international agreement. It was a PR disaster waiting to happen. The shape was completely accidental, says Willheim; it was the work of 'mapping technicians'. For others the coffin shape became symbolic of what occurred in East Timor: the massive death toll that mounted under a relentless military campaign, together with the forced relocation of the population away from the resistance army and their land and food supply. Amnesty International estimated that up to half the population was relocated into 'concentration' zones. While the negotiations were taking place, thousands of Timorese were forced to take part in a 'fence of legs' operation, marching at gunpoint in an unbroken line from one end of the island to the other in an attempt to round up the FALINTIL resistance army.

* * *

One year later, on 27 October 1989, a new, youthful and energetic foreign minister, Gareth Evans, formally announced that Australia and Indonesia had settled on the Timor Gap Treaty.[10] It was the ultimate in diplomatic comprises; 'a triumph for creative solutions to diplomatic impasses,' Evans said.[11]

In the hype that followed the signing of this agreement, reports declared that Australia was on the cusp of an oil bonanza. 'Timor Sea may make Darwin our Dallas', screamed the *Australian* in April 1989. Paul Keating was treasurer at the time of the signing, but he had forthright views on the primacy of good relations with Indonesia and he saw the treaty as the cornerstone of the relationship. As prime minister from 1991–96 he made more visits to Jakarta than the combined total of all previous prime ministers since the Second World War. He was sensitive about continued accusations that 'Australian policy was somehow shaped by Australian economic interests in the oil in the Timor Gap', and strongly rejected this notion. But he later admitted that Indonesian policy in East Timor was marked by 'insensitivity, brutality and incompetence', that the military regime developed 'significant and profitable economic interests in the province', and that not all the development funds went to the people who were destined to receive them. But he was adamant that Australia would maintain an Indonesia-first policy, notwithstanding some deference to human rights concerns. 'I had few conversations with Indonesian leaders in which I did not raise Timor or Irian Jaya, but I was not prepared to make the whole of our complex relationship with 210 million people subject to this one issue.'[12]

Critics claimed that the treaty was 'illegal' because Australia had an obligation not to recognise Indonesian sovereignty in East Timor. Australia is a signatory to two unanimously adopted resolutions of the UN General Assembly: the 1970 Declaration on Principles of International Law Concerning Friendly Relations and Co-operation among States, and the 1974 Resolution on Definition of Aggression. The 1970 declaration provides that: 'The territory of a state shall not be the object of acquisition by another state resulting from the threat or use of force. No territorial acquisition resulting from the threat or use of force shall be recognised as legal.' The 1974 resolution states that 'no territorial acquisition or special advantage resulting from aggression shall be recognised as lawful'.[13]

Professor Roger Clark, a member of the UN Committee on Crime Prevention and Control at the time the Timor Gap Treaty was signed, said the treaty was 'the same as acquiring stuff from a thief. The fact is that [Australia and Indonesia] have neither historical, nor legal, nor moral claim to East Timor and its resources.'[14] Clark wrote that the UN resolutions carry moral or even mandatory legal obligations.[15] Gareth Evans, however, told parliament that the Friendly Relations declaration had long been 'hotly contested':

> We have taken a view since 1979 that whatever the unhappy circumstances and indeed, possible illegality, surrounding Indonesia's acquisition of East Timor in the mid–1970s, Indonesian sovereignty over that territory should be accepted not only on a de factor [sic] but on a *de jure* basis.[16]

Evans' political career in Australia nosedived after Labor lost office in 1996 and he spent three unhappy and hapless years as deputy Opposition leader and treasury spokesman. In a television interview in that year he confessed to suffering from 'relevance deprivation'. He now heads the International Crisis Group, an NGO dedicated to preventing conflict that works to uphold the spirit of these UN resolutions.

* * *

The Timor Gap Treaty had to be ratified by the parliaments of both countries and did not enter into force for another 14 months, on 9 February 1991. During a visit to Indonesia at this time to finalise the treaty, Gareth Evans declared that Indonesia had made vast improvements in East Timor: 'The truth of the matter is that the human rights situation [in East Timor] has, in our judgement, conspicuously improved, particularly under the present military arrangements,' he said.[17] Nine months later the world saw the reality of the human rights situation in East Timor when British filmmaker Max Stahl captured the Indonesian military's slaughter of young Timorese people as they took part in a funeral procession at the Santa Cruz cemetery on the outskirts of Dili. Even in the wake of this appalling incident, Evans defended Indonesia's conduct in East Timor. The massacre, he told the media, was the 'product of aberrant behaviour by a sub-group within the country'. Many observers at the time, even his authorised biographer, argued otherwise, suggesting it was 'consistent with a long-standing pattern of behaviour by the Indonesian military'.[18]

After ratification, the new Australia–Indonesia Joint Authority issued the first batch of exploration licences, and Australia's biggest resource company, BHP Ltd, picked up two of the best prospects. In 1994 it struck oil and the following year it found a much bigger oil and gas field. The first oilfield, which it named Elang Kakatua (Elang for the Indonesian eagle, and Kakatua for the Australian cockatoo), turned out to have relatively small reserves of around 30 million barrels of oil. The larger oil and gas field, named Bayu-Undan (wind pelican), turned out to have 500 million barrels of light oil and 4 trillion cubic feet of gas, worth more than US$33 billion at conservative oil forward prices derived from the US Department of Energy.[19]

Portugal, which had retained some interest in the fate of the Timorese since 1975, lodged a challenge to the validity of the Timor Gap Treaty at the International Court of Justice (ICJ) in 1991, with the case being heard in January 1995. The potential oil wealth may have also motivated Portugal to mount the case. In preparing for the case, Australia's legal team drew on the best expertise they could find, travelling to Cambridge University where they went over legal precedents with Professor James Crawford, an eminent Australian academic who taught at Jesus College.[20]

In its submission, Portugal argued that Australia had infringed upon the right of the East Timorese to self-determination. Australia said in its counter-memorial to Portugal that it negotiated with Indonesia to close the Timor Gap for three reasons. It did not have an obligation of 'non-recognition' of the Indonesian occupation; Indonesia's effective occupation of East Timor meant that Australia had no other state to negotiate with; and the negotiations represented an exercise on the part of Australia of its rights under international law.[21] In its decision handed down in July 1995, the ICJ reaffirmed that East Timor remained a non-self-governing territory, but it ruled that it did not have jurisdiction, partly because Indonesia was not a party to the proceedings.[22]

Gareth Evans welcomed the fourteen to two decision as a reaffirmation of Australia's claim in the Timor Sea: 'It confirms our view that the Timor Gap Treaty is a responsible and proper framework under which Australia can secure access to its own resources in an area which we have always claimed as Australia's.'[23]

All seemed lost to most observers, although the Timorese remained optimistic that they would get their country back. In 1997 José Ramos-Horta, then vice president of the umbrella resistance organisation, *Conselho Nacional Resistência Maubere* (CNRM) and a roving international lobbyist, told the National Press Club in Canberra that East Timor would be free once President Soeharto had moved on. Within less than a year, Soeharto had departed and East Timor's independence cause began to stir. The first people whose antennae sensed the looming new order were the oil company executives.

* * *

Three months later, the leader of East Timor's resistance army who was sitting in a cell in Jakarta's Cipinang prison where he had been incarcerated for six years, received a visitor.

On most days he would paint or write poetry in his cell, but on this Sunday morning in mid-August 1998, Kay Rala Xanana Gusmão, born José Alexandre Gusmão in June 1946, received a representative from a big resource company who wanted to meet with him privately. Companies that had invested a total of more than US$700 million into Timor Sea oil and gas exploration and development wanted to protect their investments. The corporate world had already begun positioning itself for the possibility of dramatic regime change.

The visitor's name was Peter Cockcroft, a crusty Australian oilman who had lived in Asia for decades, working as a petroleum geologist. This Indonesia manager for BHP Petroleum Ltd wore a red floral shirt unbuttoned halfway but, despite the breezy appearance, was a serious operator. He had employed a succession of former DFAT officials in his Jakarta office, including one who had been an ASIS spy.

Although Cockcroft came to talk business, he brought with him a strong personal interest in East Timor, having first visited the country as a high school student in 1966. His father, John, had served briefly in East Timor during the Second World War as part of Z-Force, an elite commando unit, and he had returned with his son to write a book about Portuguese Timor.[24] The family connection could be traced back even further. From the late 1920s Cockcroft's grandfather had shipped cattle to the open pastures in the east of the country near Com for the British beef baron Lord Vesty. Peter Cockcroft also saw East Timor during the Indonesian years when he worked for the national oil company Pertamina.

In the hour-long meeting Cockcroft sought an assurance from Gusmão that rights awarded to petroleum companies under the Timor Gap Treaty would be honoured by a newly independent East Timor. Only a month earlier production had started at BHP's Elang Kakatua field in Area A of the treaty area, and plans were afoot for the development of the much bigger Bayu-Undan oil and gas field.

During the meeting, which was conducted in Portuguese and English, Gusmão enquired about the potential oil wealth of the

Timor Sea. Cockcroft told him that he thought that it was a moderately rich oil province, though nothing like the Middle East. But in giving this assessment Cockcroft asked Gusmão not to trust him. He was, after all, both an oil company executive and an Australian, he joked, but he would send him an independent study. Gusmão warmed to Cockcroft after he made this comment, saying that all his other visitors told him that they could be trusted.

Gusmão had another visitor that day, his future wife Kirsty, and there was time to snap a couple of photographs. Cockcroft walked away with a written assurance which had already been typed out, and a gift from Gusmão—a tall red rose in a marble vase. 'We encourage them to stay on, looking to help the Timorese with the oil until a resolution is reached,' Gusmão said after the meeting. The visit was promptly leaked to the media by an Australian diplomat who declared enthusiastically that East Timor, should it become independent, would honour 'during an interim period' the Timor Gap arrangements.[25] Cockcroft had not obtained permission from head office in Melbourne to make the impromptu visit. A Timorese contact had told him the previous day that the meeting could take place, and as it was the weekend Cockcroft accepted this rare opportunity to meet the Nelson Mandela of Asia. The reports of the meeting in the media were hugely problematic for the Big Australian's relationship with the Jakarta regime; the visit had bestowed legitimacy on East Timor's independence struggle. Following the visit BHP relocated Cockcroft to India and then the following year terminated his contract.

Eight months after this meeting BHP decided to bail out of Bayu-Undan. The company had been unable to reach an agreement with a joint venture partner, Houston-based Phillips Petroleum, on how to develop the field. Phillips had wanted to charge a hefty premium for using its technology to process the gas (and it succeeded in selling the technology to other partners when it took over the project). The letter from Gusmão helped BHP to offload its 42 per cent stake to Phillips in April 1999. It threw in Elang Kakatua and booked a $110 million profit on the deal.[26]

In February the following year Foreign Minister Alexander Downer met with the famous warrior poet and later claimed to have obtained a much stronger assurance. 'Mr Gusmão told me they would honour the Timor Gap treaty and that they were happy to share on an equitable basis with Australia resources that were between East Timor and Australia,' Downer said after their meeting in Jakarta.[27] Downer's comments indicated that he believed East Timor would be happy to continue the *terms* of the Timor Gap Treaty, even though under international law it might be entitled to a much bigger share than had been negotiated by Indonesia under the 'resources-for-recognition' package deal.

This assurance was exactly what Australia wanted in the event of a most undesirable outcome—East Timor becoming independent. Downer wanted a neat and tidy continuation of the arrangements that had been painstakingly negotiated with Indonesia over a period of ten years. The last thing he wanted was to have to start all over again.

These meetings were the first in a series of overtures made by western governments and companies as a UN-administered ballot for East Timor to choose between independence or increased autonomy with Indonesia came onto the horizon. For the Timorese their independence cause was simply about freedom: exercising their right to self-determination and ending 24 years of terror. For the oil industry and the Australian government, East Timor's passage to independence would be inextricably linked with Timor Sea oil.

Since 1983 diplomatic negotiations between Indonesia and Portugal under the auspices of the UN secretary-general had gone nowhere. The breakthrough came in December 1998 when Prime Minister John Howard wrote to President Habibie and proposed that his Indonesian counterpart move towards giving the people of East Timor an act of self-determination. Howard was responding to political pressure at home. In January 1998 the Labor Opposition had switched its policy on East Timor back to support for an act of self-determination, a shift single-handedly pushed through by foreign affairs spokesman Laurie Brereton, the influential power-broker in the Labor Party's predominantly Catholic, right-wing faction. His determination to change the Labor platform followed a meeting with UN Secretary-General Kofi Annan shortly after he became spokesman, and some persuasive lobbying by Catholic nuns which pricked the conscience of the convent-educated Brereton.

Howard stated in his letter to Habibie that the Australian government's preference remained keeping East Timor as part of Indonesia, and he proposed a lengthy period of autonomy followed by an act of self-determination. The model that Howard had in mind was the Matignon Accords in New Caledonia, which had deferred a decision for a decade and had then led to support for continued ties with France. In fact Howard was not advocating self-determination at all—he was simply trying to buy time—but the letter prompted a volatile reaction from the president. Habibie, an erratic and idiosyncratic successor to President Soeharto, was also operating in a rapidly changing political environment as civil rights groups pushed for a full transition to democracy. East Timor had been a source of immense international embarrassment to Indonesia, and had singularly overshadowed the great strides it had made in improving the lives of its people since independence. East Timor was a huge financial drain on Indonesia, he reasoned, and if the Timorese wanted independence then they could have it right away. As a result, on 5 May 1999, Portugal and Indonesia signed a treaty granting that a popular consultation would take place on 30 August 1999.

One critical element missing from this accord was security. DFAT had actually lobbied against a US proposal to put armed UN peacekeepers on the ground before the ballot. On 22 February 1999 US Assistant Secretary of State Stanley Roth met with DFAT secretary Ashton Calvert in Washington. A transcript of the conversation reveals that Roth pressed for a 'full-scale peacekeeping operation' and warned that without it East Timor would 'collapse'. Roth described as 'defeatist' Australia's position, as put by Calvert, which opposed having any UN peacekeepers. Calvert argued that the

Timorese had to 'sort themselves out' and he wanted to 'dispel the idea that the UN was going to solve all their problems'.[28] Australia's views on its immediate region carry a lot of weight, and on this occasion they prevailed. Anticipating the likely bloodshed after the ballot, the Australian government's only post-ballot plan, called 'Operation Spitfire', involved the evacuation of Australian personnel. Planning for Operation Spitfire began on 11 May 1999.[29]

On the polling day, 30 August, the East Timorese put red and white Indonesian flags outside their homes but in the polling booths 78.5 per cent of them rejected Jakarta's offer of special autonomy—effectively a vote for independence. Immediately after the vote was announced an orchestrated campaign of killing and destruction by Indonesian-backed militias got underway, claiming the lives of an estimated 1500 people.

The Australian government was urged to intervene by ordinary people who bombarded the offices of federal politicians with phone calls and faxes. Howard sensed the national mood and responded accordingly. Over several days in early September he lobbied international leaders to support UN intervention. Fortuitously, many world leaders had been brought together by the APEC meeting in Auckland, while Howard also telephoned others in the middle of the night, including US President Bill Clinton. The United States was reluctant to get involved after making a botched intervention in Somalia. After sixteen days of militia violence an Australian-led, UN sanctioned force, InterFET, landed in Dili on 20 September. When the Australians landed they witnessed the mass exodus of the Javanese empire in East Timor. Indonesian soldiers and civilians alike took with them everything they could possibly remove, including light bulbs, while systematically targeting Indonesian-built property as they burnt what could not be taken.

Indonesia's exit from East Timor was to be complete, even when it came to the oil and gas resources that had taken a decade of negotiations to secure. On 17 November 1999 the Indonesian government informed Australia that it was withdrawing from the

Timor Gap Treaty. Downer told the Australian parliament of Indonesia's decision to withdraw on 6 December. The treaty had had a shelf life of just over eight years; it had begun producing only a trickle of revenue before its termination. The governments of Indonesia and Australia each received US$4.45 million in royalties from the Elang Kakatua field.[30] That was all. This probably didn't cover the cost of airfares and hotels in all those years of negotiating.

The Kelp Prospect had come to nothing. Woodside drilled one well in 1994 to a depth of 2700 metres and declared it a 'dry hole'. Then in 1998 a consortium led by Mobil spent US$60 million drilling a well that went down to 5000 metres and produced a modest flow of gas—12 million cubic feet per day. This very marginal result remains uneconomic even with the recent high prices for hydrocarbons.[31] Geologists still remain hopeful and consider Kelp to be a 'very interesting' structure with geological features similar to those found in the Middle East. But for the creators of this coffin-shaped zone, the spoils proved very disappointing indeed.

4 THE GET-OUT-OF-GAOL CARD

> *'Before playing this card, Potts conjectured that the Australian Government would make a very generous and public offer to East Timor and also release the negotiating history on this issue.'*
> Minutes of a meeting between Australian and UNTAET officials, 24 November 2000

In January 2000 East Timor's capital, Dili, was swarming with military personnel and equipment, but it was almost completely devoid of locals. Most Timorese were too afraid to return home and remained camped in the mountains where they had fled. As few buildings of any significance were left standing, a cruise ship, the *Olympia*, had been brought to Dili harbour to provide temporary accommodation for the growing number of UN officials arriving to establish a civil administration.

Amid the rubble and chaos a delegation of Australian officials flew into Dili for an important mission. They came with the objective of convincing the Timorese leadership that they should accept in full the treaty that the Australian government had spent ten years negotiating with Indonesia. This followed Alexander Downer's belief that the Timorese would 'honour' the Timor Gap Treaty, even though the agreement was the result of the unlawful occupation of their country.

The get-out-of-gaol card

Led by veteran diplomat Michael Potts, the delegation of officials from DFAT and the attorney-general's and industry departments booked a conference room on the *Olympia*. This was probably the only place in Dili at the time with the facilities to hold such a meeting. In the heat and humidity of Dili's wet season, the red-faced and bespectacled Potts looked very much a reluctant visitor, like the hot and bothered colonial administrator from a bygone era. With the aid of laptops and a projected Powerpoint presentation, Potts and his team ran through the details of the Timor Gap Treaty in deadpan, humourless style. They urged the Timorese to substitute the name Indonesia with that of East Timor. In the audience was Marí Alkatiri, who as secretary general of FRETILIN had held senior positions in the *Conselho Nacional da Resisência Timorense* (CNRT, the umbrella independence council), including being in charge of Timor Sea affairs. He had returned from Mozambique to take up in July that year a cabinet position in the UN Transitional Administration East Timor (UNTAET). José Ramos-Horta, who was vice president of CNRT also attended.

At one point during the presentation, a gruff, chain-smoking international lawyer working for the UN, Miguel Galvão-Teles, stood up and told the delegation that they had omitted to explain how unfavourable the Timor Gap Treaty was when compared to East Timor's entitlement under international law. East Timor would be short-changed by signing this treaty, affording it a miserable 20 per cent share of the known resources on its side of the Timor Sea.

Even more disturbing were the economic implications of this proposal. The Australian government's offer would have set up East Timor as a beggar state upon becoming independent. Oil prices at the time were hovering around US$20 a barrel; the country's only significant source of revenue for the next 20 years would have amounted to around US$50 million a year or about US$50 per head of population. East Timor's leadership rejected Australia's proposal. As well as considering the offer inferior, they had decided that the new country would not be a 'successor' state—it would not inherit Indonesia's legal obligations.

Shortly after this meeting the former US ambassador Peter Galbraith arrived in Dili to take up the position of Minister for Political Affairs and the Timor Sea in the UNTAET administration. Galbraith, who followed the US tradition of retaining the title of 'Ambassador', came from one of liberal America's royal families. He was the son of the iconic economist, the late John Kenneth Galbraith, who served as President John F. Kennedy's ambassador to India, and then as an economic adviser to President Lyndon B. Johnson. Galbraith junior had spent most of his career serving the powerful US Senate Committee on Foreign Relations until President Clinton appointed him ambassador to Croatia in 1993, a position he held for five years. There he gained a reputation as an effective negotiator by bringing together the warring factions of former Yugoslavia. Together with the UN, Galbraith mediated the Erdut Agreement that ended the war by providing for peaceful reintegration of Serb-held Eastern Slavonia into Croatia. In this role, Galbraith emerged as an unconventional practitioner of diplomacy. Before bringing peace, he persuaded President Clinton in 1994 to allow Iranian arms to be transhipped through Croatia to aid Bosnian Muslims, thus contravening a UN embargo.[1]

The euphemism 'larger than life' does not do justice to this proud and loud American from central casting. He was emboldened by the slogan, written in meticulous red and blue cross-stitch, which was proudly hung above a large oak bookcase in an elegant sitting room in his childhood home in Cambridge, Massachusetts: 'Galbraith's First Law—Modesty is a vastly over-rated virtue'.[2] Even Americans who worked with 'Ambassador Galbraith' found his American-ness hard to take. During a meeting on permanent boundaries in 2004, Galbraith was walking through a harbourside park in Darwin with two colleagues, one of whom was Dominic Puthucheary, a septuagenarian Indian-Malaysian lawyer. Puthucheary found himself being pushed off the path by Galbraith as they walked and he asked Galbraith in a lilting voice why he was doing this, to which Galbraith barked back: 'Because I'm American!'[3]

This early fifties, high-profile American brought an immense capacity for work, a big-picture intellect and gravitas to East Timor's case. And with an aristocratic air, he also brought boundless confidence and attitude. His 2006 book on Iraq featured no fewer than six photographs of himself during his visits to that country.[4] Although he spent his career in the diplomatic world he must have missed the classes on etiquette. His abrasive style infuriated his Australian opponents to the point where they sought to remove him from his tenured position with the US government's National War College in Washington, and from his position with UNTAET. The Australian ambassador in Washington, Michael Thawley, a former foreign affairs adviser to Prime Minister John Howard, told Australian lawyer Jonathan Morrow at a social gathering in Washington that he had spent nearly all of 2000 and 2001 'trying to get rid of Galbraith'.

Galbraith was just a few years younger than the Timorese leadership, and he soon gained their respect. He and Alkatiri were both passionate about conservation and the environment. The drawing up of a list of protected places in East Timor, which became a UNTAET regulation, was one of Galbraith's proudest achievements during his time in East Timor. Both Alkatiri and Galbraith had a legal background, and so the two turned their attention to filling the legal vacuum in the Timor Sea. Under the direction of the late Sergio Vieira de Mello, the Special Representative of the Secretary-General (SRSG) in East Timor, the United Nations became directly involved in negotiating a treaty on behalf of East Timor. In due course, as the negotiations intensified, the UN's role would become a source of great displeasure for the Australian government, which made numerous formal and informal complaints about the UN's participation in these negotiations. It claimed that the UN was taking a partisan position against one of its member states.[5]

At the time of Galbraith's arrival international financial donors realised that the transitional government was in desperate need of a body of expert advisers to deal with the demands of imminent negotiations with Australia. Millissa Day, an official with the US government's development agency, USAID, began funding a handful of international consultants to work on the negotiations with money from the agency's ad hoc, 'small grants' fund. These well-remunerated advisers were joined by Timorese civil servants who earned around US$200 a month. Together they worked out of a single room in the west wing of the *Palácio do Governo*, which became known as the Timor Sea Office. USAID's funding ceased in 2003, perhaps reflecting the change of government in the United States, but other donors joined in. Major international aid organisations funded experts based in Dili and around the world, as did the governments of Norway and Portgual. The Timor Sea Office managed a diverse team made up of more than 10 Timorese civil servants and international advisers throughout the negotiations.

Some of the advisers who worked for East Timor were international experts in their field, but there was a preponderance of late-twenties, early thirties lawyers who landed some of the many adviser jobs on offer in East Timor at the time. Some of these young guns were out to prove themselves, and this infuriated Australia's team of career professionals. Downer was known to particularly dislike Jonathan Morrow, a fiery, red-head Australian lawyer who had arrived in East Timor on a Hercules aircraft in December 1999 as a 29-year-old PhD graduate and former judge's associate. 'That Morrow is very aggressive—well he has met his match with me,' Downer told Alkatiri at a meeting in November 2002. Downer was also incensed at having to encounter some of the righteous North American liberals from Ivy League universities on East Timor's negotiating team, particularly one woman who constantly scowled at him from across the negotiating table.

The preliminary negotiations resulted in an agreement by Exchange of Notes on 10 February 2000, which provided for the continuation of the *terms* of the Timor Gap Treaty. The illegal treaty itself was not continued. East Timor would not become a successor state of Indonesia; it would not accept the legal obligations of its

The get-out-of-gaol card

former occupier. A new treaty would have to be negotiated. In the interim, this agreement said that UN-administered East Timor and Australia would continue to share the central Area A of the former treaty on the same fifty-fifty basis. The Exchange of Notes was consistent with an earlier commitment to Phillips Petroleum, the major shareholder in Bayu-Undan, signed by the CNRT leadership on 20 October 1999 to make the financial terms for Bayu-Undan 'no more onerous' than those under the former Timor Gap Treaty. Phillips went on to buy a fleet of 13 Toyota SUVs for the East Timor Development Agency (ETDA) to assist with the agricultural development of Timor-Leste, although all of the vehicles soon fell into the hands of senior members of CNRT and FRETILIN, and eventually government ministers. It also made a substantial financial contribution to the Independence Day celebrations in May 2002. Despite its investment in East Timor the company refused to open an office in the country, managing its Timor Sea interests from offices in Darwin and Perth. And it employed only a token number of Timorese on the Bayu-Undan project, while engaging many more Filipinos and Indonesians. Phillips merged with Conoco Inc. to become ConocoPhillips in August 2002.

The following month UNTAET informed the Australian government that when independence occurred there would be no arrangement for oil and gas development in the Timor Sea, and that it was prepared to begin negotiations for a post-independence treaty. Ramos-Horta made clear in May 2000 that East Timor was not going to settle for the 50 per cent share of resources that Indonesia had accepted. East Timor's leadership became confident that nearly all the resources in the Timor Sea should belong to their country. Ramos-Horta quoted the figure of 90 per cent.[6]

When talks began in October 2000 between Australia and UNTAET, the two sides decided on a fast-track process to draw up a new treaty. While Australia wanted to give certainty to the companies involved, Galbraith had an eye on his legacy. He was due to leave East Timor by mid-2001 and wanted the new treaty in the bag by that time, although he claimed that the real urgency stemmed from the fact that the Timorese members of the UNTAET Cabinet would have to begin campaigning for the Constituent Assembly elections at that same time.

But by April 2001, the two parties were still far apart. The Australian negotiators were sticking to a framework that closely resembled the Timor Gap Treaty. They were offering 50 per cent of the former Area A, and they wanted equal representation and a veto on the joint authority that regulated all commercial activity in the area to be covered by the treaty. For Australia, retaining control over development was more important than the amount of revenue. This latter agenda reflected the nature of the petroleum industry in which every aspect of a project is regulated. Australia did not want to cede regulatory control to a new developing country that might impose an onerous tax burden on Australian resource companies, or insist on development plans like building pipelines to East Timor rather than to Australia. The Australian negotiators insisted that the new treaty should issue production sharing contracts to companies using the same taxation terms as the former treaty, and these included a generous 'uplift' on development costs of 127 per cent. This was the formula by which companies were able to inflate and then depreciate their development costs before tax.

Ahead of the April meeting Galbraith gave some indication of the stance East Timor was preparing to take in the negotiations:

> Marí Alkatiri has . . . asked me to remind you that the Timorese are a patient people, and, when it comes to their rights, a very determined people. For 24 years, they fought the world's fourth largest country. And, without a treaty based on international law, the East Timorese are prepared to wait patiently for their rights.[7]

East Timor pushed for up to 100 per cent of a wider area that would include the entire Greater Sunrise field and the BCL fields, together with regulatory control of the joint authority reflecting this higher revenue share. It raised concerns about the 127 per cent uplift, saying this provided the wrong incentive to companies; it provided every incentive to inflate development costs and in turn reduce the government tax take. Galbraith told the meeting that Alkatiri was alarmed by the implications of the uplift and was prepared to abolish the concession and 'repudiate' the commitment given to Phillips Petroleum of making taxation 'no more onerous' than the Timor Gap Treaty. The Australians argued that the uplift was just one element of the taxation package, and could not be looked at in isolation. The meeting ended with no progress on the three major agenda items.

* * *

In late June 2001 East Timor's negotiating team was farewelled by CNRT President Xanana Gusmão at Dili airport who told them to hold out for all of the disputed resources. 'East Timor is legally entitled to all the oil and gas resources of the Timor Gap. We will make compromises . . . but we will not accept an agreement at any price,' he said. The delegation landed in Canberra, Australia's federal capital, in the middle of a bitterly cold winter. Parliament had just risen for the long winter recess, and Alexander Downer and his colleagues, the treasurer, Peter Costello, and the industry minister, Nick Minchin, were eager to return to their electorates. East Timor would keep them waiting.

The East Timor delegation walked into a conference room in Parliament House and encountered a sea of grey, black and navy blue suits. There were up to 40 advisers in the room at any one time from departments all over Canberra. On the other side of the table was a team of just seven people, led by Marí Alkatiri and José Ramos-Horta. While attending the meeting Jonathan Morrow came to think that Australia lacked a coherent strategy to deal with this issue, and with the Howard government heading to the 2001 'boat people' election, there was no sense that Australia should conduct a negotiation with this new country in a way that was respectful, reasonable and amicable. This was hardline 'national interest' foreign policy at work. There was no room for a big picture perspective on the new country's future and Australia's reputation as an affluent, first-world nation. After helping to liberate the Timorese the Australian government was now out to plunder its resources, Morrow thought at the time. He later said: 'As an Australian citizen I was appalled by my country's leadership and their effort to stick their snouts in the trough of this country we'd liberated. They were talking about Australia's generosity. As welcome as InterFET was, it's not a gift when there's a heavy price attached.'[8]

Nevertheless the Timorese responded with equal toughness, and the Australian side just did not know how to deal with this. The Australians thought that after having 'created' East Timor the leader of this micro-state would be compliant, malleable and grateful. Alkatiri, who was about to become chief minister of UNTAET and would become prime minister of the new country, was not what they had expected. Nor was Galbraith, undoubtedly the most undiplomatic diplomat they had ever encountered.

Over the course of two days, East Timor continued to insist on a 90 per cent share of a wider treaty area to encompass Greater Sunrise and the BCL fields. The meeting was deadlocked. Ramos-Horta thought Galbraith had gone over the top as he mocked and taunted the Australian negotiators, and he passed a note to Alkatiri: 'Marí, now is the time for *you* to show leadership.'

At around this time, Downer said he had to leave the meeting and he asked Ramos-Horta to join him. In the corridor outside, Downer made an offer that clinched the deal. Australia would agree to a 90 per cent ownership of the petroleum resources by East Timor, but this would only apply to the same area as Area A of the former Timor Gap Treaty, which would later be called the Joint Petroleum Development Area (JPDA). This in turn meant that East Timor would get a mere 18 per cent of the revenue of the Greater Sunrise field. The conversation took no more than 10 minutes. Downer then came back into the meeting and reported on his agreement with Ramos-Horta, an announcement which greatly surprised some members of the East Timor delegation, including Alkatiri and Galbraith. Later that afternoon Downer invited Alkatiri, Ramos-Horta and Galbraith back to his office for a glass of champagne. There was a photographer on hand to capture the moment.

Despite failing to secure a wider area, East Timor succeeded in gaining considerable control over the regulation of oil company activities in the new JPDA. A Joint Commission comprising two Timorese and one Australian representative would govern the regulatory authority, with the executive director appointed by East Timor. But sitting above this was a ministerial council with equal representation which approved appointments to the Joint Commission. East Timor also succeeded in reducing the fixed rate of return guaranteed to onshore gas processing activities, a rate of return that means the governments, not the oil companies, bear the risk. For example, in times of low oil prices, East Timor's revenue would be cut in order to pay for the guaranteed 8 per cent after-tax return on a production facility located in Darwin and subject to Australian taxation. This was a significant burden to be placed on one of the poorest countries in the world, although it is a common feature in similar oil and gas projects worldwide. When prices rose, however, the revenue windfall would flow to East Timor. The 127 per cent uplift remained for existing contracts, but a new, much lower, depreciation system would be devised for future contracts.

The following month, on 5 July 2001, the two parties signed the Timor Sea Arrangement in Dili. This agreement would become the Timor Sea Treaty upon East Timor's becoming independent. Alkatiri signed on behalf of East Timor and as chief minister of UNTAET, and Alexander Downer signed on behalf of Australia. Xanana Gusmão and Sergio Vieira de Mello were on hand to witness the signing. 'We decided we'd give them 90 per cent on the basis of generosity,' Downer said at the signing. He was in a paternalistic mood as he played with Gusmão's baby boy, Alexandré. Downer thought the young lad might have been named after him, until he was told of Gusmão's original Christian name. Nonetheless Downer opened a bottle of Croser champagne from a famous winery in the Adelaide hills.[9]

Many politicians and community leaders in East Timor were unhappy with the outcome and, believing their leaders had sold out their sovereign rights in the Timor Sea, called on them not to sign the interim treaty. The deputy chief of the Timor Labor Party, Maria da Silva da Freitas, protested loudly at the press conference. Downer made light of it: 'We have lively negotiations, Australia and East Timor, because we're lively and interesting and entertaining people. So, we'll look forward to that.' Legal experts and ordinary Timorese feared that East Timor had paid a high price to secure 90 per cent of the area defined by the former Timor Gap Treaty. They believed that East Timor had risked surrendering its right to a much bigger claim as Australia might never agree to negotiate over the remainder of the disputed resources.

Greater Sunrise was by far the biggest prize in the Timor Sea. Based on the same conservative oil-price assumptions as used for Bayu-Undan, its 300 million barrels of oil and 7.7 trillion cubic feet of gas are valued at US$57 billion. The government revenue over the 40-year life of this field is estimated at US$24 billion, excluding tax from the onshore processing. In the agreement, East Timor had accepted a division of the Greater Sunrise field so that only 20.1 per cent was allocated to the treaty area, while 79.9 per cent went to the area outside, which was 'attributed to Australia'. (East Timor got 90 per cent of 20.1 per cent of the revenue; i.e., 18 per cent.) Annex E of the treaty stipulated that a separate Sunrise agreement would be negotiated because the field straddled the treaty area, as shown by Map 4. The parties agreed that the field would be 'unitised'—made one—and then divided up between them, thereby locking in an 82 per cent share to Australia.

East Timor's leadership believed the agreement did not constitute a permanent settlement; it retained the right to secure a bigger area of the Timor Sea under a permanent maritime boundary. The treaty was 'without prejudice' to permanent maritime boundaries, and it stated explicitly that it would cease to exist 30 years after entering into force, or if permanent maritime boundaries were agreed before that time. The 'without prejudice' clause meant that the treaty did not represent the limit of East Timor's maritime jurisdiction and rights. East Timor's claim to a maritime boundary extended beyond the treaty area.

Soon after this agreement was signed Australia moved to make it a permanent settlement by withdrawing from the jurisdiction of the International Court of Justice (ICJ) on maritime issues and the International Tribunal for the Law of the Sea (ITLOS).[10] Australia had been one of 61 countries that had submitted to the international umpire's decision on maritime disputes. It did so because Australia, with a vast maritime area, perceived this to be in its interest. Now, with East Timor about to become independent and challenge its control of Timor oil, the Australian government didn't like having an umpire.

Australia had made use of these procedures in the 1990s when it appealed to ITLOS to stop the illegal harvesting of bluefin tuna by Japanese trawlers. On 27 August 1999 ITLOS issued provisional measures to stop Japanese fishing boats from exploiting resources in violation of the rights of Australia and New Zealand under the United Nations Convention on the Law of the Sea (UNCLOS). The measures had the immediate effect of stopping the illegal fishing.[11] One legacy of the Timor Sea dispute for Australia is that it no longer has this legal recourse to prevent unlawful exploitation of its resources. In May 2005, for example, an Australian patrol boat encountered a Japanese trawler poaching the protected Patagonian tooth fish, but without the backing of ITLOS Australia's diplomatic protests were ignored.[12]

The Australian government had telegraphed its plan to East Timor to withdraw from ICJ and ITLOS at a meeting in Dili between UN and Australian officials in November 2000. Michael Potts, First Assistant Secretary, International Organisations and

Legal Division, spelled out how Australia was prepared to play very tough and avoid international law. The strategy is summarised in a confidential minute prepared by Jonathan Prentice, a political affairs officer who reported to Sergio Vieira de Mello.

First, Potts warned that if there was a threat of litigation from East Timor then Australia would not accept any temporary arrangement and, without such a legal framework, development would thus freeze. There was 'no attraction' in offering a temporary agreement that might be followed by litigation, he added. Potts then said Australia would face an 'image problem' if it agreed to acknowledge East Timor's claims outside Area A (which became the area of the new treaty). If Australia gave in to Timor's demand for 100 per cent of this area, plus a 'surcharge' for Sunrise and Laminaria, then this would 'look like a bribe or extortion'. East Timor's negotiating tactics were also undermining investor confidence, he said. One company had already signalled that it may go to Qatar, which would be a loss to East Timor and 'symptomatic' of the industry trend. Finally, Potts signalled that Australia was prepared to opt out of compulsory jurisdiction. This was Australia's 'get-out-of-gaol card', which it would be willing to use. This option had been included in a cabinet submission and no minister had objected to it, Potts revealed. He also signalled that the government would be able to deal with any negative domestic reaction by portraying East Timor as greedy.

'The more ambitious East Timor's claim, the easier it would be for the government to pursue this approach in terms of living down domestic controversy', wrote Prentice in his summary of the Potts argument.

Downer took up this option just two months before East Timor became independent. He released what seemed like an inconsequential administrative statement[13] about certain 'changes to the terms upon which Australia accepts international dispute resolution mechanisms, particularly as they apply to maritime boundaries'. The statement said these changes were directed at relations with seven countries that had maritime areas abutting Australia's. Importantly it said that 'negotiations are ongoing with New Zealand', but it did not refer to the negotiations over an interim agreement with East Timor. The Prentice minutes of that meeting held in November 2000, however, show that this decision was squarely aimed at East Timor.

Australia's official 'Declaration' to UNCLOS says the Australian government 'does not accept any of the procedures provided for in section 2 of Part XV with respect to disputes concerning the interpretation or application of articles... relating to sea boundary delimitations as well as those involving historic bays or titles'. The Declaration was signed in the name of Alexander John Gosse Downer on 21 March 2002,[14] and its announcement all but slipped under the radar of the Australian media. Hamish McDonald, who had reported from within East Timor in 1975 and in 1999, wrote a page-one story on the decision and also referred to a new legal opinion by Professor Vaughan Lowe, from Oxford University, who argued that East Timor could be entitled to 100 per cent of Sunrise and the BCL fields.[15]

Timorese-born Australian lawyer José Teixeira described the move as a 'bastard act' when asked by Alkatiri how East Timor should respond publicly. Alkatiri thought that inappropriate and they settled on calling it an 'unfriendly act'. East Timor would now have very little chance of legal recourse in the likely event that Australia proved intransigent in formal maritime boundary negotiations. The absence of any legal recourse would influence the tenor of subsequent negotiations over a permanent maritime boundary.

Australia's pre-emptive move intensified the pressure on the Timorese leadership as the May deadline for turning the Arrangement into the Timor Sea Treaty loomed. None of them had been involved in anything like this before. While they had experts such as Galbraith advising them, he did not have a background in this specialised area of maritime law. The Timorese were up against a team of professionals, many of whom had spent their careers negotiating agreements of this sort, and a government that was prepared to play very tough indeed.

Four days after the release of Downer's statement, Alkatiri flew to London to meet Professor Ian Brownlie QC, CBE, one of the world's most distinguished, and expensive, authorities in this field. Brownlie, who also taught public and international law at Oxford, had warned in a confidential opinion written in January 2002 that the joint development area created by the treaty might reinforce Australia's claims:

> The former Zone of Cooperation, now the JPDA, thus reflects the compromise solutions embodied in the original Timor Gap Treaty of 1989. As a consequence the structure of the JPDA may appear to give some degree of recognition to the Australian claim to the axis of the Timor Trough as the northern limit of Australian continental shelf rights.

He argued that East Timor would only be entitled to 100 per cent of Greater Sunrise under an 'optimistic application of legal criteria'. This involved giving a 50 per cent weighting to the Indonesian islands to the east of East Timor. The islands had the effect of swinging the lateral boundary towards East Timor and bisecting the Greater Sunrise field, whereas adjusting for their effect pushed the boundary east of Sunrise. Brownlie said there was little doubt that the horizontal boundary would be the existing median line; any adjustment northwards in favour of Australia would be very unlikely. After the meeting staff made several telephone calls to Brownlie to clarify his advice, further inflating the bill. In essence, Brownlie recommended that East Timor pursue a strategy that would allow it to 'keep its entitlements and keep the Treaty'. In other words, East Timor should go ahead with signing the treaty while very firmly setting out that it was without prejudice to a final agreement on maritime boundaries. At the same time, East Timor should publicly urge Australia to commence permanent boundary negotiations.

While Brownlie's opinion was private, Lowe wrote his for public consumption. It was commissioned by Oceanic Exploration as part of its belated attempt to have its vast 1974 concession recognised by the new government. Like Brownlie, Lowe warned that the treaty 'perpetuated' the area created by Area A, but he said that East Timor should not sign the new agreement:

> [It] therefore appears to be based upon the 1970s Australian claim to continental shelf rights over the 'natural prolongation' of the Australian shelf up to the Timor Trough. That claim is not consistent with current international law, and there is no obvious reason why any current arrangement should be based upon it.
>
> It would be very imprudent for East Timor to accept the proposed treaty if it wished to preserve a claim to a wider entitlement, particularly to any areas lying beyond the JPDA.[16]

East Timor might never be able to get more than 18 per cent of Sunrise even if it secured an agreement that swung the boundary to the east of Sunrise, Lowe warned; that is, the Sunrise agreement might override a maritime boundary covering a wider area.

The signing of the treaty had been scheduled to coincide with East Timor's birth as a new nation on 20 May 2002, the anniversary of the formation of the first political party in East Timor in 1974. As this date approached, Alkatiri was still undecided and continued pushing Australia to enter into formal maritime boundary negotiations. The decision to sign the treaty came in a very tense meeting held in his office in late April with Miguel Galvão-Teles and Galbraith. Convinced that his office was bugged by Australian intelligence, Alkatiri turned on Portuguese television and put the volume up high as the discussion proceeded. He then considered Brownlie's advice and comments by the other advisers, and decided that he would sign the treaty.

East Timor was about to become a new country in desperate need of the revenue that was expected to flow from the new Bayu-Undan development. Had it not signed, East Timor's share could have fallen back to the 50 per cent guaranteed in the February 2000

Exchange of Notes, but that would have meant aid dependency. Even with a 90 per cent share the country's first national budget was only around US$80 million a year, which in per capita terms was about $100, compared with $10 000 per head of population for the Australian federal budget alone. Australia's so-called 'generosity' amounted to a marginal future at best for the long-suffering Timorese. The World Bank's country representative Elisabeth Huybens said of the new Treaty: 'under the current arrangements in the Timor Sea, it's not enough right now . . . Timor does not have the resource base to exist as an independent state.'[17]

Immediately after the signing Alkatiri told the new National Parliament of the República Democrática de Timor-Leste that under current international law all of the known fields in the Timor Sea should come under East Timor's jurisdiction. He said East Timor would use 'all instruments and international mechanisms' to secure its rights to the resources of the Timor Sea.[18] He tabled a draft Maritime Zones Act (MZA) setting out the 200-nautical-mile claim that East Timor was entitled to under UNCLOS. Where this claim overlapped with those of neighbouring countries it would be subject to negotiation, as set out in Article 74 of UNCLOS, he said.

Asked about Alkatiri's comments, Prime Minister John Howard, who had flown to Dili for the independence celebrations, played them down and signalled a flexible approach in future negotiations:

> He was articulating his country's national interest, which is the responsibility of a prime minister of any country. We believe that the approach we have taken is very fair. We must serve our own national interest but also ensure that we are fair and generous to the people of East Timor.[19]

Senior DFAT officials, however, had a different perspective on where things would go from this point. They believed that securing Australia's national interest could involve giving East Timor absolutely nothing until it submitted to Australia's interests.

5 ANIMAL FARM

'The Democratic Republic of East Timor is a democratic, sovereign, independent and unitary state based on the rule of law, the will of the people and the respect for the dignity of the human person.' The Fundamental Principles of the Constitution of East Timor, approved by the Constituent Assembly on 22 March 2002

The *Palácio do Governo* (Palace of Government) in Dili is the most significant edifice left behind after three centuries of Portuguese colonial rule in East Timor, and a gracious and striking adornment it is. Featuring a wide, wedding-cake façade, it was built for the tropics with tall, ground-floor colonnades and a deep, first-floor balcony looking directly out to the harbour just a stone's throw away. It is grand in design and solidly built, an overwhelming statement of the Portuguese presence in an impoverished colony that at the time of its construction in the 1950s had no electricity or paved roads, and few other services, outside the capital. But the colonial administration's budget didn't stretch far enough to complete the *Palácio* with the curved tiles that were a signature touch to most colonial buildings. To this day it is crowned with corrugated metal.

SHAKEDOWN

In the colonial days it was called *Palácio do Governador* (Governor's Palace), and it looked onto the *Praça*, or main square, and then to the harbour and sea beyond. Filled with poinciana trees which yielded crimson flames in the humid build-up to the monsoon, the *Praça* was more a garden than an open square and it was here that the youth congregated in the cool of the evening after the sun had set behind the nearby Indonesian island of Alor. The Portuguese dedicated the square to Prince Henry the Navigator, *Dom Henrique*, whose legendary voyages of discovery in the 1400s along the African coast led to the rounding of the horn of Africa and the opening of trade routes to the Indies. In 1960, with the *Palácio* finally completed, the colonial administration built a stone monument resembling the bow of a Portuguese galleon in the middle of the square to mark the 500th anniversary of the death of Prince Henry. This was before the Indonesian occupiers cut down all of the flames trees and turned most of the *Praça* into a car park.

Among the young people who gathered there in the early 1970s were members of a newly formed, clandestine liberation movement. It didn't have a formal name, but this loose network of emerging leaders would meet in full view of the Portuguese administrators who at that time rounded up and exiled anyone who spoke of independence. A founding member of this movement was Marí Bin Amude Alkatiri. He had shoulder-length hair, was dressed smartly and drove a red Daihatsu convertible. Small in stature and of mixed ethnic background, this intense, intelligent and relatively well-educated individual was a natural independence leader in this tiny, half-island dominion. Alkatiri engaged another *mestiço*, the outgoing and articulate José Ramos-Horta, together with other Timorese leadership talent, most notably Nicolau Lobato and Xavier do Amaral, to champion East Timor's passage to independence.

Born in Dili in 1948, the son of a father of Yemeni origin and a Timorese mother, Alkatiri was raised as a Muslim together with nine brothers and sisters. He attended the Dili Mosque School and then the Portuguese *Liceu*, a high school for the children of the

Portuguese and the local elite. Alkatiri showed potential and in 1971 he left for Angola to study surveying, where he made contact with other anti-colonial groups in the capital, Luanda, and returned to East Timor the following year. Portugal's Carnation Revolution immediately began a process of decolonisation which became the catalyst for these young leaders to launch a fully fledged independence party. On 20 May 1974, a month after the revolution in Lisbon, Alkatiri co-founded the ASDT, the Timorese Social Democratic Association, which later became a broad political front for independence, FRETILIN. There was a small but vocal Marxist faction within FRETILIN, and the name had a distinct, leftish tone. Accusations of communist links would be used by Indonesia against FRETILIN and East Timor's independence aspirations.[1]

In the wake of the August-September civil war the Portuguese governor evacuated Dili and moved the administration to the island of Ataúro, 25 kilometres to the north. Indonesia made incursions into the border districts in October 1975, and prepared for a full-scale invasion as the Portuguese declined pleas from the FRETILIN leadership to return. More than 20 Portuguese civilians had been killed in the fighting; the colony was still regarded as unsafe, and in any event exiting Dili was in keeping with the Portuguese policy of rapid decolonisation. When it became clear that the Portuguese would not return, and Indonesia was poised to invade, FRETILIN declared independence unilaterally on 28 November. It was a fateful move, later regarded by many observers, including José Ramos-Horta, as a tactical blunder. Coming on the heels of a brief but bloody civil war, it handed Indonesia some justification for intervention. Alkatiri became Minister of State for Political Affairs, third in seniority behind President Francisco Xavier do Amaral and Prime Minister Nicolau Lobato.[2] He was just 27 years old.

On 4 December 1975 Alkatiri departed Dili with Ramos-Horta and Rogerio Lobato, the younger brother of the new prime minister, Nicolau, on a flight arranged by David Scott of Community Aid Abroad (now Oxfam Australia). Knowing full well that an invasion was imminent, they were sent overseas by the FRETILIN leadership to mobilise international support for East Timor at the United Nations and elsewhere. It was the last flight out of Portuguese Timor. Three days later, in the early hours of 7 December, the full-scale Indonesian invasion came. Alkatiri and Ramos-Horta would not return to their homeland for another 24 years, and when they did they would be two of only five of the seventeen ministers in the first government who had not died at the hands of the Indonesians.

Alkatiri lived in exile in Mozambique where he studied and practised law and worked as a consultant to the Mozambique parliament. He also remained a key player in the international resistance, which included being the minister for external relations for the government in exile. He returned to East Timor in October 1999 as the Australian-led InterFET peacekeeping force gained control of security following the 30 August ballot, and soon became a minister in the UN Transitional Administration East Timor (UNTAET). As secretary-general of FRETILIN Alkatiri began to reassert the party's role in the politics of independence. In May 2000 FRETILIN held its first major party congress in 25 years and it broke away from the Gusmão-led CNRT, the multi-party, national unity movement created to depoliticise the independence cause.[3] Gusmão founded CNRT (formerly CNRM) after resigning from FRETILIN in December 1987 and taking the FALINTIL resistance army with him. He wanted to overcome the fractious politics which had subverted East Timor's independence aspirations from the very beginning, and under the CNRT model East Timor could have had a government of national unity. The FRETILIN withdrawal from CNRT ended this dream. As a well-organised party with a grassroots network, FRETILIN won 57 per cent of the vote in the August 2001 elections and Alkatiri became chief minister of the UN administration. One of his first tasks was to draft the constitution for an independent East Timor which, significantly, made the president a figurehead with limited powers. For the first time Alkatiri found himself working inside the *Palácio*, based in a small office adjacent to the cabinet room in the central wing. He became prime minister on 20 May 2002.

In early 2004 Alkatiri commissioned extensive renovations to the *Palácio*. These included a secret emergency room in the roof cavity of the complex's west wing which could be used to command security forces in the event of riots or a more serious 'situation'. He affixed the name *Palácio do Governo* in big silver letters to the front of the building, above the windows of the cabinet room. Then in early 2006 he approved a new project to rebuild the Portuguese-era *Praça*. It seemed that very little had changed in the space of three decades; East Timor's first independence government was going back to the future.

The situation room was prompted by deadly riots that had broken out just six months after independence. A provocative speech by the new president targeted FRETILIN's domination of independence, which had undermined his national unity model of government. 'Independence serves to care for the cadres of FRETILIN ... many of whom are constantly absent,' the new president boomed. East Timor was destined to commit the mistakes made by other newly independent countries 'where the members of the Government are well off but the people live in misery', Gusmão said on 28 November 2002 in a speech marking the anniversary of FRETILIN's declaration of independence. Significantly, he called for the sacking of the interior minister, Rogerio Lobato, for 'incompetence and neglect'. The speech marked the renewal of Gusmão's war with FRETILIN. Days later, the new national police force provided the trigger to unleash the pent up frustration which Gusmão had spelled out, or indeed fomented. Officers killed a youth while trying to arrest him, and then killed several more rioters in the *mêlée* that followed. The immediate target of the mob, which may have been swelled by former militia members, was Alkatiri. They descended on his residence and torched it, together with two other properties owned by his family. Two major commercial properties across the road from the parliament, at the rear of the *Palácio*, were also torched, along with several others around the city. The riot reflected the dearth of economic opportunities since independence. Life was tougher than under the Indonesian regime which had annually doled out about US$1 billion worth of largesse. A bloated civil service 'employing' more than 30 000 people was used to buy influence; under the new regime there were half as many government jobs. But there was also deep disaffection with the new government dominated by the Alkatiri-led, Mozambique clique. This group of former exiles spread its tentacles into all of the key ministries: planning and finance, justice, interior, defence, agriculture, development and planning (later natural resources and minerals), state administration, and of course, prime minister's portfolio.

The Mozambican exiles reimposed many facets of the colonial order, most notably making Portuguese the official language. The local elite, including the Catholic Church and Gusmão, strongly endorsed the decision which defied Asia's adoption of English as a *de facto* second language and the region's three decades of global integration and economic success, and it alienated the leaders of the younger generation who had lived under the Indonesian regime and spoke English and Indonesian. Suddenly, East Timor was aligning itself with the Portuguese-speaking *lusafone* club which included the impoverished former colonies of Africa on the other side of the world. The main indigenous dialect, Tetum, was only adopted as a second official language by FRETILIN after young leaders protested at a meeting in Sydney in 1998. Some ministers still refused to speak Tetum, even when chairing meetings in the capital or visiting districts where few, if any, people understood Portuguese.

The new government showed increasingly authoritarian tendencies, and became concerned with acquiring arms for paramilitary forces operating under the interior minister, in competition with the army which was loyal to the president. It armed a new border patrol unit with 200 battlefield Steyr rifles—assault rifles used by armies—and a rapid response police unit with 66 FN-FNC semi-automatic rifles, and formed a brigade of riot police armed with tear gas and riot shields. More than 200 000 rounds of ammunition were imported under a contract awarded to a company controlled by the brother of Alkatiri. The prime minister had asked a UN security adviser, retired Australian army colonel Bob Lowry, about establishing a secret police service, just like those that had operated during the Portuguese and Indonesian years. All of these heavily armed units came under the control of the interior minister, Rogerio Lobato, who was gaining a reputation as FRETILIN's loose cannon. In November 2005 Lobato infamously pulled over a motorist and pistol-whipped him because he dared to overtake his vehicle on a highway. Lobato and Alkatiri had a very close working relationship, the former being the most frequent visitor to the prime minister's office.

The Alkatiri government was becoming increasingly undemocratic. In late 2005 it by-passed Parliament and introduced a penal code that included defamation, with heavy prison sentences. This was directly at odds with the Constitution's commitment to freedom of the press. At around this time Alkatiri also began talking about holding the next election without UN supervision. The new government imitated the former colonial regime by taking over an exclusive, waterfront precinct and turning it into a residential area for ministers. This was exactly the same place where senior colonials had resided. This initiative might not have been so bad had it not involved a plan to evict some of the local NGOs that had set up offices there during the Indonesian years. Ministers were routinely overseas on business trips to the point where it was difficult to find all the senior members of government in the country at the same time. A VIP terminal had been specially built at the airport for the comings and goings of members of government, and there was even talk among senior civil servants of buying a prime ministerial jet.

Bilateral donors, mainly the Portuguese and Chinese, lavished the new elite with opulent residences and office complexes. The Chinese government began work in 2006 on a grandiose, 6000-square-metre headquarters for the 87 *funcionários* in the foreign ministry head office. This 'Taj Mahal' of East Timor became by far the largest building in the country. That East Timor allowed the Chinese government to build its foreign ministry surprised some diplomats in Dili who knew of China's capability with listening devices; in all likelihood the complex is hardwired with bugs. Gusmão also accepted funding from the Chinese and Portuguese governments for a proposed presidential office complex, while the Portuguese funded the redevelopment of his residence in the hills above Dili in 2005. The extensive works transformed the former Portuguese governor's residence from a burnt-out shell into a Disneyland pink palace with manicured lawns and a fountain.[4] When the redevelopment began the site was shrouded by sheets of shiny-new corrugated metal roofing so that the many Timorese who had leaky roofs, and who might have put the roofing to better use, could not see in. When completed the metal roofing was replaced with a tall, pink wall. The redevelopment was so extensive that the former residence would only be used for official ceremonies; the President would reside in a massive apartment to be built beneath it. Perched above the ruins of Dili, it was the epitome of a white elephant. In a country where 70 per cent of the people live in houses with dirt floors, and where very few people received anything tangible from the new government, it all began to look very much as though the infamous elite from George Orwell's *Animal Farm* was moving in.

Alkatiri's renovations were modest by comparison, although they spoke volumes about his style. Also funded by the Chinese government, they were to a large extent inappropriate and unnecessary in impoverished East Timor. A new floor was built about 20 centimetres above the original tiles so that cables could run underneath it and carpet could be laid on top. It became the only office in this tropical country decked out with carpet. Workers erected scaffolding and began painting over the dimpled cement surface on the walls, a task that took about a week. Shortly after finishing the workers began scraping the new paint off the walls. This painstaking work took many more weeks as the blades they used were only a couple of centimetres wide. After all the paint had been removed the walls were plastered smooth and then repainted once again. When asked who had ordered the change, the foreman pointed nervously towards Alkatiri's office; the prime minister had decreed that the walls be made smooth.

When the renovations were completed the staff began walking dirt and mud into the office now adorned with smart office furniture and plush leather lounges. This was unavoidable in a city that is dusty in the dry season and muddy in the wet. No-one had thought to buy a vacuum cleaner, and it took some weeks before one could be acquired from overseas. A few months later the plaster on the walls began to crack—and these were among the many cracks emerging in this increasingly fragile democracy.

* * *

Long-time East Timor analyst Professor Noam Chomsky, who was voted in early 2007 the world's leading 'public intellectual' in a poll by the magazines *Prospect* and *Foreign Policy*, said the Timorese struggle for independence was unprecedented:

> The victory of the people of East Timor is a truly stunning accomplishment. I cannot think of a historical parallel. It is a remarkable testimony to what the human spirit can achieve in the face of overwhelming, indescribable odds, an achievement that should inspire hope as well as humility.[5]

But after the 1999 ballot exiles returned with the mindset of the colonial era and perceived the Timorese as lazy and untrustworthy.[6] Alkatiri was not the worst offender in this regard, but he did think that many Timorese had had it easy during the Indonesian years and had developed a 'dependency mentality'. He routinely complained about the demands people made on his government, as though he did not think his government had been elected to serve the people. The *modus operandi* of the FRETILIN government was centralisation and control. Government spending was highly centralised—contrary to the Constitution's statement on decentralisation of administration—to the point where ministers had to approve even the smallest allocations. The government was simply unable to spend its budget and deliver the services that the people so desperately needed. In 2005–06 half the allocated budget of US$120 million was actually spent. As ministers were often overseas, the business of government ground to a halt. The administrators in the thirteen districts that make up East Timor simply could not be trusted to manage money, Alkatiri argued. They were given a token, discretionary budget of around US$2000 a month, but all other spending was controlled from Dili.

It is not an uncommon experience in post-independence countries for the new regime to unwittingly imitate the former despots. Perhaps the most extreme case is Liberia, where emancipated slaves became slave masters.[7] Tragically, independent East Timor quickly emerged as a modern day example of this Orwellian phenomenon.

The task of building a new nation from scratch was always going to be a mammoth undertaking, and this was especially the case in East Timor with much of the physical infrastructure having been destroyed. East Timor also lost valuable human resources, with Indonesian doctors, teachers and other public servants leaving after 1999. However, some of the younger, overseas-trained ministers were impressive. The health and labour ministries were highly effective, and to some extent the ministry of agriculture. The central bank was headed by a very impressive econocrat, and while the vice minister of finance was capable, Alkatiri had appointed an incompetent crony to the senior post of finance minister.

Alkatiri's Muslim background did not help matters in a country where more than 90 per cent of the population declared themselves Catholic. He was a secular Muslim who was known to celebrate the end of Ramadan with a big party for the Dili elite at his waterfront residence. Alkatiri's blunt and insensitive public utterances, and the increasing perception of corruption associated with family companies, did not help either. An early indication of Alkatiri's authoritarian style emerged in early 2003 when he went to the premises of a metal and plastic recycling merchant and ordered his bodyguards to arrest the owner, Malaysian businessman Wong Kee Jin. In an incident witnessed by another businessman, Wong alleged that the bodyguards kicked him and called him a 'monkey'. Without a warrant, Alkatiri's bodyguards sent Wong to gaol, a move overturned some weeks later by the local court, but then he was re-arrested and immediately gaoled again after the court's decision.[8] The incident was monitored closely by the UN Human Rights Unit in Dili. It is not known whether Alkatiri's intervention was the result of a family business interest.

Just six months after independence, Alkatiri's leadership was in trouble; his torched house a suitable metaphor for what many people thought of him and his new government. But he was able to use the dispute with Australia over the Timor Sea to shore up his leadership. Australia's tactics delivered to Alkatiri a new foreign adversary to rail against; they gave oxygen to an asphyxiated political leader. Responding to Australia's intransigence, Alkatiri succeeded in rallying a wave of national sentiment against this new adversary and galvanised public support behind him and his troubled government.

In the early years of independence, with oil prices at around US$30 a barrel, East Timor did indeed face a marginal existence. Projected oil revenues from the Bayu-Undan field were approximately US$3.3 billion over a period of 20 years. This implied annual oil revenue of around US$80 million a year under a sustainable policy of saving half the revenue for future generations, which translates into US$80 per head of population per annum. Non-oil revenue at the time generated about US$20 million. There was potential for further discoveries, but the future is always unpredictable. Only three years before oil prices had been as low as US$10 a barrel; the certainty at the time was that East Timor, one of the poorest and most tormented countries in the world, faced a very uncertain existence. And it could be argued quite plausibly that Australia's tough tactics were playing havoc with its future. But in taking a defiant stand against Australia's abusive tactics, East Timor was distracted from the huge task of national reconstruction.

The new elite brought some important lessons from their time in strife-torn Mozambique. Alkatiri was an intelligent and hard-working leader who applied principle to policy decisions. He was a details man—a better technocrat than politician. When it came to oil wealth he fully comprehended the dangers of having abundant natural resources, and he had deeply embraced the concept of sustainable development. He refused to borrow from international institutions, including the World Bank and the Asian Development Bank, even when these loans were offered on very favourable terms. Alkatiri's principled views prevailed when it came to lofty, long-term goals, but the immediate losers were the ordinary Timorese who saw little evidence of any short-term development in the early years of independence. He excelled at saving money, but was unable to spend the money that was available and failed to deliver tangible benefits to the Timorese. He set up a petroleum fund to manage the revenue for future generations, with the aim of saving East Timor from becoming another Nauru, the Pacific island country which had nothing left when its phosphate bounty was exhausted. But while saving for the future there was woefully inadequate economic development in the first four years of independence. What little money was spent mainly circulated around the capital, thereby drawing hordes of new arrivals and the potential for conflict.

The shortcomings of his government that had been evident from the very beginning, but remained dormant during the developing dispute with Australia, came rushing to the surface when Alkatiri tripped up and turned a minor fracas into a national crisis.

6 TUTORIALS IN POLITICS

'We don't like brinksmanship. We are very tough. We will not care if you give information to the media. Let me give you a tutorial in politics—not a chance.' Alexander Downer telling the East Timor government that Australia would not open up negotiations over all of the disputed resources, Dili, 27 November 2002

When the Timor Sea Treaty was presented to the East Timor parliament in 2002 there was an uproar on the floor. Prime Minister Alkatiri, public servants and advisers were abused from pillar to post with unprintable insults. Parliamentarians from opposition parties, some who had links with Oceanic/Petrotimor, were the loudest, but there were also concerns within the government party about the wisdom of signing the treaty. Many feared it was a sell-out of the country's sovereignty.

This hostile political environment strengthened East Timor's hand in the subsequent negotiations. If this was the reaction to a treaty that gave East Timor a 90 per cent share, then a supplementary agreement fixing East Timor's share of the biggest and closest field, Greater Sunrise, at just 18 per cent could not go anywhere near the parliament until Australia yielded to a maritime boundary or another means of resolving ownership of the disputed resources. In overall terms the treaty delivered to East Timor about 40 per cent of the known resources located on its side of the horizontal median line. If this was to be the final settlement for the Timor Sea, then clearly the country's negotiators had failed.

For East Timor, the signing of the Timor Sea Treaty was just first base, but Australia wanted it to be game over. Immediately after the signing the respective sides began to work towards these irreconcilable objectives.

The two countries proceeded to negotiate a new agreement for the Greater Sunrise field, in accordance with Annex E of the treaty. When eventually signed, the recitals (preamble) for what became known as the International Unitisation Agreement (IUA) for the Greater Sunrise field carried these words: '*Noting* that Timor-Leste and Australia have, at the date of this agreement, made maritime claims, and not yet delimited their maritime boundaries, including in an area of the Timor Sea where Greater Sunrise lies'[1] [*original emphasis*].

This single sentence, which caused negotiations to break down when East Timor insisted that it be included, became East Timor's linchpin in the Timor Sea dispute that would threaten relations with Australia and require a further three years of difficult negotiation to resolve. It demanded that the Australian government acknowledge East Timor's claim specifically in the area where the Greater Sunrise field was located. And while this sentence may not have won the day had the dispute ended up in court, it certainly helped East Timor to win the battle for public opinion.

* * *

The Australian government had at its disposal a very powerful lever for securing the 79.9 per cent of Sunrise directly attributed to it—it could hold off ratifying the Timor Sea Treaty. Without ratification, the Bayu-Undan development would not proceed and East Timor would be starved of revenue. Ratification of the treaty had to be secured in order to provide the legal certainty for contracts to be signed with buyers of the gas.

With the treaty hanging in the balance, Alkatiri wrote to John Howard on 3 October 2002 proposing the commencement of formal maritime boundary discussions. Howard said in his reply of 6 November that negotiations would commence 'once' the treaty and the Sunrise agreement were in force. 'This remains our firm view,' Howard wrote. He had a point. The two sides had negotiated the interim arrangements, and it made perfect sense to see them put in place before moving on to a permanent settlement. For East Timor that wasn't the point. Ratifying the IUA meant giving up a powerful bargaining chip, and this was exactly what Howard wanted to achieve. Alkatiri wrote back to Howard on 18 November and feigned indignation, saying that Australia had never before said that the completion of these interim arrangements was an 'obstacle' to commencing maritime boundary negotiations. 'With no permanent boundaries between Timor-Leste and Australia, the two countries are left with maritime resources, including petroleum deposits, which are in areas of overlapping claims,' Alkatiri wrote.

The stand-off reached a climax on 27 November 2002 when Alexander Downer flew to Dili to seek East Timor's signature on the Sunrise agreement. Alkatiri said that rather than talk about this agreement, the two sides should begin at once to negotiate a permanent maritime boundary covering the disputed areas outside the JPDA. After all, Australia was already exploiting the resources—the Buffalo, Laminaria and Corallina fields—that were claimed by both countries.

Downer was in no mood for what he considered game-playing by this micro-state. The previous month 88 Australians had been killed by suicide bombers in two Bali nightclubs, and a voice recording of Osama bin Laden had linked the attack to Australia's intervention in East Timor, he said. Australia had a lot more to worry about than East Timor. It had to be concerned about 'the implications for our relations with other countries, especially Indonesia'.

Downer pounded the table as he bluntly warned that Australia could leave all of the Timor Sea resources in the ground until it got its way: 'We don't have to exploit the resources. They can stay there for 20, 40, 50 years.' Towards the end of the meeting, Downer warned Alkatiri that he had no time for his 'brinkmanship'. Downer said he was a captive of his western advisers and in need of a tutorial in politics.

A media adviser in the Timor Sea Office, Zoe Cottew, produced a full transcript of this stormy meeting. Alkatiri, while being fluent in English, chose to speak in Portuguese, which meant that the translation slowed down the exchange to the point where Cottew wrote a longhand record of the entire meeting. In early 2003, when the Timor Sea Treaty and the Sunrise agreement were still in abeyance, the Timor Sea Office circulated the full transcript on a confidential basis to a number of people in Australia. One of the recipients forwarded it to the website www.crikey.com.au, a media and political insider forum, which published it on 6 March, the day that Downer flew to Dili for the signing of the Sunrise agreement, under the headline 'Pompous Colonial Git'. The transcript's accuracy was reinforced by Australia's accusations that East Timor had secretly taped the meeting, which it had not done. Downer complained bitterly about the leaking of this transcript in every meeting he had with Ramos-Horta for the next two years. But its inadvertent release reinforced international sympathy for East Timor and perceptions of the bullying style adopted by Australia in the negotiations.

Downer is a rare breed in Australia—a genuine, third-generation member of the conservative aristocracy. Born in 1951, he is the son of Sir Alexander Downer, a cabinet minister in the Menzies government and High Commissioner to London, and grandson of Sir John Downer, one of the nation's founding fathers who in the 1890s steered the six colonies towards Federation in 1901. A suburb in Canberra is named after Sir John.

Alexander Downer Jr, like Prince Charles and Richard Woolcott, boarded at Geelong Grammar and then did his undergraduate studies in the United Kingdom, graduating with honours in arts. But it wasn't at Oxford or Cambridge or even the London School of Economics; Downer went to Newcastle-upon-Tyne University. He is distinguished by a plummy private-school accent—the subject of persistent taunts from political opponents—but he is no silver-spoon softie. He is very much the ruthless prosecutor of national interest foreign policy. As foreign minister Downer has had strained relations with the leaders of developing countries in Australia's immediate orbit, most notably Papua New Guinea, the Solomon Islands and Fiji. Downer's bullying style in his dealings with small neighbours is reminiscent of the late Professor Manning Clark's characterisation of the hard men of Australian history: 'Straiteners [sic], conformers and heart-dimmers', as opposed to the 'life-enlargers'.[2] Prime Minister Paul Keating later put it more sharply and succinctly—'the punishers and straighteners'.[3]

In 2005 Downer became Australia's longest serving foreign minister, but his links with DFAT go back 30 years. After a short stint as a bank economist after graduation, Downer went into diplomacy in 1976. While serving as a third secretary in Brussels he met John Howard for the first time and this began the long and close association that remains to this day. Shortly afterwards, in 1982, Downer began working as an adviser to Prime Minister Malcolm Fraser. A year after the defeat of the coalition government in 1983 he was back in politics as the Liberal member for the gentrified seat of Mayo in the Adelaide hills, a sprawling electorate covering 9190 square kilometres or two-thirds the size of East Timor.

In 1994, after eight years in opposition, the Liberals elected Downer as their leader, but it proved to be a disastrous venture and he lasted in the job just nine months. Downer has a wicked sense of humour and a habit of injecting this into discussions of serious matters. After launching a policy platform called 'The Things That Matter', Downer joked that the Coalition's domestic violence policy might be called 'The Things That Batter'. The media savaged him for insensitivity about the serious subject of domestic violence, and the gaffe ended his leadership. Little wonder that staffers continually advise him 'no jokes, no laughing', when giving interviews on serious matters.

* * *

By early March 2003 contracts for the sale of gas from Bayu Undan were still to be signed, and Japanese buyers had issued an ultimatum to both governments that they would walk away if the treaty was not ratified by 11 March. East Timor's economic lifeline was about to be severed because Australia was being very 'tough' indeed, as Downer had promised. The Australian government, after gaining huge international recognition for its leadership in helping to liberate East Timor, stood ready and willing to choke the new country's development in order to get control of Sunrise.

This deliberate strategy was laid out in detail by Dr Geoff Raby, a DFAT first assistant secretary (now a deputy secretary), in evidence before the Joint Standing Committee on Treaties (JSCOT) hearings on the Timor Sea Treaty in October 2002. When asked by Labor MP for Swan, Kim Wilkie, if it was worthwhile putting 'at risk' the Bayu-Undan development in order to secure ratification by East Timor of the Sunrise agreement, the exchange went:

> **Raby:** All I can say on that is that the government's position is that Australia's national interest is maximised through the development of all the fields and particularly by the development of Greater Sunrise.
> **Wilkie:** So it is the government's view that the risk is worth taking?
> **Raby:** Yes. The bigger field [Sunrise] is of great national interest to us.[4]

* * *

Late one afternoon in the first week of March 2003, the Australian ambassador to East Timor, Paul Foley, banged on the door of the Timor Sea Office, and informed two advisers working there that the Australian foreign minister wanted an urgent meeting in Dili to sign the Sunrise agreement after the conclusion of negotiations on the previous Sunday night. At this final meeting, the Australian negotiators, after breaking off the talks, had finally accepted East Timor's request to have the linchpin paragraph included in the preamble about the respective claims. The Australian cabinet had approved the agreement on the Monday, and Downer wanted it to be signed in Dili the following Wednesday before bills for the Timor Sea Treaty were tabled in parliament.

Foley was not exactly the most accomplished diplomat to have in this role. Before landing in Dili he had only served overseas as a low-level third secretary, and his position prior to Dili was assistant secretary for dealing with the Year 2000 (Y2K) computer bug. The advisers, Philip Daniel, an Oxford economist who had advised developing countries on oil negotiations for 20 years, and Jonathan Morrow, told Foley that the day chosen by Downer was in fact Ash Wednesday, a public holiday in Catholic East Timor. Ministers would be out of Dili on that day, and the signing would have to be held at another time. Foley was operating under strict instructions and did not seem to take on board the significance of Ash Wednesday. He said Downer wanted East Timor's signature on the Sunrise agreement before Australia began the process of ratifying the treaty. This was because Downer thought that East Timor's advisers would 'play tricks', Foley told them.

Later that night the ambassador went searching for other East Timor advisers and found a group in the newly built, waterfront restaurant in the tropical chic Esplanada Hotel. Foley, accompanied by another DFAT official, vented his minister's rage, telling the group that the Australian foreign minister was 'fed up' with the 'lies and dishonesty' of the new government and its prime minister and that Downer was insisting on the Wednesday meeting.

Seated at the table was Einar Risa, an agreeable and high-calibre Scandinavian who had served as a diplomat and Secretary of State for Development Cooperation in the Norwegian government, and in senior management positions in the national oil company Statoil. Risa had just been appointed executive director of the Timor Sea Designated Authority (TSDA), the joint authority established to manage the treaty area. While Foley also represented one of his employers, Risa told him that he had never before seen or heard an ambassador issue such insulting comments about his host country. While he did not know what was meant by diplomacy in Australia, he said, Foley's 'schoolyard bullying' was not the international norm. Norway and Australia, two countries ranked by the UN at the very top of its human development index, had recently clashed over human rights and tension would reverberate throughout the Timor Sea dispute. In August 2001 the Norwegian freighter the *Tampa*, captained by Arne Rinnan, was at the centre of an international storm when it was boarded by SAS troops and refused entry to Australia after rescuing 438 asylum seekers from a sinking fishing boat. In his three years in Dili the narrow 'national interest' mantra that dominated every facet of the Australian government's foreign policy constantly dismayed Risa. With strikingly similar looks to Rinnan—a weathered face, high cheek bones and a shock of silver hair—Risa developed a fascination with the mentality of the Australian government. He would talk about this at length with other Norwegians who had worked in Australia. He could not believe that Downer had released a foreign policy white paper plainly called 'In the National Interest';[5] it was something that no other sophisticated western democracy would ever do. An example of Risa's observation is that even the Australian government aid agency AusAID says the people of Australia only give aid because it is in their national interest to do so.

As Australia held off ratifying the treaty, Alkatiri wrote to Howard on Tuesday 4 March and said he would be 'submitting the IUA immediately to my Council of Ministers for its approval'. He was trying to buy time. This was not enough to satisfy Downer who wanted East Timor's signature on the agreement immediately.

The next morning, 5 March, Ash Wednesday, Howard telephoned Alkatiri from his office in Parliament House, Canberra. At the time Alkatiri was refusing to take calls from Downer, but now he was about to receive another tutorial in politics. That morning the Australian government had tabled in the House of Representatives bills for the ratification of the Timor Sea Treaty. Howard told Alkatiri that unless East Timor signed the Sunrise agreement the bills for the treaty would remain 'stalled' in the lower house, which meant that the Bayu-Undan development would collapse. 'It was an ultimatum. Howard said that unless we agreed to sign the new deal immediately, he would stop the Senate approving the treaty,' a senior Timorese official was reported as saying.[6]

Downer spoke to Ramos-Horta, and the two agreed that East Timor would call an extraordinary Council of Ministers meeting the following morning, Thursday 6 March, to endorse the Greater Sunrise deal. It was agreed that Downer would fly to Dili that day for the signing, but Alkatiri remained unconvinced, and it took the combined weight of Ramos-Horta, the president of the parliament, Francisco 'Lu Olo' Guterres, and Xanana Gusmão, who was now president of the republic, to persuade him to proceed with the signing. Philip Daniel briefed the council in the morning with both presidents in attendance. The tension in the room was so great that the meeting burst into spontaneous applause at the conclusion of the briefing. Later that day Downer signed the agreement in the same room.

Back in Canberra in the Senate that day, the Greens, the Australian Democrats and Labor spoke out strongly against the Australian government's tactics. It was evident to the opposition parties that the Australian government was prepared to sacrifice the Bayu-Undan development in order to lock in its 79.9 per cent of the Sunrise field. Senator Bob Brown of the Australian Greens launched a spirited attack on the government that culminated in his accusing Prime Minister John Howard of having engaged in 'blackmail' against East Timor. Brown told the Senate:

> I believe we are being ambushed with this legislation . . . we are being ambushed, in the interests of big oil companies, to cheat East

Timor. This is the big oil companies, with the active compliance of the Prime Minister, no less, defrauding East Timor of its resources. It is a fraud. It is illegal. Last night, as the newspaper reports tell us, the Prime Minister phoned his opposite number in East Timor to deliver blackmail. What John Howard did was coerce a poor and weak neighbour through blackmail.[7]

The president of the Senate asked Brown to withdraw the word 'blackmail' but he refused, despite being given repeated opportunities to do so. The Coalition and Labor voted to have Brown expelled from the Senate for the rest of the day. He said after being ejected, 'Blackmail is a word that has been used in the parliament a thousand times since 1981 but it is never more appropriately used than on this occasion.'

Howard claimed to have been misrepresented and made a personal explanation to the House of Representatives:

Yesterday, in another place, allegations were made by Senator Brown that I had sought to intimidate or strongarm the East Timorese leadership over the Timor Sea negotiations. Those claims are totally false. I did call the Prime Minister of East Timor yesterday to ask whether East Timor's formal approval of an international unitisation agreement could be completed in time for a visit by the Minister for Foreign Affairs today to sign that agreement. Negotiations on the key elements of the agreement were completed last Sunday. My call to Dr Alkatiri, which was totally civil and cordial in accordance with our close relationship, related solely to formal processes and not to any of the substance of the negotiated package. Might I add my very warm personal congratulations to the Minister for Foreign Affairs on his skilful guidance of this matter.[8]

Alkatiri relented and agreed to sign the Sunrise agreement, but he refused to do so personally, instead delegating this task to his justice minister, Ana Pessoa. The agreement was signed in the

Council of Ministers' room in the *Palácio do Governo*—the same place where the other Timor Sea agreements had been signed. That evening the Timor Sea Treaty bills went through the Australian Senate. The treaty entered into force on 2 April 2003 and the Bayu-Undan project stayed on the rails.

* * *

With East Timor's signature on the agreement, the Australian government's strategists thought they were finally home. But the agreement, like the Timor Sea Treaty, would have to be ratified by both parliaments in order to have legal force. East Timor could hold off ratifying the Sunrise agreement in the same way that Australia had previously done with the treaty, in order to gain leverage for the next phase—formal negotiations on maritime boundaries. Now that revenue from the Bayu-Undan project was on its way, East Timor could afford to bide its time, as Alkatiri had previously hoped. Even so, refusing to ratify an agreement signed with Australia was an audacious move for East Timor, a vulnerable new nation desperately in need of foreign investment. Denying Australia ratification would lead to accusations of 'ratting' on an international agreement.

The pressure on Alkatiri during this stand-off period intensified when in March 2004 US-based Oceanic Exploration lodged a claim for damages of US$10.5 billion in the US District Court in the District of Columbia under the *Racketeer-Influenced and Corrupt Organization Act* (RICO) relating to the concession awarded by the former Portuguese colonial administration to its subsidiary Petrotimor in January 1974. The concession awarded by Portugal at that time covered nearly all of the area from East Timor's southern coastline to the median line with production rights for 30 years.

Oceanic had returned to East Timor shortly after the UN ballot in 1999 to seek to reclaim this concession. It returned again in October 2001 and delivered to UNTAET a request not only to honour the Portuguese concession, but to widen it so that all areas within the legitimate maritime boundaries of East Timor were included. It admitted in its statement of claim that UNTAET chief Sergio Vieira de Mello told all staff not to communicate in any way with representatives of Petrotimor and Oceanic. It was at around this time that Oceanic commissioned the Lowe opinion. Oceanic wanted East Timor to hold off signing the treaty, thereby delaying the development of Bayu-Undan and leveraging its bid to have its concession recognised.

On 21 August 2001 Oceanic issued a Statement of Claim in the Federal Court of Australia in which it said the Timor Gap Treaty was invalid, but on 3 February 2003 the court ruled that it lacked jurisdiction because it involved the act of a foreign government—Portugal's granting of the concession to Petrotimor. A year later Oceanic announced that it would not pursue an appeal to the High Court in Australia. Instead, it took its case to the US District Court, lodging its statement on 1 March 2004.[9]

The defendants in this case were the major shareholder and operator of Bayu-Undan, ConocoPhillips (CoP), the Timor Sea Designated Authority, the former Indonesia–Australia Timor Gap Joint Authority, and the Indonesian state oil firms Pertamina and BP Migas. Oceanic's statement of claim reads like a detective thriller with East Timor's tragic history as the backdrop. It alleged that CoP, which had been operating in Indonesia for many years, got the benefit of information on the Timor Sea seized by the Indonesian military from Petrotimor's office immediately after they landed in Dili in December 1975. It alleged that CoP paid bribes to East Timorese politicians, including US$2.5 million to Alkatiri, in order to reconfirm the permit awarded by the former Australia–Indonesia authority with the 'no more onerous' taxation terms confirmed in a letter signed by the Timorese leadership in October 1999. It alleged that parliamentarians were bribed US$50 000 each to ratify the Timor Sea Treaty.

The statement listed the numbers of Alkatiri's bank accounts held in the Darwin branches of the ANZ and 'Wespac' (presumably

Westpac) banks where CoP allegedly paid the bribes. It quoted an ANZ account number for Alkatiri's younger brother, Ahmed, into which CoP allegedly paid monies, and four accounts at 'Wespac' under four different names: Ahmad Alkatiri, Ahmad Bin Hamud Alkatiri, Ahmed Alkatiri and Ahmade Hamute Alkatiri. The statement also alleged that CoP purchased a fleet of Toyota 4WD vehicles for the use of the Timorese leadership.

Alkatiri confirmed that his bank accounts existed, but he refused to show bank statements to the public while claiming that they never held more than a few thousand dollars. He said the bank account numbers were obtained from people who received cheques from him, such as when he paid his children's school fees in Darwin. It looked as though Oceanic had put together this dossier with the help of a private detective and some of Alkatiri's political opponents. Oceanic had engaged a professional PR firm to leak the story to journalists in the United States and Australia immediately after the statement of claim was filed with the US District Court, and it had in fact engaged a private detective in Australia. Oceanic retained high profile attorney Dale Oliver, a partner in a leading US law firm Quinn Emanuel, to represent it. Oliver represented General Motors when it won a US$1.1 billion settlement in a similar RICO action against Volkswagon for theft of intellectual property.

The legal action generated extensive publicity, engulfing Alkatiri in a cloud of suspicion and rumour at a critical time. Downer dismissed the bribery allegations made against the former Australia–Indonesia authority as 'fanciful', and East Timor's Council of Ministers put out a strong statement supporting the prime minister. Ramos-Horta wrote an article in the *Financial Review* in which he condemned the allegations and expressed strong support for Alkatiri. Still, many people in East Timor accepted the claims at face value. The East Timor government had already faced considerable criticism for signing the Timor Sea Treaty, and the lawsuit surfaced at exactly the time when the government needed to take a strong stand on Sunrise.

This wasn't the first time Oceanic had acquired a lease in a disputed area. Oceanic says that it 'engages in the acquisition of oil and gas concessions in selected locations worldwide', holding interests in the North Aegean Sea and the East China Sea, both areas being subject to maritime boundary disputes. Oceanic's 31 December 2005 annual report filed with the US Securities and Exchange Commission shows that it has nine employees and its main business expenses were $1.5 million and $1.9 million for the 2005 and 2004 years respectively, 'related to legal activities and commercial opportunities in the Timor Gap area'.[10] Despite being a small, loss-making consulting company, there is some serious money behind Oceanic. The executive chairman, Neil Blue, who controls 84 per cent of the company capitalised in September 2006 at US$15 million, also owns with his brother Linden the nuclear power research company General Atomics. Acquired from Chevron for US$50 million back in 1986, it is a significant and diversified private company. Perhaps its most noteworthy business is the production of unmanned spy-planes for the US military and NASA. Some versions of the planes carry air-to-air and air-to-ground missiles and have been deployed in combat operations in the Balkans, Afghanistan and in the Middle East. The Blue brothers' aeronautical exploits go back to the 1950s when as university graduates their epic flight in a small plane to remote parts of the Andes made the cover of *Life* magazine with a nine-page pictorial spread inside.

Blue's significant wealth indicates that Oceanic's action will be pursued vigorously. While ConocoPhillips has sought to have the matter struck out, Blue has retained Oliver and Quinn Emanuel, and has also engaged a team of private investigators in Australia that includes Alan Sing, a former Australian Federal Police commander, who has made several trips to East Timor to collect information after the US court action was taken. In September 2006 Judge Emmet Sullivan of the US District Court dismissed the Timor Sea Designated Authority as a defendant in the case, but, significantly, the ruling left standing Oceanic's claims under the RICO law.[11]

* * *

Pressure on East Timor over the Sunrise agreement was also coming from the operator of the project—Woodside Petroleum Ltd. Woodside is Australia's biggest dedicated energy company, and while it is a medium-sized player on the global stage, ranked about 40th in the world, its development of the North West Shelf off Western Australia in the 1980s turned the company into a national icon. One field alone, North Rankin, is three times the size of Sunrise, and the total area is believed to hold more than 100 trillion cubic feet of natural gas—more than ten times the known reserves of the Timor Sea.[12] With a significant number of individual shareholders, the company has been treated by successive federal governments as though it were a national oil company. In 2001 Australia's conservative government blocked a hostile takeover by Royal Dutch Shell. As with most other large-scale petroleum projects, Woodside had reduced the risk and capital cost of the development by inviting other major oil companies to join the project as joint venture partners, while retaining overall control as the project operator. Woodside's 33 per cent stake in Sunrise was joined by ConocoPhillips with 30 per cent, Shell with 26.6 per cent and Osaka Gas with 10 per cent. Woodside's leading role in developing Greater Sunrise was a key factor in the Australian government's engagement in the dispute with East Timor. Without a significant Australian commercial interest, the government may have shown no willingness whatsoever to get involved.

From late 2003 and throughout 2004, a steady stream of Woodside executives began beating a path to Dili, including Paul Kitson, the Perth-based leader of the Sunrise project, and James Kernaghan, a Darwin-based lobbyist who was known to fly to Dili to hand-deliver correspondence. They were joined by Gary Gray, a former national secretary of the Australian Labor Party who famously nicknamed Prime Minister Paul Keating 'Captain Whacky' during the ill-fated 1996 election campaign. The enduring contribution of this proud son of the labour movement was a speech to the National Press Club in which he described the preponderance of former union bosses and party apparatchiks among Labor's ranks in federal parliament as 'whitebread politicians'. Gray left the Labor Party in 1999 and in 2001 joined Woodside as its 'Principal Strategic Adviser'. He was ranked in the company's top fifteen senior executives. Woodside went a step further in fostering links with Australia's political elite with the appointment to its board in September 2005 of Ashton Calvert, the recently retired secretary of DFAT. In March 2007 Gray returned to the Labor fold when he was officially endorsed as the candidate for the safe Labor seat of Brand, succeeding the former Labor leader Kim Beazley.

When Gray came to Dili he gave a fireside chat on the dispute to anyone who would listen, explaining that the two countries had to have a 'project' before they could fight over the division. Without ratification of the Sunrise agreement, Woodside did not have 'title' and it could not take the project from the drawing board to the development phase. The ongoing dispute was undermining its efforts to market the gas—securing these agreements was necessary for the joint venture partners to invest in the project. The argument got a cool reception in East Timor as the leadership knew full well that if they ratified the agreement then they would only ever end up with 18 per cent of the project.

In tandem with Gray, Kitson and Kernaghan commenced a series of regular engagements in Dili. They met with the East Timorese leadership, with parliamentarians, advisers, civil society groups and aid donors. And they met regularly with Ramos-Horta as they perceived him as accessible, pragmatic and realistic. Alkatiri seemed impenetrable to them. Woodside's lobbyists hired the biggest 4WD they could find—a Toyota LandCruiser—to get to their Dili meetings even though a modest sedan would have sufficed. They handed out copies of a glossy brochure that showed a slight increase in projected revenue to East Timor from its 18 per cent share of Sunrise to around US$2 billion. That equated to a nominal sum of about US$50 million a year for the 40-year life of the project.

Kitson and Kernaghan also gave briefings on the marketing of liquefied natural gas (LNG), which operates under decades-long contracts. In an elaborately crafted argument, they said the development of Sunrise was aimed at a marketing 'window' in 2010 when an opportunity would arise from the expiry of many long-term contracts. Unless ratification was forthcoming, Woodside would not be able to sign those contracts and the $5 billion capital investment for the offshore development would be shelved. At the same time, the Australian government's commodity analyst, the Australian Bureau of Agricultural and Resource Economics (ABARE), predicted that demand for LNG would continue to run well ahead of supply for the medium to long-term as a result of growing demand in Asia, and new demand for this energy source in the United States. This analysis did not indicate that the window proclaimed by Woodside actually existed.[13]

In April 2004 Kitson turned up uninvited to a conference of East Timor's aid donors. At that time about 40 per cent of East Timor's national budget was financed directly by donors as oil revenue had not yet begun to come on stream. He told the donors that East Timor's demand on aid money would be lessened, somewhat, by immediate ratification of the Sunrise agreement. Kitson's objective was to get the donors to add pressure to the East Timor government to ratify the Sunrise agreement.

Woodside's lobbying effort was not totally one-sided. It applied pressure to Canberra, and this is what motivated the Australian government to begin looking seriously at resolving the dispute. But with East Timor holding out on ratification, most of Woodside's attention was focused on Dili.

In the same month Woodside acquired a new chief executive, American Don Voelte, a former executive at Mobil and Atlantic Richfield. Under his leadership, the company began to take a firm line. In late July Voelte flew to Dili and met with Alkatiri. This straightforward early fifties oilman, distinguished by an oversized diamond ring, told Alkatiri that unless East Timor ratified the

Sunrise agreement by the end of the year, development would be scrapped. Alkatiri told Voelte that Woodside could do whatever it wanted. Woodside's deadline made no impression on him.

In an attempt to apply more pressure, Woodside publicly canvassed its strategy with the media. A few days after the Dili meeting Keith Spence, the chief operating officer and second in line after Voelte, went public with the Christmas deadline. Unless East Timor ratified the Sunrise agreement before Christmas 'we can't proceed . . . the harsh reality,' he said, 'is we will not invest billions of dollars without fiscal and legal certainty. So we can't proceed.'[14]

While using the media to its advantage, Woodside attempted to impose a muzzle on East Timor. The company warned East Timor that potential buyers of Sunrise gas were unnerved by what they had been reading about the dispute between East Timor and Australia, and were reluctant to enter contracts with the project. The media coverage of the dispute was highlighting Woodside's lack of secure title. This concern prompted Woodside to attempt to impose on the East Timor government a media 'protocol' that involved a script of agreed 'messages', and the requirement to obtain prior approval by the other side before making public statements in relation to Greater Sunrise. This oil company thought that it could bind East Timor, an independent sovereign nation, on what it could say publicly, while it did not attempt to impose such a protocol on the Australian government. East Timor did not flatly reject the protocol, but when Woodside officials asked about it they were told that it had been sent to the prime minister for consideration. The company remained hopeful that it would succeed in securing the protocol, and continued to ask about it throughout 2004.

Woodside's lobbying did not impress the East Timorese leadership or its advisers, many of whom had significant international experience and were unaccustomed to having deadlines imposed on hem by oil companies. Einar Risa told executives from one multinational that he liked dealing with them because 'unlike another company you don't impose deadlines'. Nor did it impress the considerably vocal and active network of NGOs in Dili. In mid-2004 Woodside briefed the NGO Forum, an umbrella group for interest groups in East Timor. Later that year, as negotiations appeared to be moving close to a resolution, the same network put out a statement that condemned the pressure applied by Woodside on an issue of national sovereignty. 'Greater Sunrise should be East Timor's territory, development cannot be started until a boundary or IUA is in place. We condemn pressure exerted by Woodside Oil Company to quickly begin exploitation in this area,' the statement said.

As an Australian icon, Woodside worked hand-in-hand with the Australian government throughout the negotiations. In late 2004 Kitson telephoned Risa to speak about the talks that were taking place that week in Dili. Kitson had called Risa's mobile phone and did not hang up properly. He then picked up another telephone and called one of the Australian negotiators, relaying everything that Risa had just told him. Risa was aghast. He had never experienced anything like this in his long career in government and in the oil industry. East Timor really was getting tutorials in a very peculiar brand of politics.

7 THE CREATIVE SOLUTION

> *'Australian officials said yesterday this was unrealistic as the history of establishing maritime boundaries suggested such negotiations could take up to 30 years to complete.'* DFAT officials dismissing East Timor's request for a prompt resolution to the dispute, and revealing their strategy to drag out the negotiations for 30 years; reported in the *Australian*, November 2003

Prominent in many towns in East Timor are impressive colonial residences built by the Portuguese administration. Known as *pousadas* (guest houses), they served as the homes of officials of the colonial administration or as guest houses. The symbolism of the colonists residing high above the local population was deliberate, and so was that of the massive foundations supporting these buildings. Using forced labour, mammoth earthworks were undertaken to produce an extensive level area on a hilltop where a promenade was built so that the colonials could observe life below. It is not difficult to imagine the small Timorese men hauling loads of earth onto those hilltops. The foundations sent a very strong signal: the Portuguese administration believed it was here to stay.

The creative solution

With the invasion of East Timor in 1975, many of these residences were immediately occupied by the Indonesian military. The senior officers resided in the homes while buildings at the back were turned into places of interrogation, torture and grisly death. Near the lighthouse on the Dili waterfront, on Avenida Sergio Vieira de Mello, stands a row of six, solidly built colonial homes which look out to a park and the sea beyond. Senior Indonesian officers lived in these waterfront residences during the occupation, and most were torched when they departed in 1999. When in late 2005 renovations began on one, now the residence and office of the New Zealand embassy, excavation work unearthed the remains of at least three people in shallow graves directly beneath a side window. More remains were found as digging for an in-ground swimming pool was begun in the yard. It was difficult to tell how many sets of remains were uncovered but the loose bones overflowed from four garbage bags.[1] At no point did the construction work stop, or was consideration given to building a memorial to these unknown victims or to halt proceeding with the building of a veranda and in-ground pool on these grave sites.

In late 2003 a group of consultants and civil servants from the East Timor government held a three-day retreat at the *Pousada de Baucau*, formerly the thriving Hotel Flamboyant, a destination favoured by honeymooners who flew in on direct flights from Darwin during the Portuguese time. Perched high above the main street, the hotel looked over the top of palm trees to the sea beyond. The intensive meeting was held to map out a strategy to negotiate with Australia over a permanent maritime boundary in the Timor Sea. The group met in a conference room that looked onto a courtyard and to derelict rooms at the back that had been used as torture chambers.

With the Timor Sea Treaty now ratified by both parliaments and the Sunrise agreement signed, East Timor was pressuring Australia to move quickly onto negotiating a boundary in the Timor Sea. Australia's active depletion of the BCL fields, and its issuing of new licences in the disputed area, provided the impetus for East Timor to press for an expeditious settlement. Alkatiri had written to John Howard in March 2003 asking for the formal commencement of boundary negotiations, but Howard did not reply for another five months. When he did send a reply, Howard apologised for its lateness and confirmed that his government would open talks on a maritime boundary in the Timor Sea.

Seated around the table at the Baucau retreat was a formidable assembly of expertise—people with decades of experience in foreign and defence ministries, in maritime law and in the petroleum industry. They were joined by José Teixeira, at the time a secretary of state—a third-level minister—in Alkatiri's government, together with Timorese civil servants who had been educated in Australia, Portugal, Macau and Indonesia, and a couple of serious young Ivy League lawyers. The team came from around the world—from the United States, the United Kingdom, Norway, Canada and Australia. Some of the internationals had been associated with East Timor for several years and were strongly committed to the country; others had just flown in to work on six-figure, tax-free salaries while having scant knowledge of the country's history. One of the lawyers, a Harvard graduate, knew so little about East Timor's traumatic past that they said 'What was that?' when someone mentioned the 1991 Santa Cruz massacre.

Firmly entrenched at the head of the table was Peter Galbraith, who had retired from his teaching position and had gone to work in Kurdish Iraq, among other places, as a freelance adviser. Alkatiri had asked Galbraith to become involved in the boundary negotiations given his role in the treaty negotiations. Einar Risa was there along with a fellow *éminence grise*, Philip Daniel, who had left an academic career to travel the world advising developing countries on their dealings with multinational oil companies while based in the Sussex hills south of London. Daniel wrote with a gold-nibbed fountain pen, spoke in perfectly rounded vowels and sang bass in a choir, while also being a capable economist.

The creative solution

As this strategy session progressed over three days it became a platform for some of these high-calibre, over-achieving experts to show their expertise. It was called a negotiating team, but throughout the negotiations it operated more like a collection of individuals with their own agendas, or like rival fiefdoms. It was a microcosm of how international development agencies work, or fail to work, around the world.

Jonathan Morrow gave the opening presentation—an overview of the history of maritime arrangements in the Timor Sea. A month earlier Morrow, together with Galbraith, had briefed the Council of Ministers on East Timor's maritime boundary strategy, but his overview quickly became something akin to a university tutorial dominated by an irrepressible and highly demonstrative Portuguese naval officer who had recently completed a PhD on maritime boundaries in the Timor Sea.[2]

Angolan-born Nuno Antunes had migrated with his family to Portugal in the mid-1970s as the civil war in Angola engulfed the abandoned former colony. Speaking with an Angolan accent, he immediately found himself treated as an inferior, but he later gained entry to the Portuguese navy and studied at the college in Sagres, the port city from where explorers had sailed to discover the new world and its treasures more than half a millennium ago. Antunes spent the best part of two decades at sea, and as a navigator he worked in the early hours of the morning to take readings from the stars. Upon returning to dry land he found himself still waking early, so he started studying law in Portugal and then at the University of Durham in the United Kingdom.

Antunes was one of the few experts in the world who could give advice on Timor Sea maritime boundaries, but he was dropped from East Timor's negotiating team back in 2000 after an email from Ian Brownlie, the professor of law from Oxford University who had advised East Timor on the Timor Sea Treaty. Brownlie told Galbraith he had received a memo from Antunes which was not very helpful. 'In particular, he draws my attention to a number of cases in which in fact I was Counsel. None of those cases bears any resemblance to the geographical circumstances of the present case,'[3] Brownlie wrote. Galbraith told Antunes that he no longer wanted him involved. Returning two years later, Antunes was determined to make a strong impression. As the only expert on maritime law on the team he saw fit to preface his remarks with the comment, 'I am going to speak at some length.' While he came to Portugal as an outsider, he certainly adopted the tendency to speak with supercilious formality.

Morrow did not have a background in maritime law but he had worked closely with Galbraith on the treaty negotiations, which Antunes no doubt deeply resented. Antunes' main contribution to this three-day discussion was to repeat the concerns that had already been raised about the wisdom of signing the Timor Sea Treaty. Antunes was less worried about the treaty than by the signing of an agreement attributing 79.9 per cent of Sunrise directly to Australia which might be interpreted by a court as a surrender by East Timor of its rights. In other words, even though East Timor succeeded in getting that clause in the recitals about both sides having claims in the area around Sunrise, the act of signing off on the 79.9 per cent could dominate any court's view of this dispute.

Galbraith had taught strategy at the US government's National War College in Washington and talked at length about what he called the BATNA—the 'best alternative to a negotiated agreement'. This meant obtaining the same amount of money as would be derived from having a boundary without actually having one. The meeting agreed that Australia would probably never accept a maritime boundary that followed the median line because it feared the reaction of Indonesia. This concern, however, was based on supposition rather than a real threat from Indonesia, which had relinquished completely its interest in the Timor Sea immediately after the 1999 ballot. As John Dowd, the former NSW attorney-general and president of the Australian branch of the International Commission of Jurists put it, 'They haven't said a word, and if they did they are 30 years too late.'[4]

The creative solution

Instead, what Galbraith called the 'Creative Solution' emerged. This wasn't an original name. It was exactly what Gareth Evans had called the Timor Gap Treaty at its signing in 1989. It meant that East Timor would accept an expansion of the JPDA, or a bigger share of the Sunrise field, together with compensation for the BCL fields, to achieve its revenue objective. East Timor would still press Australia for a boundary, and it would insist on its right to a boundary as a means of achieving its revenue goal, but it would be prepared to accept a revenue share without the invisible line on the seabed.

The meeting discussed doing a deal with Indonesia to add leverage to East Timor's negotiating position. It could trade East Timor's potential maritime jurisdiction north of Timor, where it projected into the Indonesian archipelago, with areas in the south. If this was achieved, then East Timor could conceivably secure a wider area to the north of the 1972 boundary, and use this to pressure Australia to agree to the same adjustment below this line. This was a long shot but one worth exploring, Galbraith reasoned.

One outcome of the Baucau meeting was the drawing of a map that set out the maximum area of overlap between the claims of East Timor and Australia outside the treaty area. It was a good device to focus on exactly what was at stake. In these areas East Timor called on Australia to exercise 'restraint' under UNCLOS Articles 74 (3) and 83 (3). These articles say that pending an agreement on maritime boundaries, states shall make every effort to reach provisional arrangements and shall not 'jeopardize or hamper' the reaching of a final settlement. East Timor argued that Australia's unilateral exploitation of the BCL fields and the continuing issuances of licences were exactly the sort of actions prescribed as unlawful by UNCLOS.

East Timor called the areas the red zones (see Map 5). A perpendicular line drawn from East Timor's land border with Indonesia, passing through point A18 in the Indonesia–Australia seabed agreement, and then stopping at the median line defined the western zone. In the east, the median line extended in a straight line until it met the 1972 boundary. The intersection point coincided with a lateral boundary that gave only a 50 per cent weighting to the Indonesian islands, a discount that eminent international lawyers said East Timor might be entitled to in a court ruling.

The outer edges of shaded areas in Map 5 were not what East Timor expected to achieve as a boundary, but they defined the maximum area of overlap not covered by the Timor Sea Treaty. The perpendicular line in the west represented an optimistic reading of the law. While InterFET had adopted this line for military jurisdiction, courts in the past had tended not to decide on such boundaries. The Brownlie opinion says there was 'no basis, in the context of geographical circumstances and equitable principles, for the use of a "perpendicular"'. A court might arrive at a boundary that went close to this perpendicular line by discounting for the effect of the Tanjong We Toh cape, thereby giving the BCL fields to East Timor, but there was no guarantee of this outcome.

In relation to the eastern area, the Lowe opinion predicted that East Timor could secure the entire Sunrise field by discounting for the effect of the Indonesian island of Leti:

> Modern international law . . . does not permit small islands to have a disproportionate and inequitable effect upon maritime boundaries. The law requires that small islands that would disproportionately affect a maritime delimitation be given only a proportional effect— perhaps one half or three-quarters effect.
>
> This approach is now very firmly established in the practice of international courts and tribunals. ICJ and arbitration cases routinely discount the effect given to small islands that would inequitably or disproportionately affect the delimitation. This was done, for example, by the arbitral tribunal in the *Western Approaches* case (1977) between France and the United Kingdom, where the United Kingdom's Scilly Isles were given half weight, and by the ICJ in the *Tunisia/Libya* case (1982), in which the Tunisian Kerkennah islands were given half weight. In the *Dubai/Sharjah* case (1981), Sharjah's island of Abu Musa was in effect ignored.[5]

Lowe was confident that a court would discount the effect of Leti, although he did not mention the other islands, thereby pushing the eastern lateral east of Sunrise and giving all of it to East Timor. But Brownlie's private opinion was far more cautious on the eastern lateral: East Timor would only be entitled to 100 per cent of Greater Sunrise under an 'optimistic application of legal criteria'. Antunes had written publicly that a fifty-fifty division of Sunrise, together with awarding the BCL fields to East Timor, was a likely outcome because it 'entails an equitable access to resources'.[6]

The median line shown on Map 3 seemed firmly entrenched as the fisheries boundary agreed between Australia and Indonesia in 1981 had affirmed it as the horizontal boundary, and this was reinforced when they settled on their Exclusive Economic Zone in 1997. But the threat of moving it northwards was used by Downer and senior government officials in DFAT and the Attorney-General's Department. The Jesuit lawyer and civil rights activist Frank Brennan gave these arguments a fair hearing when he said Australia could point to the 1984 Gulf of Maine ruling in which the International Court of Justice said the boundary should reflect the length of Canada's coastline, 206 nautical miles, relative to the greater length of the United States coastline of 284 nautical miles, giving a ratio of 1:1.38. The ratio in the Timor Sea was far greater: 148 nautical miles of East Timorese coastline to 327 nautical miles of Australian coastline, or 1:2.21.[7] Brennan's influential paper came about after the East Timor government briefed the Catholic Bishops' Committee for Justice, Peace and Development, and Caritas on the dispute in December 2003. Brennan went out of his way to present the arguments of all parties, speaking privately to senior figures in both governments and from Woodside, but in his conclusion he decided against moving the median line towards East Timor. He thought a fair settlement might involve giving 90 per cent of the Sunrise field to East Timor, while awarding the BCL fields to Australia.

In the landmark Libya–Malta case the court moved the equidistance line towards Libya, but this reflected a coastline ratio of almost 10:1 in favour of Libya. The southern edge of the Bayu-Undan field is just 12 nautical miles from the median line, so even a slight adjustment could bisect the field or even move the boundary north of it so that it fell into Australia's hands. Downer warned East Timor during the dispute that it could be left with a median line further to the north 'without any share of the Bayu Undan gas field, rather than the 90 per cent share East Timor currently enjoys'.[8] All of this was hypothetical, of course, because Australia's withdrawal from international arbitration meant that the dispute would never go before a court. The strength of East Timor's claim to the median line was underscored by Australia's decision to withdraw from the international umpire.

* * *

East Timor's public prosecution of its case was the final element discussed at some length at the Baucau strategy meeting.[9] East Timor was up against an Australia where increasing xenophobia among some sections of the community could be used against it in this dispute. This had loomed large in the 2001 election when John Howard won with a slogan, printed in white letters on a sinister black background, that read: 'WE DECIDE WHO COMES INTO THIS COUNTRY AND THE CIRCUMSTANCES IN WHICH THEY COME.' The Australian government had also fabricated claims during the federal election campaign that refugees had thrown their children overboard, thereby demonising them for political gain. There was an increasingly tabloid political culture in Australia. And in the Timor Sea dispute it was the tabloid newspapers, together with Murdoch's broadsheet the *Australian*, that aggressively ran with comments by Downer defending Australia's national interest in this dispute.

The meeting agreed with a recommendation from an Australian adviser that East Timor adopt a very strong international focus in its campaigning, rather than initially trying to cut through the noise of the daily domestic news cycle in Australia. Indeed East Timor was advised to focus almost entirely on international exposure. This strategy was based on the premise that there is very little international news coverage of Australia, and so getting even a small amount of global coverage with this story would have a magnifying effect and turn the issue into something that defined Australia's image abroad. Australian politicians pay a lot of attention to international coverage and the impact it has on Australia's reputation. After achieving prominence in the international press, the Australian media would take the Timor Sea dispute more seriously, or so strategy went.

This strategy was also likely to be more effective in grabbing the attention of the one individual who really mattered in this dispute, and that was John Howard. East Timor was a big part of Howard's legacy after the role he played in putting together the InterFET force in 1999. In order to succeed, East Timor had to take this issue away from the control of DFAT. In late 1998 Howard decided to review Australia's policy on the issue of the self-determination of East Timor, setting up an inter-departmental review run by his own Department of Prime Minister and Cabinet rather than one controlled by DFAT.

The meeting agreed that East Timor would seek to expose Australia's intransigent position by making the reasonable request that Australia do one of the following three things:

- Enter into good faith negotiations to agree to a boundary within three to five years.
- Cease the exploitation of the disputed resources or put the money into escrow.
- Submit to the jurisdiction of an international arbiter.

At the conclusion of the Baucau retreat Galbraith gave the team strict instructions on secrecy. He predicted that Australian intelligence would intercept all of the team's emails and telephone conversations. He was speaking from his considerable experience in the US departments of state and defence, although he refused to elaborate on what he knew. The team decided on a password—based on the name of one of the key cases—that would be used to protect documents that were to be emailed among the group.

* * *

The first meeting on maritime boundaries between the two governments took place on 12 November 2003 in Darwin, at the height of the hot and humid build-up to northern Australia's wet season. From the Australian perspective this meeting was not building up to anything, precipitation or otherwise. Letters exchanged in advance made clear that this was to be the first of a formal series of meetings to sort out the dispute. When East Timor's negotiating team of ten people assembled in full, they met just three negotiators on the other side of the table in a conference room in a Darwin hotel. This first meeting was to be a 'scoping' meeting to talk about future talks, but the Australian delegation gave a clear indication that the resources outside the JPDA were not to be on the agenda. Australia simply did not recognise that East Timor had any claim whatsoever.

Prior to this meeting the Australian government showed its real intent with regard to the negotiations. In background comments to the media, officials sought to play down expectations of a resolution of the dispute. This was to be the start of a drawn out saga that might take 30 years and would probably achieve nothing, they explained. Australia was hoping to wear down a tiny country that had very limited resources, while continuing to exploit oil from the disputed areas. A story in the *Australian* gave the game away when it reported a government response to East Timor's request for a three to five year timeframe to resolve the dispute: 'But Australian officials said yesterday this was unrealistic as the history of establishing maritime boundaries suggested such negotiations could take up to 30 years to complete.'[10]

Negotiations over the 1972 treaty with Indonesia, for an area many times greater than the Timor Sea, took just over 17 months to complete. And more recently negotiations with New Zealand took just four years.

The creative solution

Australia's active depletion of the BCL fields provided a springboard for East Timor to mount a persuasive argument for a fair and expeditious resolution of the dispute. East Timor had protested about Australia's exploitation of these fields during the Timor Sea Treaty negotiations. Now that the negotiations had moved to maritime boundaries, they were to become pivotal in East Timor's public campaign which claimed that Australia had pocketed since 1999 a total of more than US$2 billion.

When East Timor asked for monthly meetings, the Australian delegation made the unbelievable claim that the Australian government did not have the 'resources' to negotiate at this pace. The cost of a more committed Australian involvement would have been a negligible proportion of the US$1 million per day that it had collected from the BCL fields since 1999. In making this argument the Australian team provided East Timor with immensely valuable capital in its battle to win public opinion.

Immediately after the Darwin meeting Alkatiri wrote to Howard and expressed his 'dismay' at the statements by Australian officials that 'Australia does not even acknowledge that Timor-Leste has maritime boundary claims outside the Joint Petroleum Development Area (JPDA), and that Australia is therefore free from a legal obligation of restraint with regard to the exploitation of resources in the disputed area'.[11] Alkatiri wrote that he was very concerned that Australia was unwilling to consider more than two meetings a year given that it was already earning billions of dollars from the disputed areas.

Five days after this meeting the Council of Ministers formally adopted a strong position on maritime boundaries, based on the results of the Baucau retreat and the Darwin meeting. The submission from Alkatiri, made on 17 November 2003 and approved unanimously, said that East Timor should pursue negotiations with Australia over a permanent maritime boundary that would follow the median line and include all of Sunrise and the BCL fields. This was East Timor's starting point. Alkatiri and the cabinet knew they would end up with a 'creative' outcome that would mean accepting much less.

8 THE RELUCTANT PRESIDENT

'This is not right. The country which steals from us then organises conferences regarding transparency, anti-corruption.'
President Xanana Gusmão, quoted in Portugal's *Publico* newspaper, April 2004

In late 2003 the government of East Timor began a process of privately asserting its rights in the disputed area. In September the foreign ministry sent a formal diplomatic note to the Australian government in which it outlined the country's 200-nautical-mile claim and Australia's obligation to exercise restraint in the areas of overlap. The note challenged Australia's authorisation of licences for exploration and the exploitation of petroleum in these areas. The Australian government made no public comment about the note.

The Australian government's written response came almost three months later, following the November meeting in Darwin. It formally rejected any claim on the part of East Timor to the areas outside the JPDA. It formally rejected any claim on the part of East Timor to the area outside the JPDA. The response said that Australia does not accept that East Timor has claim over any of the deposits referred to as they lay within areas over which 'Australia has sole sovereign rights'. The letter emphasised the fact Australia has exercised sovereign rights over these for 'an extensive period of time', and therefore it cannot be in breach of international law. It said East Timor was merely making an ambit claim and that this did not raise for Australia any obligation of restraint. 'Australia will continue to exercise its exclusive sovereign rights in the relevant areas,' the letter concluded.[1]

The following month the East Timor government wrote privately to the companies that were operating the BCL fields, including BHP Billiton and Woodside, and informed them that they were:

> ... conducting petroleum activities in areas under Timor-Leste jurisdiction—most notably, relating to the Corallina and Laminaria fields. Those activities have not been authorized under Timor-Leste law. Failure to comply with relevant laws governing petroleum activities will render [the company] liable to civil and criminal prosecution. [The company] may have incurred tax and other financial liabilities in relation to these petroleum activities.[2]

The Uniting Church's Victorian and Tasmanian Synod, which owned a not insignificant holding in Woodside and BHP Billiton through its pension fund, asked the companies at around this time to explain why they were not paying tax on the Laminaria and Corallina fields to East Timor. In a letter signed by Gary Gray, Woodside said it was operating 'under properly issued titles authorised pursuant to the laws of Australia. We do not accept that the joint venturers have any liabilities in relation to those oilfields under other laws.' The Uniting Church kept up the pressure at meetings with senior Woodside and BHP Billiton executives, and it actually got a sympathetic hearing from BHP's vice president for 'sustainable development', Dr Ian Wood. In November 2004, following a year of bad press about these fields, BHP Billiton announced that it would sell its 32.6 per cent stake in Laminaria and 25 per cent stake in Corallina to the London-listed Paladin Resources plc.

SHAKEDOWN

East Timor had begun to assert its claim to the disputed resources with its private communications to the oil companies. The actions of the Australian government prompted prominent figures in East Timor to go public.

In late March 2004 the Australian government tabled bills[3] for the ratification of the Sunrise agreement. The explanatory memorandum said Australia had sole jurisdiction outside the JPDA, a claim that contradicted what the agreement actually said about both countries having claims in the area around Greater Sunrise. In response, the East Timor government issued a press release in which it challenged these claims. Under the headline 'Australia is Undermining Greater Sunrise Development', the release said these statements and actions 'contradict the International Unitisation Agreement and undermine prospects for its approval'.[4] East Timor for the first time signalled that it was prepared to take the bold step of rejecting ratification of the agreement.

On the day it tabled the legislation the Australian government advertised new blocks for exploration in the disputed areas near Sunrise and the BCL fields. East Timor responded with a second strong statement in which it protested this latest move, saying for the first time that Australia was unlawfully 'occupying' the Timor Sea.

> A permanent boundary is also an integral part of Timor-Leste's right to self-determination and will end the illegal occupation of its territory. As long as Australia continues to illegally occupy this area of the Timor Sea, it is undermining our territorial integrity.[5]

This was a direct reference to the production licences issued by Australia for the BCL fields prior to 1999, and its continued issuing and advertising of exploration licences in the disputed areas subsequent to East Timor becoming independent. In 2003, after the signing of the Sunrise agreement, the Australian government had issued an exploration permit adjacent to the Sunrise field, and then it had issued another in early 2004. Now it was advertising even more, as shown in Map 6. This was a deliberate strategy on the part of the Australian government to completely cover the disputed areas with its permits. East Timor's statement took aim at investor confidence—it bluntly told companies not to apply for the permits: 'Companies considering bidding for these blocks should be aware of the potential risks of investing in disputed territory as Timor-Leste will take all lawful steps to prevent unlawful exploration and exploitation of resources within its maritime zone.'

On this occasion even the Murdoch press saw the injustice of East Timor's rights being disregarded. In an article titled 'Release taunts Timor', Nigel Wilson said Australia had issued permits in an area claimed by East Timor, and that an 'unrepentant' Resources Minister Ian Macfarlane said defiantly in his raspy voice: 'We can't leave these resources unexplored and undeveloped.'[6] The unfairness of Australia's unilateral licensing of disputed resources lying twice as close to East Timor as to Australia was illustrated by Woodside's reactions to oil spills at its Laminaria facility. Woodside reported a small spill to the Australian government in October 2004, and then in February 2005 reported another spill of around 300 barrels. Woodside claimed, without providing independent verification, that the oil had evaporated. It did not report the incident to the East Timor government, which wrote to Woodside seeking an explanation and expressing its concern that there had been no independent assessment of these incidents.

East Timor's press statements elicited an official protest from the Australian ambassador, Paul Foley, even though it was doing exactly what was required under international law—the country had to act in accordance with its claim to the resources. An article by Dean Bialek, a Melbourne University academic who later joined DFAT's negotiating team, and Professor Gillian Triggs, also of the University of Melbourne, said it would be 'prudent' for East Timor to protect its claims by reaffirming its non-recognition of any interests granted by Australia that were inconsistent with East Timor's rights to a maritime jurisdiction under international law.[7] East Timor was simply reinforcing its rights.

* * *

The Australian government's response to the September 2003 diplomatic note, its subsequent tactics at the November meeting, its release of more licences in the disputed areas, and its public statements provoked and fuelled a very assertive international lobbying campaign by East Timor. A strategy of 'good cop bad cop' had been planned. Initially Galbraith had wanted to play a very high profile role in speaking on behalf of East Timor, but the Timor Sea Office decided that having a campaign led by a hired gun was very likely to be counter-productive. It was difficult to see how Galbraith could win Australian public opinion, particularly with his grating, Bostonian accent; having Timorese figures leading the campaign made more sense. After all, East Timor had a star-studded line-up of figures who had gained an international reputation during the independence struggle.

The prime minister, while not having a high profile, would be the bad cop, the forceful advocate of East Timor's case, and it was hoped that President Xanana Gusmão would join him. Gusmão, however, is a very independent individual and his involvement would depend on his own disposition. The foreign minister, José Ramos-Horta, was to be the good cop, together with the first lady, Australian-born Kirsty Sword Gusmão, whom Ramos-Horta described as East Timor's 'secret weapon'.[8]

Gusmão was initially very reluctant to take part in the Timor Sea debate. His advisers had a keen interest in the issue but the president initially believed it was a matter for the executive; he believed that his role was one of oversight and review of the executive.

Gusmão is the reluctant hero of East Timor's resistance struggle. A minor player on the fringes of the 1970s independence movement,[9] he eschewed direct involvement with the FRETILIN party.

In late 1975 he was made a member of the party's governing body, the Central Committee, when the party leadership submitted his name and told him the decision was final. He was editing the FRETILIN newspaper *Journal do Povo Maubere*[10] (Journal of the Maubere People) when he saw his name on a list for publication of the 50 members of FRETILIN's governing body. He tried unsuccessfully to have it removed.[11]

Gusmão rose to prominence only after most members of the first ministry and the Central Committee were wiped out by the end of the 1970s, and then in December 1987 he resigned from FRETILIN because he believed East Timor needed a broader, multi-party independence movement. Exactly one year later he founded the *Conselho Nacional da Resistência Maubere* (CNRM), which later became the CNRT.

After 16 years on the run in the mountains, and eight years in Jakarta's Cipinang prison, he did not covet high office. He said he would prefer to write, paint and take photographs. But as independence approached he was press-ganged into standing for the presidency. He won with 82.7 per cent of the vote. His rival, the first president Francisco Xavier do Amaral, said he only became a candidate to give the appearance of a democratic contest. The vote for Gusmão underscored his role as figure of national unity during difficult times.

In October 2003 Gusmão travelled to the United Kingdom on an official visit. He took with him a set of talking points on the Timor Sea dispute prepared by the Timor Sea Office, which also set up an interview in London with the *Guardian*. Gusmão's comments were unremarkable: 'We're not asking too much from Australia. What belongs to us is ours. We hope Australia can understand that.' There wasn't a story in these comments, but the *Guardian* linked them with the announcement in Dili of budget cuts as a result of delays in the start of production at the Bayu-Undan field. The first paragraph read: 'Australia, which led an international peace force to help East Timor become independent last year, has become the greatest barrier to the country's hopes of breaking free from reliance on foreign aid, according to stark budget figures released yesterday.'[12]

The *Guardian* article demonstrated the potency of international coverage. Until this time the Australian government had never responded to any public comments on the dispute from the East Timor leadership. Yet the response to this article was swift. Downer's man in London, High Commissioner Michael L'Estrange, who in early 2005 became secretary to DFAT, wrote in a letter to the *Guardian* that the Timor Sea Treaty and the Sunrise agreement amounted to a 'win-win package' for East Timor and Australia. The 90 per cent share was 'very generous' compared with the 50 per cent that Indonesia received. Addressing Australia's withdrawal from compulsory dispute resolution, he said this reflected a desire to settle such disputes through negotiation rather than arbitration, and that 'we are looking forward to engaging with East Timor on these issues soon'.[13] This statement, which had undoubtedly been prepared with help from Canberra, suggested that Australia was willing to hold genuine negotiations with East Timor to resolve the dispute.

Despite having achieved a very effective intervention, Gusmão still remained reticent about playing a prominent role in the dispute. Later in 2003 he attended an investment conference in Japan and took a briefing note from the Timor Sea Office which linked East Timor's oil and gas potential with the need to bring about the rule of law in the Timor Sea. But instead of raising the issue the president talked about the country's potential as a diving destination.

By this time, however, the Gusmão household had become well briefed on the dispute. Gusmão's wife, Kirsty, began preparing for a national speaking tour of Australia planned for mid-2004. With Kirsty Sword Gusmão now involved, it was hoped that the story would reach a wider audience. East Timor's strategists thought that Sword Gusmão might succeed in grabbing the attention of female politicians, or politicians' wives, most notably the very influential Janette Howard, the wife of the prime minister.

Sword Gusmão is a compelling advocate for East Timor. She was a ballerina as a child, and this perhaps explains the grace and poise that she brings to the speaker's podium. This is exactly what East Timor needed in this campaign, and it would need even more of it after her husband had finished making his contribution.

For Xanana Gusmão, the tipping point came when he fully comprehended the extent to which Australia had disregarded East Timor's rights in the Timor Sea. Just before the first formal meeting between East Timor and Australia in April 2004, Gusmão received a briefing note from the Timor Sea Office which outlined Australia's issuance of new licences and the offending statements attached to the Sunrise bills. The briefing note repeated the characterisation of 'illegal occupation' used in the 31 March press release.

All of this was weighing on Gusmão's mind one day in April 2004 as he drove up the windy mountain road south of Dili en route to the district centre of Ailieu. At the top of the mountain he passed a dilapidated school at Laulara which had part of its roof missing and chicken wire for windows. What he saw angered him and he decided he wanted to speak to the children directly. He told his driver to stop, and then, with the children assembled around him, he said in a loud, angry voice:

> Today we are still begging. They give us money with a smile and say 'take it'. We have no money. You might have heard that we have oil, oil and gas in our sea that people want to steal. They are the resources that can help us to fix everything.
>
> Australia is a rich country. A rich country which recognised our past integration. After that, Ali Alatas and Gareth Evans flew over East Timor drinking champagne and signing the agreement to steal our oil. You don't understand what I'm saying. This petroleum zone is mine and that is yours. Understand?[14]

Cameraman and journalist José Belo, who had turned his hand to making films while serving in the resistance army in the mountains, captured the address and sent the footage to the SBS *Dateline* television program. The host, Mark Davis, noted that until very recently it was the prime minister who had presented the Timor Sea dispute to the public, but now the president had suddenly taken carriage of the issue.

Now that Gusmão had finally latched onto the dispute there was no holding him back. Later that month he travelled to Portugal on an official visit which coincided with the first formal maritime boundary meeting in Dili. He expanded on the theme of 'occupation'. The BBC reported:

> East Timor's President Xanana Gusmão has launched a fierce attack on Australia's attitude in its dealings with the fledgling country. Mr. Gusmão said there was an unequal struggle with Australia to secure oil and gas resources. In a speech in Lisbon, he said that the battle was only comparable to the Timorese fight to free themselves from Indonesian domination.[15]

Four days later, in an interview with the newspaper *Publico*, Gusmão said that Australia was 'using all the dirty tactics it can' in the dispute, and he alluded to the hypocrisy of its adherence to the fashionable 'good governance' agenda in its aid program while at the same time it refused to follow the rule of law in the Timor Sea. 'This is not right. The country which steals from us then organises conferences regarding transparency, anti-corruption.'[16] If Australia was really concerned about stability and good governance in East Timor, then justice in the Timor Sea was the first place to start. He warned Australia that this new democracy was at risk because of its hardline approach in the Timor Sea negotiations:

> Without money, democracy can fail. When you go to bed hungry, how can you think, 'no, it's all right, I am democratic?' I say to people, 'calm down, calm down', but I don't know how long I can maintain stability. We are losing a million dollars a day but currently we have no schools, no roads, no jobs.[17]

The drawing of a parallel with the Indonesian occupation was not an easy proposition to make—Gusmão appeared to have overplayed his hand in making this statement. The Indonesian occupation led to the deaths of at least 180 000 people. Australia's intransigence in the Timor Sea could not be compared with that. However supporters in Australia picked up the notion that their government was indirectly contributing to the abject poverty and high mortality rates in East Timor. This would become a key theme in the TV advertisements run by an Australian businessman, Ian Melrose, which in mid-2005 included the confronting line 'stealing from a third world country kills their children'.

Gusmão's intervention echoed a comment made by Greens' Senator Bob Brown during the dispute: the Australian government's actions were turning a country that should be Australia's best friend into a potentially hostile neighbour.[18] Gusmão demonstrated the commitment and determination of East Timor's leadership to fight and win this battle. He showed that Australia was up against formidable opponents who would not go away quietly. Australia's plan to drag out the dispute interminably would not succeed. The president's intervention put this two-year-old nation on the brink of completely rupturing its relationship with its affluent neighbour and would prompt Alexander Downer to send in a heavy hitter. The need for high-level, hard-hitting diplomacy was only reinforced when the first formal maritime boundary meeting was held in Dili.

9 THE SECRET ENVOY

'If we don't do this, as David, we will die.' Prime Minister Marí Alkatiri on why East Timor would defy Australia's ultimatums to cease public comment in its 'David and Goliath' struggle over the Timor Sea, April 2004

One of the positive legacies of East Timor's long resistance struggle is a highly effective support network that extends from the grassroots to the highest levels of the United Nations, the US Congress and the European parliament. In the lead-up to the first formal maritime boundary meeting that commenced on 19 April 2004, an international lobbying effort swung into operation.

The Washington-based East Timor Action Network (ETAN) began working at Capitol Hill to get US Congressmen to send a letter to Prime Minister John Howard urging Australia to act justly in the forthcoming negotiations. Set up in the wake of the Santa Cruz massacre, ETAN is a shoestring but highly effective operation with Professor Noam Chomsky as its high-profile patron.

A letter from high-ranking Democrat Barney Frank was co-signed by 52 members of Congress.[1] It called on the Australian government to negotiate in a timely manner to settle the dispute and, significantly, to put the money derived from disputed resources into an escrow account, thereby recognising East Timor's rights to resources outside the JPDA. This concept drew support from one of the few Australian academics who sided with the Australian government on the dispute. Professor Gillian Triggs from the University of Melbourne said there was a 'very good argument for putting the funds in escrow for a period' if East Timor's claims about the western lateral had 'any credibility'.[2]

The letter from the 53 members of Congress was very effective in building the international case against Australia's actions. The signatories were not lowly backbenchers, and they included a number of heavyweights on Capitol Hill, most notably: Nancy Pelosi, the highest ranking Democrat in the House of Representatives who in late 2006 became the first woman speaker of the House; Chris Smith, the Republican vice-chair of the powerful International Relations Committee; Tom Lantos, the highest ranking Democrat on the International Relations Committee and a survivor of the Holocaust; James Jeffords, the highest ranking Democrat on the Environment and Public Works Committee; and, Barney Frank, the highest ranking Democrat on the Financial Services Committee.

In the lead-up to the four-day April 2004 meeting East Timor's advisers briefed international media and NGOs around the world on what would be a crash-or-crash-through moment in the dispute. East Timor needed to generate widespread international support for its rights, and condemnation of Australia's tactics, if it was to win. The ABC's *Four Corners* and SBS's *Dateline* programs in Australia sent television crews to cover the meeting. As East Timor's advisers were drafting the prime minister's incendiary opening address, the Australian section of the International Commission of Jurists, a global law and human rights lobby, condemned the government's tactics. It described Australia's withdrawal from international arbitration as 'unconscionable', and added a very effective sporting metaphor:

> Australia is not only depriving its poverty-stricken neighbour of the opportunity to have law determine the issue, Australia is also

exploiting its present economic advantage by depleting the resources which are the subject of the dispute. We kicked out the umpire before East Timor existed.

Surely it is in Australia's interest to have a viable near neighbour in East Timor, rather than take from it, by hard commercial bargaining, the only cash earner it has. We ask the Australian government to return to the negotiating table in good faith or let the law or independent arbitration determine the result.[3]

East Timor needed all the support it could muster. It was up against a team of professionals, many of whom had spent their careers negotiating treaties and similar agreements—and standing firmly behind them was a government determined to be as tough as was required. East Timor's team comprised a core group made up of one member of the government, José Teixeira, and three full-time staffers, plus a collection of fly-in consultants who were working on other projects. Most of the consultants did not arrive until a few days before the meeting. Galbraith swaggered into Dili on the noon flight from Bali on the Thursday before the Monday morning meeting at the Hotel Timor, and spent the rest of the day writing a 6000-word opus on the Iraq war for the *New York Review of Books*, later published under the headline 'How to get out of Iraq'. Antunes came straight from his full-time position with the Portuguese navy and spent most of the weekend before the meeting locked in his room at the Hotel Timor writing what would be East Timor's definitive presentation.

* * *

East Timor's strategy for the April 2004 meeting transformed it from what would have otherwise been a tedious, behind-closed-doors meeting of officials, to a media spectacle. With all of East Timor's team assembled, an intensive series of meetings took place over the weekend in a converted garage in the backyard of the Timor Sea

Designated Authority's waterfront office in Dili. Galbraith's work in Iraq made him dislike working in this room because it had double-glass doors at one end facing a busy street, presenting a perfect target for a would-be terrorist. Over the next two days East Timor planned in precise detail for the four-day meeting. When a list of the Australian delegation came through Jonathan Morrow saw a familiar name, a former Melbourne academic who had only two years before publicly supported East Timor's position. Some archival research to retrieve the academic's public position on the dispute was required. Galbraith conceived of the dramatic opening, the traditional welcome and the presentation of *tais* to the officials by the teenage girls. There were also logistics and protocol to be arranged to ensure that the cameras would be in the conference room to film the opening speech. It was possible that the Australians would refuse to attend a meeting with cameras present, notwithstanding East Timor's 'home ground advantage'. This had to be raised in a low-key manner without giving anything away. The writing of the speech was a team effort, although Galbraith produced the line accusing Australia of profiting from 'a crime'. Some of the Galbraith lines smacked of Hollywood—'this is too much pain for us to bear'—and had to be removed. Galbraith insisted on keeping a line about East Timor offering to pay Australia's expenses to negotiate expeditiously, and when this was read by Alkatiri the head of the Australian delegation, Chris Moraitis, who had been listening attentively up to that point, shook his head in disbelief and began to smirk. There was so much haggling amongst team members over the speech that it was not sent to Alkatiri until 1 p.m., an hour before he was due to read it. The speech lasted less than two minutes but it spelled out East Timor's plea for justice with tenacity and simplicity. Journalists who were there in the room, including veteran reporters from the ABC and SBS, were greatly impressed by this audacious statement.

After the Australian delegation had recovered from Alkatiri's opening presentation—and all of them had removed the *tais* that the teenage girls had given them—they quickly got down to business.

First, the Australians laid down some ground rules about the meeting. There would be no record of anything said, not even one that could be used inside the meeting only. Everything that occurred in this meeting was to disappear into thin air—instantly. Members of the East Timor delegation did take notes throughout the course of these negotiations, but when they referred back to them later the Australians retorted, Orwellian-style 'There is no record'.

The Australian delegation strongly reaffirmed their government's position that the areas of overlap not covered by the Timor Sea Treaty were not up for negotiation. Bill Campbell QC, a general counsel within the Attorney-General's Department, was Australia's top legal adviser on international legal negotiations. He used the word 'benefit' repeatedly when presenting Australia's case. He argued that Australia had secured a treaty with Indonesia and derived *benefits* from it, and should not be expected to give up that *benefit*. In Australia's view, the disputed resources that fell within East Timor's 200-nautical-mile claim were not up for negotiation, Campbell said, citing Australia's 'active jurisdiction' while East Timor was occupied. Campbell had conveniently forgotten the essential fact that the end points of the 1972 seabed boundary should have been negotiated with East Timor as well, as the agreement's Article 3 plainly says. These benefits were derived from a two-party agreement whereas in fact a third party, East Timor, should have been involved. As general counsel Campbell, together with DFAT's senior legal adviser Chris Moraitis, gave advice to the Howard government in 2003 on the invasion of Iraq. Campbell also gave advice on the Tampa refugees in 2001 and the incarceration, without trial, of terror suspect David Hicks.

Galbraith, the head of the East Timor delegation, forcefully told the Australian side that this position amounted to Australia's negotiating in bad faith—a very serious charge. Australia was attending a formal negotiation without having the disposition to negotiate. Antunes argued succinctly and powerfully that there were over 60 cases around the world in which similar overlaps—where opposite states were less than 400 nautical miles apart—had been settled by drawing either a simple median line or one that varied only slightly from equidistance. There was only one case where an overlap had been resolved with reference to the shape of the seabed, and that was the 1972 agreement between Indonesia and Australia.

Struggling to counter Australia's intransigence, Galbraith resorted to theatrics. When the Australian negotiators, slouched back in their chairs, repeated their arguments about East Timor not having a claim outside the JPDA, Galbraith said that he would pay that argument, taking a United States quarter-dollar coin from his pocket and putting it on the table (at this time East Timor used US coins). When they repeated the assertion yet again Galbraith asked the most attractive women on East Timor's side to take the quarter across no-man's land and hand-deliver it to the Australians. Reluctantly, the adviser followed Galbraith's instructions as eyes rolled and cringes broke out all around.

As the Australian side dug in East Timor capitalised on public support it had received from an unexpected quarter—a member of the Australian delegation sitting in the room. This presented Galbraith with a platform for more theatrics as he read submissions and evidence to an Australian parliamentary committee in 2002 by Dean Bialek who at the time was a Melbourne University academic. Bialek had also helped write a submission for Oxfam Australia on the Timor Sea Treaty that strongly supported East Timor's rights. After joining DFAT, Bialek had been appointed to the Australian negotiating team, presumably because he would have been one of the few officials in the department with a background in maritime law. Bialek said nothing during this meeting, but his previously published papers and submissions were quoted extensively by the East Timor delegation.

On the pivotal issue of the median line, Bialek had questioned Australia's reliance on the 'natural prolongation' of its continental shelf. He wrote in his 2002 submission to the Joint Standing Committee on Treaties:

While the principle of natural prolongation remains valid at international law to support Australia's claim of a shelf out to the Timor Trough, it is increasingly subject to the preference for a median line where there is less than 400 nm between opposite states.[5]

In his submission Bialek also challenged the notion that the Australian government could drag out the talks interminably, saying that Australia had an international obligation under UNCLOS to negotiate in good faith. 'The Australian Government should remain mindful of the need to engage meaningfully in negotiations for the settlement of permanent maritime boundaries with East Timor.'[6]

Most damning of all in this submission was Bialek's statement that Australia should not be licensing production in the areas of overlap. This statement underpinned East Timor's key assertion that Australia had been unlawfully collecting $1 million a day on average since 1999 from the BCL fields.

> There is at least a good faith requirement to seek to discuss a proposal to explore an area subject to conflicting claims . . .
> Australia should avoid the unilateral pursuit of petroleum development in areas now known to be subject to overlapping claims. Such action would serve to heighten diplomatic unease that complicates the movement forward of plans to exploit the lucrative resources of the Timor Sea for the mutual benefit of Australia and East Timor.[7]

Bialek had also indicated that East Timor might be entitled to a bigger share of Greater Sunrise. While working as an academic he had contacted Morrow to inform him of a case between Indonesia and Malaysia that supported a discounting of the Indonesian island of Leti, thereby buttressing the case for an eastern lateral that gave all of the giant field to East Timor.

After the second day of talks Bialek sat with his bags in the foyer of the Hotel Timor waiting to be taken to the airport for a flight back to Canberra. Apparently, he had to leave early in order to attend a training course.

* * *

On the final day of the talks, local NGOs held a vigil outside the Hotel Timor. A coalition of NGOs had formed the 'Movement Against the Occupation of the Timor Sea' after Alkatiri had put the word 'occupation' into a press release in late March.

Dili is a city that barely has what most people would think of as a main street. It is a city where, aside from a handful of exceptions, the streets have no names. Nor do the houses have numbers, making it impossible for a postal service to operate, or for anyone living there to declare a residential address. The city's postcard feature is the waterfront, along which is strung out the main government buildings, colonial residences, embassies and some restaurants. The Hotel Timor, called the *Mahkota* in the Indonesian time, was wrecked in 1999 and substantially renovated by *Fundacão Oriente*, which runs casinos in Macau. Despite the makeover, cracks from earthquakes and tremors routinely appear in the building's walls and the US embassy will not allow staff to stay there. It sits on the waterfront road opposite the port, looking directly onto the place favoured by the Indonesian military for summary executions in December 1975. The downtown area consists of a few banks, hotels and shops on the streets abutting the *Palácio do Governo*. Some members of the Australian delegation found during their visits to Dili that they could find nothing to buy.

During the three days of talks, protestors had gathered outside the Australian embassy, which stands isolated on the dusty, one-lane *Avenida dos Martires da Patria* linking the town centre with the airport, before moving down to the Hotel Timor. (Nearly all of the other embassies are located on the prestigious waterfront road and look out to the sea.) Some protesters stayed on at the Australian embassy after the talks had finished and staged a hunger strike.

It was a steamy afternoon at the tail end of the wet season, and protestors lit candles outside the Hotel Timor and put them on the bitumen, as though they were attending a wake. Gathering on the road in between the hotel and the port, they sang a stirring independence anthem with a slight change to the lyrics. Instead of the chorus 'East Timor is Ours', it became 'The Timor Sea is Ours'. Senator Bob Brown flew up especially and addressed the rally. The April talks might have achieved nothing inside the negotiating room, but outside the meeting East Timor's rallying of national and international support was clearly taking off.

After the talks Alkatiri cancelled all engagements and did a marathon series of interviews that culminated in favourable coverage of East Timor's case in *The Wall St Journal*, *Time*, the *Sydney Morning Herald*, the *Far Eastern Economic Review*, and on the BBC, the ABC's *Four Corners* and the SBS *Dateline* program. All of these news organisations had sent their reporters and news crews to East Timor—such was their level of interest in the dispute. The impact of Alkatiri's opening speech continued to reverberate for weeks after the meeting, prompting more journalists and news crews to fly to Dili. The BBC featured the dispute on its *Newsnight* program hosted by Jeremy Paxman, which included an interview with an angered Alexander Downer. In an interview with *Time* Galbraith said of Australia's tactics: 'It is like dealing with the Krajina Serbs.'[8] In television interviews Galbraith displayed affected disappointment at learning that his perception of Australians as people who were like enlightened Scandinavians of the Asia-Pacific had been sadly let down by the Australian government's tactics in the dispute.

The *Wall Street Journal*'s reporter Timothy Mapes spent weeks on his story. When it was published in June it was 2100 words long, starting on the front page, with a map and picture of Alkatiri, and then spilling inside. Mapes picked up the 'dual struggle' notion that had been first raised, rather provocatively, by President Gusmão: 'Tiny East Timor fought for nearly a quarter of a century to free itself from Indonesian invaders. Now it faces a struggle with this region's other giant, Australia, over lucrative oil fields critical to its economic survival.'[9] The article infuriated Downer, who immediately dispatched a letter to the *Wall Street Journal*, which in turn carried a reply from Ramos-Horta as the lead item in 'Letters to the Editor'—a rare exception given that it was company policy not to publish letters in response to letters.[10]

The ABC's *Four Corners* program had sent a crew to Dili to produce a 45-minute documentary, 'Rich Man, Poor Man', on the dispute.[11] In committing to the project *Four Corners* found compelling the argument that the Indonesia lobby within DFAT didn't really have a strong interest in seeing the newly independent country becoming prosperous and successful. In fact, if this new state failed, then their long-held advice that an independent East Timor was unviable would be vindicated. This lobby had a lot of baggage when it came to East Timor. The former head of DFAT's Indonesia desk, Bruce Haigh, says that after becoming independent East Timor did not have the full support of the Australian government.

> The most tragic thing in East Timor has been to have the Howard Government in power. The East Timorese needed to have a really supportive Australian Government behind them. They did not have that and we now have the precondition for a civil war. Instead, Australia made East Timor vulnerable and open to manipulation and influence.[12]

Australia's aid commitment to East Timor of around $40 million a year was another reflection of this sentiment, although this is part of an overall global aid program valued at a 0.28 per cent of national income—one of the lowest ratios of any western country and less than half the UN target, despite promises to increase it. The *Australian* newspaper took the unusual step of advocating a significantly bigger aid program for East Timor. Given Australia's considerable commitment of more than $2 billion in military and humanitarian aid to East Timor since 1999, it simply made no sense to have such a modest aid program, the paper argued.[13]

Attempting to turn the tide of public opinion against East Timor, Downer appeared on *Four Corners* and portrayed East Timor as ungrateful. He incessantly used lines he had prepared for the interview about East Timor's tactics in the dispute. Reporter Jonathan Holmes, a highly experienced, former executive producer of the program, told Downer that the program could only screen the line once or twice at the most, as the repetition would be edited, so he should think of something else to say. Downer was visibly angered throughout the interview:

> I think they've made a very big mistake thinking that the best way to handle this negotiation is trying to shame Australia, is mounting abuse on our country, um, accusing us of being bullying and rich and so on, when you consider all we've done for East Timor.[14]

These words, wrote the *Sydney Morning Herald* columnist Richard Ackland, were delivered with a 'pained expression' as he 'moaned' about East Timor's tactics. Ackland made the obvious point about what Australia had really done for East Timor—supporting Indonesia's brutal occupation for 24 years.[15]

* * *

While East Timor had achieved nothing inside the negotiating room, the April talks had gone badly for Australia in terms of public opinion, and this became even more obvious as the strident criticism from Gusmão and Alkatiri was broadcast in the Australian media and around the world following the meeting. Downer showed his frustration when he publicly criticised his department for having been slow to challenge East Timor's public statements.[16] And to show them how it was done, he came up with a new rhetorical flourish in which he claimed that East Timor was asking Australia to cede territory on the basis of it being a poor country:

It's an argument that Mexico, being a poor country, might try with the US to take over Texas with rather more historic claims than East Timor has with us. But I wouldn't fancy Mexico's chances. For us, the East Timor argument could be applied to PNG, Indonesia and New Zealand, and would still fail in international law.[17]

The basis of East Timor's negotiating position had always been rights rather than need. In any event, Downer was starting from too far behind. Conservative opinion was seriously questioning the government's tactics, and with an election to be held by the end of the year this spelt bad politics for the incumbents.

The *Australian*'s political editor Dennis Shanahan, a 25-year veteran correspondent who is close to Howard and read avidly by the conservatives, spelled out the implications in his weekly column:

> There is a similar 'David and Goliath battle', as John Howard puts it, right now and Australia could end up with a public black eye. Worse still, it could sour one of Canberra's most popular initiatives in decades—the creation of the independent state of East Timor. It is no exaggeration to say that Australia's bilateral relationship with East Timor is in danger—that's what Australia told East Timor recently. East Timor is fighting for its future and Australia is playing hard ball with its fledgling ward, for which there is an inordinate fondness and sympathy within the Australian public.[18]

Cartoonists also picked up the injustice in the Howard government's stance in the dispute and a steady stream of opinion-page cartoons began appearing from early 2004 which portrayed the Australian government, and Alexander Downer in particular, as greedy, glutinous and hypocritical. Bruce Petty of the *Age* showed Downer and an emaciated Timorese in a hotel room bed with a sign that said 'Timor Sea Bed', and as room service delivers a large meal the Timorese is kicked out of the bed by Downer. Alan Moir of the *Sydney Morning Herald* portrayed Downer as a child, sitting on the floor, gorging himself with what looked like honey pots but instead had 'oil, gas and $' written on them. A small Timorese child holds out a bowl and Downer asks 'MORE!!?'. The dispute captured the interest of Peter Nicholson of the *Australian*, who produced a steady stream of cartoons throughout 2004 and into 2005, as well as an animation which was featured on the paper's website.

The Australian media was now almost universally convinced that the Howard government's tactics were manifestly unfair and that it was endangering East Timor's future by 'playing hard ball with its fledgling ward', as Dennis Shanahan put it. One of the few exceptions was conservative columnist Christopher Pearson who wrote a scathing attack on the Timorese, 'How to strike political crude'.[19] Repeating Downer's lines, Pearson said their tactics of publicly condemning Australia were doomed to fail. Pearson was then and remains a member of the Foreign Affairs Council which was established by Downer in 1997 so that in developing foreign policy he could 'draw on the expertise and views of a range of individuals working in business, academia and the media'. But the council, which also includes the *Australian*'s editor-at-large Paul Kelly and columnist Janet Albrechtsen, is designed to influence elite opinion. Downer's briefing on the Timor Sea dispute led to columns by both Pearson and Kelly. Pearson had at the time a working relationship with Downer. DFAT paid a recruitment firm which engaged Pearson for more than $11 000 from 2004 to 2006 to write speeches for the minister. Appearing before a Senate estimates committee when the matter was raised, Doug Chester appeared to defend the arrangement: 'There's no-one in his [Downer's] office designated as a speechwriter.' Labor's Senator John Faulkner described it as 'scandalous'.[20]

The Labor Party realised that it was time to break ranks with the Howard government. Earlier in the year the party's national conference had passed a resolution that established the basis for a different approach on this issue. This resolution was not binding on the parliamentary party, but nonetheless it provided a useful platform for Labor to differentiate itself from the government should the opportunity arise. The resolution began by recognising the rights of the people of East Timor to:

> ... secure, internationally recognised borders with all neighbouring countries. A future Labor Government will negotiate in good faith with the Government of East Timor, in full accordance with international law and all its applications, including the UN Convention on the Law of the Sea. In Government Labor will do all things practicable to achieve a negotiated settlement within 3–5 years.[21]

A crucial element missing from this resolution, however, was a commitment to return to international arbitration in the event that an agreement could not be reached. Labor had followed Downer's lead of ducking the international umpire. This was the result of some last-minute footwork at the conference by then foreign affairs spokesman Kevin Rudd, who like Downer is a former DFAT officer, and the Northern Territory's chief minister, Clare Martin.

The Labor Opposition had a new leader, Mark Latham, who was being advised by right-wing powerbroker Laurie Brereton, the former foreign affairs spokesman who had changed Labor's policy to support an act of self-determination in East Timor. Latham's resource spokesman and close friend Joel Fitzgibbon had consistently labelled the Howard government a bully for its treatment of East Timor. Labor's strategy in engaging sympathetically with this issue was deliberately aimed at winning back the voters who had gone to the Greens in 2001 over Labor's refusal to take a principled stand on the refugee issue.

The secret envoy

In late July Latham sent Brereton to Dili to meet directly with the East Timor government. When asked during a meeting what sort of deal Labor would deliver should it win office, Brereton said it would be something quite 'generous'. Timorese civil servant Manuel de Lemos hit back instantly and said words to the effect, 'we're not asking for generosity—we just want what's fair'. Brereton had used the same language as Downer.

Latham had scored a couple of early wins against the government but Downer turned the tide against him after Latham's first intervention in the dispute. On 22 July Latham made his first—and last—comments on the Timor Sea dispute when he said in a radio interview:

> If we come into government, I think we'll have to start again because, from what I can gather, there's been a lot of bad blood across the negotiating table and you never get it right in these sensitive areas unless you're doing these things in good faith.[22]

Latham was tacitly siding with East Timor. It was his attempt at signalling, or 'dog whistling', to the Left, but Downer succeeded in portraying his comments as a betrayal of the national interest.

Downer wrote a private letter to Latham with the intent of leaking it to the media. His office gave the letter to the *Australian* and it immediately switched into demolition mode. A front-page lead story[23] headlined 'Latham "threat" to East Timor' claimed 'Latham's pledge to start new boundary talks with East Timor is threatening the tiny country's economic future'. The story quoted unnamed East Timor officials as being 'alarmed' by Woodside's threat to pull out of the Sunrise project if the agreement was not ratified, and it quoted a paragraph in the Downer letter in which he accused Latham of betraying the national interest: 'Obviously if the Labor Party has a different position to the Government, then East Timor will be able to play one side against the other and this will be very damaging for the national interest.'

The *Australian* followed through with an editorial that said Latham had recklessly walked into the issue 'like a bull in a china shop'. Denying that East Timor had any rights at all, the editorial claimed that if Australia wanted to help East Timor it should do so through aid rather than 'giving way on maritime boundaries and ceding bits of Australia'. With a historical flourish, Latham's comments were likened to the intervention by Richard Nixon who in 1968 'cruelled the Johnson administration's peace talks in 1968 by telling the South Vietnamese they'd get a better deal under him'.[24]

Downer had demonstrated how the conservative government could strike back with deadly accuracy on this issue and turn it into a political 'wedge', forcing Labor to toe the government's line. With the election less than four months away, the government was deliberately smothering East Timor's support with the blanket of national interest.

* * *

At the top of the crumbling tile staircase leading to the office of the prime minister of East Timor on the first floor of the *Palácio do Governo* there was a whiteboard. And, in an apparent recognition of political mortality, the name at the top of the board—*Primeiro-Ministro Alkatiri*—was written in marker ink that can be erased with a single swipe. Each morning a member of staff wrote up the PM's agenda for the day.

One morning in early May 2004 the agenda on the whiteboard was left mysteriously blank. The prime minister had a meeting with a special visitor, and he had acceded to a demand that it be kept absolutely confidential. Alkatiri would meet with a 'secret envoy' from DFAT. The Australian government had decided it was time to get tough and Alexander Downer had just the man to deliver a very blunt message to this newly independent country that in his view owed its very existence to Australia. The secret envoy was Doug Chester, a deputy secretary in Downer's department.

In his mid-fifties, Chester appeared more of an ordinary personality relative to his sophisticated contemporaries in DFAT. He could be a suburban solicitor, or even John Howard's younger brother. Or he could be one of Paul Keating's 'punishers and straighteners'. This driven individual had a slow way of speaking that disguised a fast-thinking mind, and intense eyes that flickered as he absorbed every nuance. His ordinariness, like that of John Howard, masked tenacity and ruthlessness. Chester is an exception in his elite institution because he joined the department very late in his career, after working for many years in the patents office within the Department of Industry. He had come to DFAT as a 40-something middle-level bureaucrat because his skills were needed for the Uruguay round of trade talks. He was soon promoted and branched out into staffing and corporate management, where he proved dependable, followed by a posting to Washington as a commercial attaché. But, like an increasing number of officials who have moved into senior executive roles in DFAT over the past decade, Chester had limited experience in Asia. His only experience of this region was a year spent as high commissioner to Brunei Darussalam for the 2000 APEC meeting. In 2003 he made it to DFAT's second highest rung—deputy secretary—just one level below the position of permanent head of the department.

His rise and ambition were resented by some of his contemporaries who had spent their entire working lives in DFAT. An early riser, he often gets to work before others in the department and collects press articles and briefings that have come in overnight. At the morning meetings Chester would be the one fully briefed on overnight developments and able to show up his rivals. Senior officials within the department regard him as someone who promoted himself as a fixer. East Timor was a problem that needed to be fixed.

This secret mission to Dili came about because Downer had been angered by the president's offensive remarks in Portugal, and the tactics and public commentary employed by East Timor during and after the April 2004 meeting. Chester indicated that if this did not stop then dire consequences would follow. Chester met privately and separately with the prime minister, the president and the foreign minister. In his meeting with Gusmão Chester said the Australian government was 'dismayed' by his comments in Portugal in which he likened Australia's occupation of the Timor Sea to the Indonesian occupation. He told each of them that the Timor Sea dispute could not be isolated from the bilateral relationship, meaning that it could seriously undermine the relationship. He didn't tell them that the Australian government had already decided to cut East Timor's aid budget by 10 per cent, while increasing aid substantially for other countries in the region. This warning shot would be delivered in two weeks' time with the release of Australia's 2004–05 federal budget.

The government had begun trying to turn opinion-makers in Australia against East Timor by backgrounding them on its unruly negotiating tactics. The *Australian*'s Dennis Shanahan called Alkatiri's office shortly after Chester's departure from Dili. He was well versed on the delicate state of the bilateral relationship, and broke the story of the Chester visit with a neat description of him as Downer's 'secret envoy' to Dili.

At the conclusion of these secret meetings, Chester returned to the Hotel Timor with the ambassador, Paul Foley. There, in the cafe of the hotel, he encountered to his horror a group of Australians who were lobbying on behalf of East Timor in this dispute. Chester looked aghast as Foley explained who was seated at the table on the other side of the room. Oxfam Australia's public policy and advocacy director, James Ensor, had come to Dili to speak to the East Timor government and others about a report he was to publish that said East Timor was destined to become another failed state if it did not get a fair deal.[25] Ensor wanted a briefing on the oil revenue projections and a meeting had been arranged in the cafe with Bruce Taplin, an adviser working on an AusAID program who had taken leave from his position with the Australian Treasury. Keryn Clark, the country manager of Oxfam's program, who had been coordinating

Oxfam's lobbying effort from Dili, was also present together with an adviser from the Timor Sea Office.[26] The briefing had just started when Chester and Foley walked into the cafe. Taplin handled it admirably. He turned his head, acknowledged the ambassador with a nod, and continued with his briefing.

The blunt warning delivered in person by Chester in May 2004 caused East Timor to dig in and take an even stronger stand. It simply enraged Gusmão. When the *Sydney Morning Herald*'s political editor Peter Hartcher stopped over in Dili on his way back from Indonesia later that month, his 20-minute interview with Gusmão went for more than an hour as the president railed against Downer's tactics. Gusmão said the Australian government had failed to respect the legitimacy of East Timor's claim, and threatened to make his country a permanent beggar: 'We will be like the Solomon Islands, like Libya, like Haiti. Alexander Downer, I like him very much, but on this issue—aaagh! I do not accept my friend Alexander Downer saying "no, it's not yours". We have a legitimate claim. How can we behave like beggars?'[27]

Alkatiri confirmed that his government had been pressured by Australia to stop speaking about the negotiations. He likened the campaign to an epic David and Goliath battle, and told Hartcher, 'If we don't do this, as David, we will die.'

Chester's visit to Dili marked the culmination of a series of official Australian protests. The Australian ambassador Paul Foley had been to see Alkatiri on at least three occasions between November 2003 and April 2004. Downer's message just wasn't getting through. As his frustration grew, he decided he would have to take matters into his own hands.

10 THE CONSUMMATE DIPLOMAT

'Sorry mate, we're not interested—it's all kissy kissy,' ABC *7.30 Report* producer after the meeting between Ramos-Horta and Downer on 11 August 2004

In mid-2004 Alexander Downer began to roll out a strategy to neutralise the Timor Sea dispute ahead of the forthcoming federal election. The dispute had become lodged in the pre-election sound bites and had been picked up by a high-profile challenger in his own electorate of Mayo. In late June Downer attended a four-day ASEAN ministerial meeting in Jakarta, and he took the opportunity to propose what seemed like a casual breakfast meeting with his counterpart, José Ramos-Horta, at his hotel in Jakarta. Arriving at the meeting with the head of his department, Nelson Santos and his ambassador to Jakarta Arlindo Marcal, Ramos-Horta encountered a phalanx of advisers seated around the Australian foreign minister. This was not going to be a friendly chat while crunching on muesli. Ramos-Horta had walked into an ambush.

The conversation was fast and furious. Downer complained loudly and bitterly about East Timor's tactics, and he especially singled out the conduct of Peter Galbraith. Downer said Galbraith's involvement would make it difficult for Australia to move forward.

He was furious with East Timor's tactic of revealing details of the negotiations to the media, which he blamed on Galbraith. He warned that there was very little support for East Timor on this issue in Australia, aside from 'a few leftists', and said that the country could not count on the support of opposition parties. He implied that the government had conducted some private polling of the Australian electorate's views on the dispute by saying that the 'majority' of Australians believed the government had been 'generous' to East Timor.

A meticulous record of this meeting was produced by Nelson Santos, who wrote furiously throughout the meeting to the point where he had no breakfast that morning. Santos, a mid-thirties mathematician who had served for four years as a Macau-based Interpol officer, concluded that Galbraith's style did not suit the current negotiations: 'If this continues Australia will dig in and the process of resolving the dispute will not move forward.' Downer's broadside was deliberately aimed at having Galbraith removed from East Timor's negotiating team, and he had convinced some in the East Timor government that this was necessary.

Downer opened a way forward. He said there were avenues for resolving the dispute—a 'political solution'. Downer proposed that he and Ramos-Horta should meet again in Canberra for a more formal dialogue. Naturally Ramos-Horta accepted the invitation.

The following month a proposal aimed at putting a lid on this noisy issue was discussed in the Australian Cabinet. This was part of the government's pre-election 'clearing the decks' strategy. The proposal was based on East Timor's concept of the 'creative solution', although it went much further in terms of securing Australia's interests. In delivering this proposal to the East Timor government, Downer had already lined up a friendly target: his old friend and counterpart in East Timor, the Nobel laureate and foreign minister, José Ramos-Horta.

On 11 August Downer invited Ramos-Horta to the place where he would have the home ground advantage—a grand, modern-day palace built not on a hilltop, but in place of one. The construction of Australia's national parliament in the 1980s in the federal capital, Canberra, required earthmoving works on a scale that the Portuguese colonists in East Timor could never have imagined. It involved removing an entire mount and then replacing it with an elaborate set of interconnected, symmetrical buildings encased in an enormous concrete shell. Topped with a four-legged flagpole that flew an Australian flag the size of a double-decker bus, the complex stood as a symbol of 'people power'. The Australian people could walk on the manicured and heavily watered lawns rising up over the complex and look down into the places where their politicians governed on their behalf. Well before the age of terrorism, however, demonstrators were barred from the entrances used by ministers and politicians, and in the post 9/11 world people were prohibited from walking over the top.

The Commonwealth of Australia Parliament is believed to be unique in the world because it not only houses ministers, parliamentarians and their staff—who number more than 6500[1] when parliament is sitting—it has a section that is dedicated to the national media. More than 250 journalists occupy an entire floor of the Senate wing.

Downer's engagement on the Timor Sea issue was heightened by a campaign that had emerged in his own electorate. A former South Australian magistrate, Brian Deegan, whose son Josh was one of the 88 Australians killed in the 2002 Bali bombings, had announced that he would stand against Downer in his seat. Downer had previously got close to losing Mayo when a high-profile musician, John Schumann, stood against him in 1998. Deegan, a feisty and articulate campaigner, had cited Downer's poor conduct in the oil dispute as part of a litany of failings in Downer's handling of foreign policy. When Deegan's campaign was raised at a media doorstop in April, Downer suggested that his opponent was not on Australia's side.

Journalist: Mr Downer, Brian Deegan's nominated the East Timor issue with the oil and gas reserves as one of the issues he'll be pursuing as part of his election platform.

The consummate diplomat

Downer: That's not a big issue in Mayo but ... well maybe those people in Mayo who are interested in oil and gas will be pleased to know that as their local representative, I'm on Australia's side.[2]

* * *

Throughout the bruising campaign over the Timor Sea resources, Ramos-Horta had remained on good terms with the Australian government; this made him a natural focus for Downer's overtures. He kept open the lines of communications and prevented what might otherwise have been a complete breakdown in diplomatic relations. He was the natural good cop in the Timor Sea dispute.

A consummate diplomat and compulsive dealmaker and networker, Ramos-Horta's skills as an advocate for East Timor earned him numerous references in the 1974–76 Department of Foreign Affairs cables. A submission from the department to the foreign minister in December 1975 refers with great dissatisfaction to the highly successful activities of Ramos-Horta and FRETILIN in soliciting moral and material support from groups in Australia.

While being exceptionally well connected internationally, Ramos-Horta is a remarkably unpretentious, self-deprecating and idealistic individual. The noble tenets of peace, friendship and reconciliation can be found throughout his written and spoken words. His lifelong mission has been to forge alliances and friendships, unlike some of his contemporaries in government who sought to divide and rule. This sentiment led to his resigning in October 1989 from the FRETILIN party which he had co-founded to join Xanana Gusmão's multi-party umbrella group, the CNRM. And after independence he remained an independent while serving in the FRETILIN government as senior minister of foreign affairs and cooperation. But this diplomatic maestro has a tendency to over-achieve, prime examples being the palatial foreign affairs head office in Dili and the opening of an incredible fifteen embassies and two consulates around the world.

Acknowledging past mistakes has been prominent in his pursuit of peace, particularly in relation to the events of 1975—the civil war and the unilateral declaration of independence—even though Indonesia had a campaign of destabilisation which provoked the civil war. Ramos-Horta's suave diplomacy and sincere advocacy of peace and reconciliation culminated in his jointly winning the Nobel Prize for Peace in 1996, with Bishop Carlos Ximenes Belo, although there have since been many twists and turns in his practice of diplomacy.

A firm believer in the value of what he emphatically calls 'PR', Ramos-Horta can be a slick propagandist who, as a very gifted speaker and writer, sometimes knows no bounds. In the mid-1990s he put out a press release which described in precise detail the bombing of a village in East Timor by one of the 24 British-made Hawke jets that were sold to the Indonesian military. The story generated worldwide headlines, and it inspired a group of four women in north England to hatch a daring plan to break into the British Aerospace factory at Warton, Lancashire, where the aircraft were being made. On 29 January 1996 they used hammers to destroy one of the planes painted with Indonesian insignia. After offering themselves up for arrest they became known famously as the 'ploughshare women'. The charges brought against them were later dismissed in a court case that kept the wheels of publicity spinning. But there was just one problem with the story—the bombing raid described by Ramos-Horta was fictitious. While the jets were deployed in East Timor by the Indonesian military, Ramos-Horta had invented the details used in the press release, proving yet again that in war the first casualty is the truth. He was mortified when he learned that the women could go to gaol for a very long time as a result of a very creative propaganda exercise, and he went to Liverpool, United Kingdom, to give evidence on their behalf in the proceedings.

After independence Ramos-Horta, together with Gusmão, crafted a policy of taking a soft line on pursuing justice for the Indonesian atrocities in 1999, and over the previous 24 years. But the spin made no impression on the vast number of Timorese who had lost multiple family members during the occupation and hoped that independence would also bring justice. It also set a very bad precedent for the Indonesian military's ongoing human rights abuses in West Papua and Aceh. It seemed that now East Timor was free its government was not going to lift a finger to help its neighbours living under the Indonesian yoke. Under Ramos-Horta's stewardship East Timor created with Indonesia a toothless 'Truth and Friendship Commission'. Aderito de Jesus Soares, a highly respected human rights lawyer and former FRETILIN member of the East Timor parliament, noted in an opinion article in the *International Herald Tribune* in 2005 that the commission appeared to exclude further justice processes, and that Ramos-Horta had in a joint declaration with Indonesia publicly rejected the recommendations of the report by the UN secretary-general's commission of experts on justice in East Timor. The report called for an international tribunal and it urged international donors not to fund the Truth and Friendship Commission. 'Instead, both governments have said that the Commission on Truth and Friendship ... is meant to bring "definitive closure" to the events of 1999. No one doubts that reconciliation between Indonesia and East Timor is extremely important. However, justice is indispensable to the success of true reconciliation,'[3] concluded de Jesus Soares.

Ramos-Horta often brings mischief and humour to his diplomacy. As a tireless promoter of East Timor's organic arabica coffee, he invented a novel marketing pitch claiming it contains 'certain Viagra-like qualities'. During the Timor Sea negotiations, Ramos-Horta gave Doug Chester a packet of the coffee and told him of its special qualities. Some months later he met Chester and his wife at a function in Canberra and asked the couple about the coffee's effects.

Fundamentally pro-American, he renamed the Dili street where he lives Robert Kennedy Boulevard. While professing to be a pacifist, he strongly defended the invasion of Iraq in 2003 because it stemmed genocide and ethnic cleansing.[4] These comments earned him the gratitude of John Howard, who described him as a 'courageous man'. In early 2006 the US government floated his name as a possible replacement for Kofi Annan as UN Secretary-General, as did the former US ambassador to the UN, Richard Holbrooke, in an article in the *Washington Post*.[5] The ongoing turmoil in East Timor sparked by the armed forces dispute, however, is likely to keep Ramos-Horta at home for some years to come. It was during these months that his skills and courage as a diplomat came to the fore as he criss-crossed the country in a bid to broker peace deals with armed and dangerous rebel soldiers. At this time other senior members of government went into hiding.

In February 2007 he took his role as a unifying figure to another level, announcing that he would stand for president as an independent candidate.

The son of a Timorese mother and a Portuguese *deportado*, José Manuel Ramos-Horta was born the day after Christmas 1949. His father was a sergeant in the Portuguese navy who had taken part in the Tagus River Mutiny in 1936. The crew had attempted to commandeer their frigate with the intention of sailing to Spain to join the Republicans in the fight against Franco. The military crushed the mutiny and as a result his father, Francisco, was deported to East Timor. He was the fifth of his parents' ten children, three of whom were killed by the Indonesians. He boarded at a mission school in the remote and spectacular mountains of Soibada. Here he studied the languages that would help him in his future career as a diplomat: English and French, as well as Portuguese. He now thinks in English. As a boy, Ramos-Horta was bright, confident and he stood out from the crowd. James Dunn, Australia's consul-general in Dili in the early 1960s, remembers meeting him as a young teenager when a tree had fallen in front of his parked diplomatic car. Ramos-Horta offered to help and made an immediate impression on Dunn. It was Ramos-Horta's first diplomatic encounter, and it began a long friendship with Dunn who later wrote the definitive history of East Timor.[6]

By the time Ramos-Horta was 20 he was again stepping out of the crowd to lead the march towards independence. He first worked as a journalist for *A Voz de Timor* (the Voice of Timor) and in January 1970, together with Alkatiri, co-founded a clandestine, anti-colonial group. After he made a public attack on Portuguese colonialism the secret police interrogated him and asked him to leave East Timor.[7] Allowed to go to any Portuguese country of his choosing, he landed in the leftist, anti-colonial hotbed of Mozambique, where he linked up with the independence front FRELIMO (the Mozambican Liberation Front). He returned to East Timor in 1972, just in time to become a founding member of FRETILIN, and at the unilateral declaration of independence on 28 November 1975 he became Minister for Foreign Affairs, a month before his 26th birthday.

Ramos-Horta has always maintained a good disposition towards Australia, and now regards it as a second home. His mother migrated there in 1990 and lives in the western Sydney suburb of Liverpool. In the late 1990s, just before the UN's popular consultation, he filled out an application form for an Australian passport but he never submitted it. He has a permanent resident visa, however. In his address at the independence ceremony on 20 May 2002 Ramos-Horta acknowledged Howard's 'invaluable' support and declared him a 'friend of East Timor'. His warmth towards Australia exists in spite of his being treated as a virtual terrorist for several years after the Indonesian invasion. From 1977 to 1982 he was barred from entry into Australia. When he was awarded the Nobel peace prize in 1996 the Australian ambassador, Judith Pead, refused to attend the ceremony, despite attending other award ceremonies in Stockholm.[8]

During the Timor Sea negotiations, a key tactic employed by this good cop was to criticise, or even publicly admonish, his own side. When the prime minister and president accused Australia of stealing oil from East Timor, or of illegally occupying East Timor's maritime 'territory', Ramos-Horta kept the diplomatic relationship intact by publicly rebuking his leaders. Asked about the demonstrators outside the Australian embassy who brandished anti-Australian placards like 'Aussie Aussie Aussie—Oil Oil Oil' and 'F—k your petrol arrogance', Ramos-Horta said, 'They've picked up the mood from some of our leaders who should be a lot more calm. I would prefer to be more prudent, more cautious.'[9]

Ramos-Horta's good relationship with Australia meant that it was he, and not Alkatiri, who opened East Timor's first embassy in Australia in late 2003. The Australian government had bluntly refused to issue an official invitation to Alkatiri, who had been expecting to officiate at the opening. Alkatiri could have gone to Australia uninvited but without any diplomatic protocol. He was a stickler for protocol, so Ramos-Horta saved face and went instead.

During this visit to Canberra Ramos-Horta demonstrated his unique ability to prosecute his country's case while also employing humour in order to remain on good terms with Australia. In a televised address to the National Press Club, Ramos-Horta mocked Australia's claim at the November 2003 meeting that it could only afford to meet twice a year. In lines delivered with perfect tone and timing, he said he was a straightforward person who usually accepted what people said at face value. If Australia did not have the resources to negotiate then an organisation called the United Nations Development Programme, which worked on capacity building in East Timor, could be brought to Australia to assist DFAT. Immediately after the Press Club address he met with Downer who feigned indignation over Ramos-Horta's drawing on what had been said inside the negotiating room.

* * *

At the 11 August meeting Downer was joined by Doug Chester with another adviser from his office at his side, while José Teixeira—a secretary of state reporting directly to Alkatiri—accompanied Ramos-Horta. Downer wanted to keep the meeting small and efficient and on this occasion Nelson Santos had to wait outside in the corridor. There would be no copious notes produced at this meeting.

On offer was a 'financial settlement' to resolve the dispute, and in making this offer Downer acknowledged for the first time East Timor's rights outside the JPDA. As a gesture of goodwill, he proposed an intensive series of meetings, commencing on 20 September, with the aim of resolving the dispute by the end of the year. Downer accepted the notion of the 'creative solution' when he said the negotiations would look at alternatives to a maritime boundary. He did not explain how this settlement would work, and gave away remarkably very little. What he actually had in mind was the concept of what he would later call 'financial assistance' in return for East Timor's surrendering its sovereign rights in the Timor Sea.

After almost an hour Teixeira came bounding out of the meeting and signalled to an adviser from the Timor Sea Office to follow him down the corridor to the men's toilet.[10] There he explained breathlessly his interpretation of Downer's offer. Teixeira believed that Australia was willing to enter into 'resource sharing' in the disputed area—exactly what East Timor wanted. He mentioned that Downer had talked about widening the treaty area to the east and west.

At the conclusion of the meeting Downer proposed a joint press conference. He wanted to appear before the media with his 'old friend', the Nobel laureate, to make a dramatic public display of Australia's friendly relations with East Timor, the country he often claimed to have brought into being.

Under the studio lights of the television networks, East Timor's strident campaign evaporated as two old pals rubbed shoulders at the lectern and exchanged fond glances. The press conference was held in the 'Blue Room' located next door to the Cabinet room and the prime minister's office—a presidential-style press conference room usually reserved for significant ministerial statements. Downer shrewdly avoided giving away the details of what Australia was to offer, but he played up Australia's concerns over sovereignty and East Timor's 'needs', as though East Timor had needs only and no sovereignty in the Timor Sea. Downer presented himself as Father Christmas when he said the deal might mean a big Christmas present for the Timorese. In so doing, he signed on to Woodside's ultimatum to achieve an agreement by the end of the year if the project were to be kept alive. The headline message in Downer's comments, delivered in his usual avuncular style, was that the settlement would be another case of Australian generosity. 'And it would be good if we could do that, if we can have a Christmas present for everybody, for all the people of East Timor and a slightly smaller and more modest Christmas present for the people of Australia,' Downer said.

One journalist, who seemed well briefed, asked Ramos-Horta if this 'creative solution' meant East Timor would give Australia the 'line on a map' that it wanted in return for revenue. Ramos-Horta said it was a nice try but refused to give away details.

Downer had publicly foreshadowed a 'cash for sovereignty' deal that would never be acceptable to East Timor, but this was not fully understood by the East Timorese. Journalists interpreted this meeting as having produced the genesis of a 'deal', if not a deal in its own right. Such was Downer's control of media spin, even when up against a lifelong practitioner. East Timor had been put back in its box.

In keeping with this new era of constructive dialogue, East Timor did not brief the captive media after the press conference. As soon as the conference ended Downer's chief of staff, Innes Willox, ushered Ramos-Horta and the rest of the East Timor delegation to one of the side doors of Parliament House and out to a waiting car. Half an hour later a producer on the ABC's flagship current affairs program the *7.30 Report* cancelled an interview with Ramos-Horta for the program that evening. The producer, Jeremy Thompson, said the program was no longer interested in interviewing him because he had seen the press conference and it was now 'all kissy kissy'. The next morning newspapers carried smiling photographs of Downer and Ramos-Horta.

The 11 August meeting had achieved the Australian government's objective of putting a lid on East Timor for the election. The momentum in support of its appeal that East Timor had built throughout the year in the international community and the Australian public was deflated by Downer at this press conference. But immediately after this meeting an adviser from the Timor Sea Office flew to Melbourne to meet with a businessman who was willing to bankroll an advertising campaign to change the Australian government's policy on the Timor Sea dispute.

* * *

About a week after the Canberra meeting José Teixeira received a call from Doug Chester while having lunch at his favourite Dili restaurant, the Golden Star.[11] Sounding like Sir Humphrey in *Yes Minister*, Teixeira recounted what Chester had said: 'Some things our minister said might have come across differently to what he meant to say, and some things he said he didn't mean to say. He meant to say that permanent maritime boundaries were one thing that we might want to negotiate.'[12]

This was at odds with what had been discussed at the 11 August meeting, when Downer had explained that the accelerated round of negotiations would be aimed specifically at finding a solution that did not involve a permanent boundary. Downer had discussed having two sets of negotiations running parallel: one set to deal with the financial settlement and another, which might take much longer, to deal with boundaries. 'We are so far apart on agreeing to a boundary—let's talk about resources,' Downer had said.[13]

It was evident that the bureaucrats had thought about the implications of this meeting afterwards, and did not like where they were leading. They decided to try to shift the goal posts. Their agenda was in fact to have a boundary at the Timor Trough—to close the Timor Gap. They wanted to succeed where their predecessors had failed a generation earlier. In return, East Timor would get 'financial assistance'. This would achieve one of the objectives of Australia's foreign policy—keeping an impoverished near-neighbour on a tight financial drip.

East Timor got a clear understanding of where this bureaucrat-driven process was heading when in early September it started receiving calls from Labor politicians. The government had called a 9 October election, and this meant the 20 September talks would be held right in the middle of the campaign. Labor was pushing for representation at these talks as a potential future government. Downer said he would agree to this on one condition—Labor had to support the government's plan to propose a boundary at the Timor Trough in return for offering financial assistance to East Timor. There was to be no widening of the treaty area or a greater share of Greater Sunrise for East Timor. Labor, fearful of being monstered by Downer yet again, tried to have the talks postponed until after the election. Labor's then foreign affairs spokesman, Kevin Rudd, called Teixeira and Brereton called a Timor Sea Office adviser.[14] Brereton, who had changed Labor's policy to support an act of self-determination and had no time for Rudd, warned that 'others' in the Labor party had little sympathy for East Timor and that if the party supported closing the Timor Gap at the election then this position would be 'very difficult to unwind' in the event that it won. With very forthright language, Brereton warned of dire consequences for East Timor if his advice was not followed.

Teixeira was rattled by these approaches. He sought advice from Janelle Saffin, a politically savvy former Labor member of the NSW Upper House who now worked for Ramos-Horta. She gave him good counsel: 'They are the ones in a tight spot—not you.' It looked as though Downer was turning the government's position on the Timor Sea to an election advantage. Instead of the government's handling of this issue potentially costing votes, he was applying the pressure of the campaign to force Labor to side with the government. Not only was he projecting the government as a strong defender of the national interest, he would inflict long-term damage on East Timor's negotiating position. As Brereton had warned, Downer's locking in of bipartisan support for closing the Timor Gap at the 1972 boundary would be very difficult to unravel.

East Timor had no choice but to go ahead with the 20 September meeting. After calling for accelerated talks for the past year, it could not walk away.

*　*　*

East Timor's negotiating team started to drift into Dili to prepare for the next round of talks in early September, just as it began to emerge that the Australian side was planning to propose the unthinkable at the 20 September meeting. The reaction of some of the key advisers to this was even more surprising—they thought that an expected offer of financial assistance at the meeting was the best East Timor could hope for. East Timor's leadership wasn't going to rule out a cash settlement in the first instance. If the Australian government offered a princely sum—US$10 billion, for example—then it would have to consider it seriously. But the notion of exchanging sovereign rights for cash was always going to be the most difficult solution to sell politically in East Timor, a country that had paid an inordinate price for its sovereignty. The primacy of sovereignty is enshrined in the East Timor constitution, which prevents the state from alienating any part of the territory or giving up its sovereign rights.

Peter Galbraith was in a buoyant mood because he'd had another article published in the *New York Review of Books*,[15] which had now been cited on the front-page of the *New York Times* by US Democrat presidential candidate John Kerry. Not only on the front page, the reference to his article was printed 'above the fold', as an excited Galbraith pointed out to anyone who would listen. However, when it came to the negotiations, Galbraith was decidedly downbeat. 'Let's not be consumed by our own propaganda. The most attractive option is a cash settlement,' was his well-rehearsed opening line at a planning meeting. East Timor's legal case was not as rock solid as the East Timor government had been telling the world for the past few years, he said. The cash settlement that Australia would put on the table was East Timor's best and the only option that could be hoped for.

Galbraith put the case for taking the payout rather artfully. East Timor was a poor country and should therefore avoid if possible relying on volatile oil revenue, even though at this time oil prices had spiked at over US$50 a barrel and were now hovering at around US$40. Having a guaranteed income stream from Australia—an amount equivalent to the current national budget paid every year—would create for the country a 'balanced portfolio'. It was like any investment portfolio that had a spectrum of investments: cash, capital-guaranteed bonds and equities. East Timor was about to create a permanent Petroleum Fund for the long-term investment of its revenues, and Galbraith argued that with his proposed deal it could effectively create such a fund because the money would drip into it every year. The proposed deal would create a fund that could never be raided, he said emphatically.

Nuno Antunes, the Portuguese maritime lawyer, also believed that if East Timor could get US$5 billion paid over the life of the fields this would be an acceptable outcome. The rest of the negotiating team, however, believed that East Timor should persist in seeking a widening of the JPDA or a bigger percentage share of Sunrise, plus compensation for the estimated US$2.7 billion to be collected by Australia over the life of the BCL fields. This was the total estimate of the revenue collected to date, and what remained to be paid.

In preparation for the 20 September meeting Doug Chester flew to Dili for meetings with senior members of the East Timor government. At a meeting with Alkatiri on 13 September he noted Australia's close alignment with Indonesia on maritime boundaries. In other words, even though the 1972 agreement had greatly disadvantaged Indonesia, the two countries may have reached an understanding that would not give any leverage to East Timor. There had been rumours of a recent Paris meeting between the two countries on maritime boundaries. Chester's comment sounded like a warning shot. Alkatiri made clear that East Timor could not agree to a solution that prejudiced its sovereign rights, meaning the cash for sovereignty deal was a no go.

Chester said repeatedly that in the following week the two countries would agree to a political solution to boundaries. Expanding the treaty area was not in Australia's view a solution, but Australia wanted a final settlement—it wanted to achieve what it had mistakenly hoped would be achieved with the Timor Sea Treaty. 'Australia wants to come up with an agreement that Timor-Leste is happy with and Australia can live with,' he told Alkatiri. Chester signalled that there might be some flexibility; Australia was 'not necessarily looking for an A16-A17 solution', meaning the closing of the Timor Gap by continuing the 1972 boundary. Australia would look at other alternatives to closing the Timor Gap in exchange for cash, he claimed.

East Timor's negotiating team discussed in great detail Chester's preliminary proposal. Australia's tactics displeased Ramos-Horta immensely. He considered that Australia's raising the Timor Trough boundary backtracked from the 11 August understanding. But East Timor's leadership was not going to close off completely the idea of a cash agreement. A dollar amount could be converted into a percentage share, and creative ways of ensuring that their rights were preserved could be found. Any economic package would have to be 'without prejudice' to East Timor's right to claim a maritime boundary, Alkatiri made very clear to the team. However he was also interested in seeing just how much money would be on offer.

The value of the disputed resources and the potential for other finds in the disputed area were also an important focus of East Timor's preparations. Just before 20 September Alkatiri and Ramos-Horta received a briefing from a geologist, Alistair Gray. Outfitted in baggy khaki shorts, a fisherman's vest and hiking boots, he carried under his arm a bundle of huge maps. As he rolled out the maps on a coffee table he explained how the rock formations in the Timor Sea resembled formations in the Middle East, particularly a large structure in the middle of the Timor Gap area known as Kelp High. 'Quite an interesting feature,' he noted in his strong Scottish brogue.

Gray explained to Alkatiri that the eastern disputed area around Greater Sunrise was definitely worth fighting for, whereas the western area near the BCL fields had little potential. A giant oil and gas field lies beneath Greater Sunrise in the Permian layer, the next layer of rock. Gray said that, based on his analysis, there was a strong probability that the Sunrise Permian field had reserves many times greater than those of Greater Sunrise, reserves worth a mind-boggling sum, in fact—that is, if the field could be developed. Gray noted that Woodside had drilled down to 5000 metres, reaching the top of this structure.

Gray's briefing signified that there was potentially much more at stake, and that certainly an expansion of the JPDA or at least a bigger percentage share of the disputed resources was the only way to go. If Sunrise Permian was developed it would come under a separate contract, and East Timor would only have control of it under two scenarios: first, if one corner of it straddled the JPDA, as the field above it did, or second, if East Timor could expand the JPDA to the east in order to cover it.

Galbraith made the point that Gray's analysis was relevant to a deal that involved a percentage split, but it was not relevant to a cash payout. Incredibly, however, the findings did not persuade him that his proposal for a fixed sum with no provision for an upside should the value of the resources increase might not be a good idea.

At its last meeting before the team left for Canberra Alkatiri said firmly that he and the president should be kept closely informed of the progress of the talks. He insisted that East Timor would not be giving up its right to a boundary. Its sovereignty was not for sale. 'All negotiations are without prejudice to permanent maritime boundaries and we are to explore all creative solutions. If they come with a substantial offer call me immediately,' he said.

Alkatiri also announced that Teixeira would be elevated to the position of head of the delegation, with Galbraith his deputy. Teixeira had achieved what he had been working towards for more than a year.

* * *

José Fernandes Teixeira gained a rare insight into the stirrings of East Timor's independence while growing up in Dili in the 1960s and 1970s. Born in East Timor in 1964, the son of a Portuguese father and a mother of Portuguese, Timorese and Chinese descent, his uncle and godfather, Alarico Fernandes, was the first secretary-general of the FRETILIN party and a senior minister in the first government. He took the young Teixeira to political meetings, including the one that launched FRETILIN. The effects of Teixeira's early exposure to Timorese politics stayed with him over the years, and eventually brought him back to Timor.

After the 1975 invasion Alarico Fernandes fled to the mountains with the FRETILIN leadership and the FALINTIL resistance army, where he soon gained a reputation as a war criminal. Three weeks later, on Christmas day 1975, Fernandes is believed to have ordered the execution of about 150 political prisoners, according to Gusmão, after having shown a 'frenzied thirst for vengeance' during the August civil war.[16] In 1978, as the Indonesians tightened their net around the resistance army, Fernandes cracked under the pressure and began advocating surrender. He was gaoled by his own side, but then during an attack in December he surrendered to the Indonesians and took with him FRETILIN's only radio.[17] Fernandes had previously worked as a radio operator at the Baucau airport and so the loss of the radio and his operational skills were a serious blow to the resistance army. But to this day Teixeira remains loyal to the uncle who showed him so much; he maintains that Fernandes was 'captured'. Fernandes cooperated extensively with the Indonesians and since independence has not returned to East Timor. He lives in Bali and is believed to have lost his mind.

When the Indonesian invasion of East Timor was looming in 1975, Teixeira and his family left for Australia and settled in the western Sydney suburb of Cabramatta, a low-income area that also attracted a massive influx of Vietnamese refugees. He spoke some English upon arrival, but got plenty of practice translating for family members who spoke none. He went to government schools in

Cabramatta from 1976 until he finished year 12 in 1983. He did well enough at school to go to university where he studied arts and law. He joined the law firm Deacon and Milani Solicitors in downtown Brisbane where he became a senior associate. While in Brisbane he joined the Australian Labor Party, worked as an adviser in the Goss State Labor government and became a serious political aspirant. He sought to gain pre-selection for a Queensland state seat but was unsuccessful.

After this setback, the vote for independence offered Teixeira the opportunity to start a new life with a new government. He gained a position as a UN volunteer and then with the formation of the first government in May 2002 became a secretary of state with a wide-ranging portfolio encompassing environment, tourism and investment. While his position was ranked 30th out of 31 in the government, Teixeira was on the way up and was someone worth getting to know. Shortly after arriving back in Dili, he was befriended by a former ASIS agent with extensive Southeast Asia experience who now worked in East Timor for an international aid agency. The former agent became one of Teixeira's best friends. When told of his former affiliation, Teixeira was stunned and admitted to having confided in him at some length about the government. He believed that what he had told the former agent had made its way back to the Australian government, 'Those guys never stop being spies,' he lamented.

When former Midnight Oil frontman Peter Garrett, now Federal Labor MP for Kingsford-Smith, met Teixeira during a visit in mid-2004 Garrett said he strongly reminded him of Graham Richardson, the Machiavellian powerbroker of the Hawke and Keating Labor governments who called his autobiography *Whatever it Takes*.[18] Teixeira was not officially a member of the FRETILIN party but he worked assiduously to cultivate a role as a loyal acolyte of Alkatiri and his Mozambique clique. Like Richardson, he practised a brutal brand of tribal loyalty and was often preoccupied with running wars against anyone whom he perceived as a threat, most notably Alkatiri's main rival, Ramos-Horta.

Teixeira was at Alkatiri's side throughout the crisis of April–June 2006, even though the president, foreign minister, church leaders, and at least half the country, were calling for Alkatiri's resignation over his mismanagement of a minor dispute that put the new country on the brink of another civil war. When Alkatiri's press secretary departed in the middle of the crisis Teixeira stepped into the breach and served as his spokesman. Just as Teixeira's loyalty to his disgraced uncle was immutable, he repaid Alkatiri for his patronage with unswerving loyalty until the bitter end, when on 26 June the prime minister was forced to stand down amid allegations that his government had armed civilian hit squads.

In 2003 Alkatiri had appointed him one of three commissioners for the joint East Timor-Australia authority—the Timor Sea Designated Authority (TSDA)—that administers all activity in the treaty area. In mid-2005 he was made a vice-minister with responsibility for oil and gas, serving under Alkatiri who held onto this crucial portfolio. Alkatiri sent Teixeira to hold secret discussions with the Kuwaitis and Chinese on potential oil deals, and with some of the world's biggest oil companies, most notably the French multinational Total. With Alkatiri's departure in June 2006 he became a minister with the same portfolio.

In returning to East Timor Teixiera had left behind a comfortable suburban life for a job in Alkatiri's government that paid US$350 a month. His move back to East Timor had enabled him to 'gain a new country', as he told a friend. While not having been a player in the independence struggle, he had assiduously manoeuvred himself into a pivotal role in the development of East Timor's vast oil wealth. He had gained infinitely greater responsibility than he could ever have dreamt of while growing up in western Sydney, or while working as a Brisbane solicitor. He had gained more influence than money could buy.

11 PEOPLE POWER

'You don't know me. I'm Ian Melrose and I got your name from the web because of the work you're doing on the Timor Sea. I plan to spend quite a bit of my own money on this issue. It would be good to speak.' Message left by Ian Melrose on Dan Nicholson's mobile phone when he was on holiday in Queensland, late 2004

In October 2003 12-year-old Julmira Babo died a slow and painful death. The young girl from the coffee-growing mountains of Ermera had collapsed a few days earlier and lay unconscious as her family applied traditional medicine. Julmira would have been just another anonymous statistic in the horrific death toll from preventable illnesses among East Timor's children had it not been for the work of a UN doctor and an Australian journalist.

Dr Nurul Islam worked for the UN's Serious Crimes Unit in Dili where he had established a mortuary and new autopsy procedures. Julmira's body was brought to Dili and Dr Islam quickly uncovered the shocking cause of her mysterious death—asphyxiation. Her stomach, oesophagus, trachea and throat had become swollen with 25-centimetre roundworms that choked her as they moved through her body in search of food. 'In my entire career as a pathologist in the Third World, I have never seen anything like it,' Dr Islam said.

Five months later Rochelle Mutton, a young freelance journalist from Western Australia, landed in Dili in search of stories she could send back to newspapers in Australia. During her two weeks in East Timor, Mutton met by chance forensic anthropologist Caroline Barker who was studying the remains of victims of the 1999 violence at the Serious Crimes Unit. Barker invited Mutton to visit the unit so she could write a story on this work. During this visit, Mutton saw a large jar that contained the roundworms extracted from Julmira's body.

In early May 2004 Melbourne businessman Ian Melrose was reading the *Age* over breakfast. He noticed on page 19 a short article by Mutton with the headline 'Girl, 12, Chokes to Death on Worms'. It was a headline and a story that defied one of the iron laws of journalism—that it takes a significant death toll in a developing country to generate news coverage in the western media. 'The worm-ridden body of a 12-year-old girl, who suffered suffocation by hundreds of parasites, has alerted authorities to the spectre of worm infestations in East Timor,' read the lead paragraph.[1] The girl's life, and perhaps thousands like her, could have been saved by a 10 cent tablet, the story added.

The story distressed Melrose. He had a young daughter not much older than Julmira. He walked around his living room, and then read the article again, and then a third time, wondering what he could do. Melrose had also been reading about the ongoing dispute over Timor Sea oil and gas, and how Australia had been collecting disputed taxes at the rate of US$1 million a day since 1999. He made a connection. Australia's negotiating tactics were depriving East Timor of revenue that could save lives, he thought.

Melrose knew that his business gave him considerable political clout. His network of 37 optometry businesses were largely located in marginal seats in regional Australia. He thought about running a campaign on behalf of East Timor to support its position in the negotiations with Australia.

He called the head office of Oxfam in Melbourne and spoke to James Ensor, the director of public policy and outreach, and talked about spending a lot of money—millions of dollars—on an advertising campaign to help East Timor get a fair outcome. He met Ensor and showed him some drafts of his scripts for advertisements. Ensor hoped that Melrose would make a big donation to support Oxfam's work in East Timor, but Melrose had other ideas.

Three months later Melrose and his wife, Margaret, came to hear Kirsty Sword Gusmão speak at Melbourne Town Hall. Sword Gusmão, then six months pregnant with her third child, was at the tail end of a week-long national speaking tour on the Timor Sea dispute. She had generated a lot of interest in the first couple of days. The letters page of the *Sydney Morning Herald* had lit up with supportive comments after it reported her remark that the Australian government's conduct in the Timor Sea dispute made her ashamed to be an Australian.

Sword Gusmão is one of the generation who went through university in the 1980s as the Asian economic miracle was unfolding and interest in the countries to Australia's north was becoming more widespread. Born in 1966 and raised in a comfortable, middle-class Melbourne family, she studied Italian, Portuguese and Indonesian at university and met several East Timorese students. Upon graduating she was determined to focus her career on Asia. In 1990 she worked in West Papua on a film called *Arrows Against the Wind*, and then in 1991 she worked as a producer for Yorkshire Television's *Cold Blood: The Massacre of East Timor*, a documentary which included footage of the Santa Cruz massacre. After this experience, Sword Gusmão found work in Jakarta so that she could assist East Timor's clandestine resistance operation. It was in this capacity that she encountered her future husband while he was in prison. Sword Gusmão now lives in Dili where she and her president husband raise their three young boys, all of whom were delivered in Dili National Hospital, without any western drugs. In 2001 Sword Gusmão launched the Alola Foundation which is dedicated to caring for women in East Timor and has made a major contribution in improving maternal and infant health. She is a powerful advocate for the people of East Timor, and in 2006 emerged as an outspoken critic of the East Timor government's handling of the dispute in the armed forces.

As Sword Gusmão's week-long tour wore on it had become more difficult to maintain the momentum. A federal election was looming and Australians were being made to focus on interest rates. At her last public engagement Sword Gusmão appeared 'in conversation' at Melbourne Town Hall with the Reverend Tim Costello, the Baptist minister, leading social justice activist and elder brother of the man slated to become the next conservative prime minister of Australia, the federal treasurer, Peter Costello. It was a coup to have the Reverend Costello sitting next to the first lady of East Timor at the Melbourne Town Hall, but nonetheless public and media interest was waning. Most of the people who came were long-time East Timor supporters.

At the end of the week, a Melbourne advertising magnate, Harold Mitchell, hosted a Saturday lunch at a pub with a group of about 25 Melbourne business identities. The purpose of the lunch was to bring together an influential group for a briefing on the Timor Sea dispute. One of the guests, a leading businessman who had a Rolls Royce parked outside, said he had already raised his concerns about the dispute informally with Downer during a chance encounter in the Qantas Chairman's Lounge. East Timor's campaign was clearly having an impact if leading business people were, of their own volition, agitating at the highest level of the government. At this time former US president Bill Clinton was visiting Australia and he also was talking about the dispute. In an informal, off-air chat with television host Andrew Denton, Clinton said of the dispute: 'You guys can cut them a little slack and, you know, a little bit of money will go a long way there.'

Harold Mitchell had been a generous supporter of East Timor and of Sword Gusmão's work for a number of years. He expressed interest in funding an advertising campaign and putting serious money behind it. The offer from this advertising magnate was there, but Ian Melrose, a complete novice got off and running before anyone else had a chance to make a move.

* * *

East Timor had gained significant public support in Australia during the long years of Indonesian occupation. The conduct of successive Australian governments had pricked the conscience of a nation that felt uneasy about the way a near neighbour and a Second World War ally had been betrayed.

East Timor's overwhelming 78.5 per cent vote for independence in the 30 August 1999 ballot defied an Indonesian campaign of intimidation, but without the presence of peacekeepers, an orchestrated campaign of militia violence ensued after the result was announced. The militias singled out the media and most journalists left immediately. There was no live coverage of the campaign of violence, but the little information that trickled out horrified the world and the Australian public especially. Phone calls and faxes urging the Australian government to intervene inundated the offices of federal MPs. Downer said that 'people were ringing up, crying over the phone, we had more calls on that issue than I've ever had in my life on anything'.[2] Churches, trade unions, East Timor support groups and Amnesty International joined together to stage mass rallies in Sydney and Melbourne. Ships bound for Indonesia were prevented from loading cargo and passengers were barred from boarding Garuda flights. Howard, a wily politician who has an acute sense of the national mood, worked around the clock to speak to world leaders, including President Bill Clinton, to enlist their support for an international peacekeeping force for East Timor (to be called InterFET). On 7 September the Australian government dropped its evacuation-only plan, Operation Spitfire, and began to develop a new plan for restoring order in East Timor. Under Operation Warden,[3] a contingent of SAS soldiers landed in Dili on

20 September, followed by up to 5000 Australian troops over the next two and a half years.

In the subsequent fight for its economic independence, East Timor fell back on the same networks and the same sense of goodwill and 'fair go'. Public support in Australia for East Timor has always been at odds with opinion in the media, and among the diplomatic and academic elite who made up the 'Jakarta/Indonesia lobby'.[4] This is the lobby that took a very sanguine view of the leadership of President Soeharto—named by Transparency International as the most corrupt dictator in history[5]—and Indonesia generally.

One of the fruits of the Jakarta lobby was the creation of the Australia–Indonesia Institute (AII), which had a secretariat in the Indonesia section of DFAT and direct funding by the department. Australian foreign minister Gareth Evans and his counterpart Ali Alatas launched AII in 1989 at a time when Indonesia's conduct in East Timor was generating strong anti-Indonesian sentiment in Australia.[6] Its mandate was to give positive exposure of Indonesia to key 'opinion-makers' in Australia, most notably journalists, by paying for study tours and the like.[7] Two former departmental secretaries, Richard Woolcott and Phillip Flood, have chaired AII and in 2005 Downer appointed Allan Taylor, the counsellor in the Jakarta embassy in 1975 and the former head of ASIS, as the AII chair.

It was an article of faith for this lobby that East Timorese independence was a lost cause; members believed that Indonesian excesses were exaggerated and in any event should be airbrushed out of existence because there was no possibility of revisiting independence for East Timor. Jakarta correspondents and Australian-based editors in the mainstream media played a role in ignoring or even killing negative stories about East Timor. There were a few exceptions, mainly at the Fairfax newspapers and the Australian Broadcasting Corporation, but even in these institutions the lobby had loyal acolytes.

Following the Santa Cruz massacre in 1991 the ABC's bureau in Darwin produced a story on the deportation from East Timor of journalist Dennis Schultz who had visited sites where bodies had been dumped after the massacre. The story was not broadcast. The ABC's Jakarta correspondent Michael Maher argued a technicality, saying the incident could not be described as deportation, and that in any event the story would create problems with the Indonesian government. Other prime examples of self-censorship include the refusal of the Australian media to publish reports of a massacre at Alas in November 1998, and a story about Australian-trained Indonesian soldiers turning up on the frontline in East Timor at the same time.

East Timor needed more than the opinion-makers in the media during the occupation, and the same applied to the Timor Sea dispute. While East Timor's campaign succeeded in generating very favourable coverage in Australia and internationally, it was ordinary people in Australia who drove the message of 'fair go' home to John Howard's government.

The place in Australia from where this groundswell came was Melbourne, the centre of East Timor's support base in Australia, where many aid organisations and other non-government organisations and the largest concentration of Timorese immigrants are based. With a European climate and culture, it is a place where people meet indoors in pubs, bars and cafes and talk. Melbourne's daily broadsheet, the *Age*, still retains a social justice edge. Its sister newspaper, the *Sydney Morning Herald*, rejected Rochelle Mutton's story about the death of Julmira Babo.

In early 2004 a grass roots campaign to support East Timor's rights in the Timor Sea sprang up in Melbourne, the initiative of a handful of university graduates who had worked or travelled in East Timor. They called it the Timor Sea Justice Campaign (TSJC). Dan Nicholson, a lanky, unassuming law graduate, and Natalie Bugalski, a smart and vivacious lawyer who was writing a PhD on East Timor, conceived of it during a visit to East Timor in December 2003. The two came to East Timor to look at the issue of access to housing, but they soon realised that achieving a fair settlement in the Timor Sea dispute would be far more significant than anything they could achieve on housing rights.

After returning to Australia, through word of mouth and a few well-placed advertisements, Nicholson and Bugalski proposed a meeting at Melbourne's Trades Hall for anyone interested in forming this group. Around 40 people attended the first meeting, and the group started meeting fortnightly. In March, just two months later, Nicholson, then 25, travelled to Canberra at his own expense to give evidence to the Senate Economics Committee on East Timor's rights in the Timor Sea.

The government had tabled legislation in the House of Representatives for the ratification of the Sunrise agreement in order to mount pressure on East Timor to ratify the agreement.[8] The legislation had been referred to the committee by Labor, not out of concern for East Timor's rights to these resources, but because an accompanying bill gave the operator of the field the right to import duty-free capital goods. Labor was concerned that Australia would miss out on business from the construction of the project.

In his evidence to the Senate Economics Committee, Nicholson outlined the implications of Australia's withdrawal from international arbitration. The TSJC's submission proposed an amendment to put the revenue from the disputed fields into a trust fund until the boundary dispute was resolved. Nicholson told the committee:

> This bill gives the Government the opportunity to stall on negotiations. It creates an incentive for that, because whilst the stalling is going on, they collect 82 per cent of the revenue. Even if boundaries were finalised, there's nothing to actually ensure that the petroleum would be redistributed in accordance with those boundaries.[9]

Asked by the committee chair, Senator George Brandis QC, if he was saying that a future government could act in bad faith, Nicholson made very clear that he was talking about the current government's conduct. 'I think there have been some indications that this government is currently acting in bad faith,' he said, adding that Prime Minister Alkatiri had released a statement that morning accusing Australia of undermining the Sunrise agreement.

His presentation was flawless. His only mistake that day was leaving Bugalski sitting behind him in the visitors' seating and not next to him as another witness.[10] Woodside executives also looked on from these seats as the company did not make a submission. The following morning Gary Gray, the former national secretary of the ALP and chief lobbyist for Woodside, took Nicholson and Bugalski out to breakfast at the Canberra Hyatt.

The Labor Party had opted to support the government's Sunrise legislation—it was unlikely to do anything else in an election year. But anticipating a hostile reaction from its left wing, Labor senators claimed that Alkatiri had told Labor's foreign policy spokesman, Kevin Rudd, that he had no problem with the bills being passed. This was the result of a telephone conversation between Alkatiri and Rudd the previous month. Rudd used his interpretation of the conversation to justify Labor's position, a version disputed by Alkatiri. Rudd later disputed Alkatiri's statement.

Labor's Senate leader, John Faulkner, said in the debate on the bills that no representative of the 'Democratic Republic of Timor-Leste' had asked that they not be passed. Victorian Left heavyweight, Senator Kim Carr, had the job of spelling out Labor's justification during the debate:

> The Australian Opposition has sought to talk directly to the government of Timor-Leste, and the Prime Minister, Mr Mari Alkatiri, spoke with Mr Rudd and Mr Jull[11] [sic] last week. Specific questions were put on the issue of whether or not there were problems with the Opposition in this country supporting this legislation, and the response was no. So we feel that the issue of this particular legislation, which should be the subject of this debate, is worthy of support—and I will explain the reason for that—and that is the view that the Government of Timor-Leste is putting to us.

We are not relying on hearsay here. We are not relying on press reports, We are not even relying on the Australian Government. We are getting it directly from Dili.[12]

Labor, just months away from a federal election, was never going to oppose these bills. Its resources spokesman Joel Fitzgibbon said Labor was 'as keen as anyone' to see these bills passed so that the development of Sunrise could occur in the 'national interest'. The minor parties, the Greens and the Democrats, urged the government to put all revenues in escrow until a permanent maritime boundary was settled. Even the anti-immigration One Nation Party said that all the revenues from Sunrise should 'go directly to Timor-Leste'.

As with independence, the only support that East Timor could really depend on in Australia was from ordinary people and the minor parties.

* * *

As Ian Melrose began working on his first batch of television advertisements and leaflets he heard about the TSJC and got in contact with Dan Nicholson who was on holiday at Stradbroke Island. In September 2004 Melrose put some information about the dispute on the back of his company's eyeglass catalogue which was mailed out to 524 000 households around Australia. Most of the recipients lived in regional areas and some of the major cities that had a high prevalence of marginal seats, most notably Downer's home city of Adelaide. Using a full A4 page, Melrose highlighted Australia's exploitation of the BCL fields, the withdrawal from international arbitration, and he copied the Mutton story in full. He wrote that he was 'ashamed of Australia's conduct' and urged customers to contact their federal MPs: 'Please make John Howard and Alexander Downer act honestly for Australia.'

Ian and Margaret Melrose brought a no-frills, novice approach to their involvement, in keeping with their own personal style. He was a mid-fifties former accountant, she a former dietician. Both drove white Holden sedans bought secondhand at government auctions. Improvements on their home in the outer suburbs were left unfinished. A typical dinner at the Melrose home was steak and vegetables followed by apple pie and ice-cream.

Running for a minute and broadcast on regional networks, the first television advertisements showed pictures of Timorese children with the following voiceover:

> East Timor, one of our nearest neighbours, is a country so poor that eight out of every 100 children die before they are five. A deplorable situation.
>
> Two months before East Timor became a nation, Australia withdrew recognition of the international court which would have determined who *owns* the gas and oil so close to East Timor. While Australia continues to take the oil revenue the East Timorese continue to suffer.
>
> Since 1999 the Australian government has received more than $2000 million in taxes from East Timor oil, and has returned more than $400 million in aid.
>
> Australia, let's be fair in dealing with oil and gas. Give the East Timorese the entitlements that would be due under international law so that they can build hospitals and schools and feed their children.
>
> Australia is not being fair to the people of East Timor.

A second advertisement took direct aim at Howard and Downer:

> An important message to John Howard:
>
> East Timor, one of our nearest neighbours is a country so poor that eight out of every 100 children die before they are five. A deplorable situation.
>
> John Howard and Alexander Downer, let's be fair . . .
>
> John Howard and Alexander Downer we are not being fair to the people of East Timor.

Upon learning of the advertisements, Downer sought an urgent meeting with Melrose. They met for almost two hours in Downer's electorate office on 17 September, just three days before the first of the intensive meetings aimed at settling the dispute. Melrose told Downer that he liked the government's economic management and was a nominal Liberal voter, but he could not abide its treatment of East Timor. Downer suggested that Melrose spend his money on humanitarian projects in the impoverished country. Melrose replied that he could not fix all of East Timor's problems with his money, but if he used it to achieve a fair outcome in the division of Timor Sea resources then perhaps he would make a real difference. Downer said he and Ramos-Horta had already agreed on a 'framework' to achieve a settlement, with a commitment to resolve the dispute by the end of 2004. Melrose was not going to accept Downer's word; he would only withdraw the advertisements if Downer gave an undertaking that Australia would return to independent arbitration if a settlement could not be reached by the end of the year. Downer knew he could not give Melrose any such commitment, and the advertisements continued throughout the election campaign.

After this meeting Melrose realised he needed some professional political help. He hired Ben Oquist, who had advised Senator Bob Brown since 1996. Melrose had linked up with a very astute political professional who just happened to be available after returning from extended travel. Oquist suggested that Melrose commission a Newspoll about the commitment that Downer had refused to give at that meeting. It produced a stunning result—77 per cent of Australians believed that the dispute should be taken to the International Court of Justice if it could not be resolved amicably. The Australian sense of 'a fair go'—of heeding the 'umpire's decision'—clearly prevailed.

* * *

Late in 2004 Melrose began directly funding the TSJC. The Melrose war chest, enthusiasm and ideas together with the group's grassroots activism and tactical skills made for a formidable combination.

The TSJC first targeted people who were familiar with East Timor. The core membership went to suburban areas and spoke about the issue with the aim of mobilising people to contact their local politicians in the same way the public had done in 1999. They wanted to create a lot of noise out in the electorates, giving the impression of widespread community disquiet over the government's conduct. The campaign focused on the network of 'friendship cities' that had been set up since 1999. In the state of Victoria, sixteen cities and towns had friendship city relationships with towns in East Timor, far more than in any other state. This network provided fertile ground for grassroots activism.

The TSJC rallied other NGOs, churches and unions in Melbourne. The group produced information kits on the issue for these organisations and for all federal politicians. Regular meetings to plan the lobbying effort, attracting representatives from more than 20 organisations, were hosted by Oxfam Australia, the Uniting Church and the Australia East Timor Association. After kicking off in Melbourne, the movement spread across the country, with branches in other capital cities—Sydney, Adelaide and Darwin—and as well in the smaller cities of Newcastle and Alice Springs. The TSJC hosted a national speaking tour on the eve of the federal election. One night in the remote desert centre of Alice Springs, more than 200 people attended a dinner to hear a forum on the dispute that included politicians from opposition parties and Manuel de Lemos, the third-generation Timorese civil servant who had been a member of East Timor's negotiating team since 2000.

* * *

In early 2005, as overtures were being made to restart negotiations, Melrose produced a new set of advertisements to run on 26 January,

Australia Day. He bought cheap television advertising time during the post-Christmas hiatus, which coincided with the Australian Open tennis tournament in Melbourne. Advertisements that cost him around $30 000 ran in the middle of top-rating games featuring Lleyton Hewitt, and in the fourth-round match between Alicia Molik and Venus Williams. They ran with this script:

> The spirit of Australia has been shown in our generosity to the tsunami victims.
> In East Timor eight out of 100 children die before the age of five.
> They don't want our charity—they just want justice.
> Under international law the Howard Government has stolen $2 billion in gas and oil royalties which East Timor needs to create a working health system.
> Let your Liberal politician know Australia must stop stealing East Timor's gas and oil.

Again, the advertisements showed still pictures of Timorese children, but when the words 'has stolen $2 billion' were spoken a picture of Australia's Parliament House flashed onto the screen. In all of the advertisements Melrose underquoted the estimated level of child mortality, which at the time was that twelve children out of every 100 children would die before their fifth birthday. (In Australia it is 0.6 out of every 100.) Melrose had taken the wrong figure from a Ramos-Horta speech and decided to continue using it after being told it was inaccurate. The mistake enabled the East Timor government to distance itself from the advertisements. When Australian government officials complained about them they were told that had East Timor been directly involved then the child mortality rate given would have been 50 per cent higher.

The Melroses visited East Timor in early 2005 to look at a potential aid project on the remote south coast and for part of the journey Ramos-Horta arranged for them to fly in a UN helicopter. Doug

Chester learned of this and complained bitterly to the East Timor government. The Melroses had transferred $1 million into the Dili branch of the ANZ Bank and this money was quickly dispersed among a range of health and nutrition projects. Despite following Downer's advice and supporting humanitarian projects, Chester accused Ian Melrose of betrayal during a telephone conversation at this time. Melrose was reminded that he was an 'Australian citizen', meaning that his loyalty should be with the Australian government.

Melrose and the TSJC continued the campaign with a series of full-page newspaper advertisements and they distributed free postcards around Australia that summarised the dispute. The advertisements focused on the great needs of East Timor but, importantly, they avoided turning the dispute into a charity case. East Timor's poverty was not the basis of its claim, but it underscored the injustice resulting from Australia's tactics. In one TV advertisement Dr Barry Mendelawitz, an obstetrician, said that during a period of three months working as East Timor's sole obstetrician he had delivered one dead baby every day. He saw ten women die of childbirth compared with just two during his 30 years working in Australia. He concluded, 'Building a viable health system takes a long time and a lot of money. East Timor needs money now and for a long time.'

The campaign became unpalatable for some elements of the mainstream media when a version of the TV advertisements finished with this very confronting line: 'Stealing from a third world country kills their children. Please complain to your federal politician.' It was the last line in an advertisement to mark the anniversary of Australia's withdrawal from international arbitration. Drawing a parallel with the evasion of justice by a disgraced businessman, the late Christopher Skase, it said: 'The Australian government has done a Skase on the East Timorese. On 25 March 2002 Australia withdrew East Timor's right to take the oil and gas ownership to the international court. East Timor needs their stolen 2000 million for hospitals.'

It was too much for the Seven and SBS networks; they refused to run this version. However, they did broadcast less confronting versions in later months.[13] Nonetheless he had caught the attention of popular morning-show presenter, Seven's David Koch, who, in spite of the management sensitivity, decided to make the dispute his 'issue of 2005'. Later that month, Koch travelled to East Timor with Melrose to produce a TV special on East Timor and the oil dispute. After just six months' campaigning, a complete amateur had turned the Timor Sea dispute into a celebrity cause.

12 THE BRAINSTORMING TRAP

'There must be a price.' Doug Chester pressing José Teixeira during the early October 2004 negotiations

When East Timor's negotiating team departed for Canberra in September 2004 they took with them an extraordinary instruction from the prime minister and the president. Fearful of Australia's tactics to secure its line across the Timor Trough, the two told the team not to actively engage in negotiations. They were to go to Canberra and 'listen' to what the Australian government had to say—nothing more.

On the morning of 20 September East Timor's ten-member team began last-minute work on José Teixeira's opening statement. Peter Galbraith had taken a presidential suite at a Rydges hotel on Canberra Avenue which featured an atrium design that reminded fiscal adviser Philip Daniel of his travels to the Soviet Union. The group met in this spacious room, drafting the opening statement on a laptop. Galbraith proposed a statement that said East Timor was here to negotiate a permanent or long-term agreement covering three main points: Australia's concerns about sovereignty, East Timor's concerns about the issues of natural resources, and the need to formulate an agreement 'without prejudice' to permanent maritime boundary claims.

This immediately sounded odd to some in the room, and it sounded particularly odd to Dominic Puthucheary, the Indian-Malaysian constitutional lawyer who had been put on the team by Alkatiri because he wanted a stronger focus on issues of sovereignty. The presence of this erudite septuagenarian brought a touch of Gandhi to East Timor's negotiating team. Puthucheary asked in a lilting accent why the draft only mentioned Australia's concerns about sovereignty, as though East Timor had no rights in the disputed area. Galbraith insisted on keeping his original outline and after a drawn-out discussion the group decided to cite both countries' concerns.

At the formal opening of talks in the afternoon Doug Chester was uncharacteristically affable—a far different persona to the one seen in Dili only four months earlier. Chris Moraitis, the current deputy head of Australia's delegation, also displayed good humour as he welcomed the 'famous Dili Allstars' to Canberra. This was a reference to a name given to East Timor's negotiating team by *Time* editor-at-large Tom Dusevic in a detailed article on the April 2004 talks. It was a rather poignant appellation because a Melbourne-based rock band of Timorese and Australian musicians with the same name has as its frontman, Paul Stewart, the younger brother of Tony Stewart, the youngest of the five newsmen killed at Balibo.

The two sides sat around an enormous oval conference table in the Doug Anthony Room in DFAT's 'gazebo' head office. Hollow in the middle, the table was big enough to seat 30 people. Doug Chester opened by proposing, in avuncular style, that the two sides enter into something akin to a game. He suggested that East Timor think of the meeting as a 'brainstorming' session rather than a negotiation. This was, after all, the spirit of the 'creative solution'.

Under this guise Bill Campbell QC, Australia's most senior government expert on international law, moved straight into his proposal for a treaty between Australia and East Timor that would close the Timor Gap at the Timor Trough in return for regular financial payments to East Timor. The Australian government would be willing to commence paying East Timor for these rights from January 2005, even though the Greater Sunrise field was still on the drawing board, and it would continue to pay compensation even if Greater Sunrise did not go ahead. East Timor had failed to have this unacceptable proposal taken off the table at the meetings with Chester in Dili. Teixeira made the point firmly that there appeared to be 'fundamental misunderstanding here . . . one thing that was made clear was the significance to Timor-Leste of our resources. We are not going to settle for aid in exchange for territory.'

Moraitis suggested that he think of it as a revenue transfer rather than aid and East Timor asked for a break so that the group could discuss how to respond. The delegation moved into a smaller room which they thought was in all likelihood bugged, but there was no alternative. Galbraith argued that Australia was not serious about the proposal; it was simply going through the motions. Bureaucrats had to demonstrate to their superiors who in turn had to demonstrate to their political masters that they had fought the good fight and had tried hard to achieve their institutional priorities, he explained. He believed Campbell had couched the proposal along these lines. Campbell had said to the meeting that he had gone to all the trouble of drafting this proposal and so asked that he be allowed to present it.

Nonetheless, despite Galbraith's argument, the Australian government had constructed the offer in a way to make it look very attractive. The money could start flowing in within four months, long before Greater Sunrise came on stream.

In the small room the East Timor delegation quickly devised a response to the proposal. If Australia wanted to talk about financial assistance, East Timor would do the same by discussing how much financial assistance would be paid to Australia under East Timor's boundary proposal which took in all of Greater Sunrise and the BCL fields. This novel idea came from Peter Galbraith and Philip Daniel who thought it was an effective way of increasing the amount of money on the table. There were smirks all over the faces of those on the Australian side of the big table as Daniel explained his estimate of

US$20 billion[1] in disputed government revenue, and how under East Timor's boundary proposal it could pay Australia a regular stipend. Campbell went along with the ploy when he asked whether East Timor's definition of non-petroleum seabed resources included living creatures, but Moraitis firmly made clear, yet again, that Australia was completely unwilling to look at any boundary proposal outside the JPDA. In terms of what Australia understood by the 'creative solution', Moraitis explained that East Timor's concept of a maritime boundary was 'far from being in those parameters, not in the ballpark'.

At the end of the first day DFAT released a brief statement saying that the talks were making progress. This was aimed at sending the signal in the middle of the election campaign that all was well inside the negotiating room and that the Howard government was playing fair.

Although it responded creatively to Australia's buy-back proposal, East Timor's team was struggling and caught off-guard. On the second morning it asked for an adjournment and met in the sculpture garden of the Australian National Gallery, a location chosen in order to avoid the suspected bugs in the hotel, for a long and tedious discussion on how to respond. Galbraith instructed that all mobile phones—potential receptors for eavesdropping devices—be put in a bag which was placed about 100 metres away from the group on the other side of the garden. This worked for some time until a security guard came along and enquired about the bag. One clear option was to simply go back to Dili, but this would involve a public condemnation of Australia's negotiating tactics and would be seen as trying to tip the election, Galbraith argued. It could earn 'strong enemies' should the conservatives be re-elected, he warned. Antunes thought it was worthwhile trying to see if there was another boundary proposal that Australia would agree to. The discussion eventually concluded that East Timor had to go back into the meeting and kill off Australia's proposal for closing the Timor Gap.

That afternoon Teixeira told the Australians that since August it had been made clear by East Timor that closing the Timor Gap between points A16 and A17 was not acceptable. He rejected the notion that a maritime boundary should be limited to the borders of the JPDA. By the end of this day East Timor finally knocked Australia's boundary proposal on the head, but the concept of a cash settlement for Greater Sunrise to go ahead persisted.

The following morning, when the two sides met again, Galbraith gave the cash option a whole new lease of life. He proposed what he called a 'Hong Kong solution'. By this he meant an arrangement in which Australia purchased or leased East Timor's rights for a century, yet he had never discussed this extraordinary proposal with the negotiating team or the East Timor government. 'We could think about an arrangement that does not involve a maritime boundary. We'd like to accommodate Australia's desire for permanency—a Hong Kong solution,' he said.

Naturally Moraitis responded positively to the idea, though he expressed neither surprise nor delight at a proposal that was very favourable to Australia's interests. It was an 'interesting idea . . . [we are] more than willing to have a listen to what you mean by that'. Galbraith knew immediately he had overstepped the line. 'This is really in the nature of brainstorming,' he said. 'I'm not making a formal proposal.' It was too late. The idea was out of the bag and the Australian side would run with it for the next month. Galbraith had used the word 'permanency'. The notion of a 99-year deal that involved cash for a suspension of East Timor's rights was completely at odds with the negotiating team's instructions. Alkatiri had repeatedly emphasised that any deal was to be without prejudice to East Timor's rights to a maritime boundary.

While Galbraith was convinced that the cash option was the only one acceptable to Australia, Einar Risa, the Norwegian oil and political veteran, pressed for other options to be considered, such as the widening of the JPDA. In a meeting in Galbraith's presidential suite Risa declared that the cash settlement was 'defeatist'. Galbraith exploded into a rage. Standing over Risa and wagging his index finger at him, he thundered that he would not tolerate 'name calling' and that he was the only person on the team with negotiating experience and therefore his judgements had to be accepted.

For Australia, this meeting had gone exceptionally well. After beginning with the ploy of brainstorming, the negotiations on the third day were careering at a frightening pace towards exactly the result that it wanted. While Downer had said a resolution might be reached by Christmas, Chester was on track to deliver his boss an outcome right in the middle of the election campaign. It was all going so well that Australia proposed another meeting for the end of September.

* * *

The Australian and Timorese negotiating teams met again in Darwin on 27 September 2004, as the election campaign continued. It was here that Chester and Galbraith came up with a formula to decide how the compensation would work. They would add up the value of all the government revenue from the disputed area, including the JPDA, and divide it by two. Australia would then pay compensation to East Timor to make up the shortfall between what it would get under current arrangements, and what it would get under the fifty-fifty split. To Galbraith this sounded fair, but for others it made no sense to include the treaty area in this calculation because East Timor had already secured a 90 per cent share. This formula, crucially, required making an assumption about oil prices for a field that might not be in production for another ten years at the earliest. The offer to East Timor had now reached US$4.35 billion but this came from a very low oil price assumption of US$23 a barrel, compared with the prevailing market price of around US$34 a barrel. Under this proposal East Timor would be paid US$125 million for 35 years.

In East Timor's backroom meetings Galbraith pressed forcefully for a quick settlement. The offer was as good as East Timor could hope for, he argued. The alternative of court action could take years and might not result in a better outcome. The time value of money dictated that it was better to secure a deal now, he said. Alkatiri, who was interested in seeing how much money would be offered, thought little of the current proposal. 'They are playing with me,' he told Teixeira over the phone when he was briefed on the negotiations.

Daniel thought that East Timor needed to get Australia to agree to indexation for inflation in order to make it acceptable. If it could achieve this East Timor would have 'an extremely good deal'. There was some discussion of linking the indexation to energy prices. Teixeira thought this might help 'bring it closer to genuine resource sharing'. But the reality was that the emerging deal was looking so much like quasi aid that Daniel and Galbraith proposed getting a commitment out of Australia not to reduce its aid program as part of the overall deal. Antunes thought the proposed deal was compelling to Australia, and the government might be prepared to pay a lot more. 'This deal gets them everything they want. They have money. What they don't have is power. Very simply it resolves all sorts of problems for them,' he said.

With the momentum building towards a deal, a third meeting was proposed for Dili at the end of October. On the eve of this meeting Chester told journalists he was within 'inches' of clinching a final settlement for the Timor Gap.

* * *

Back in Dili there was time for a stocktake. Alkatiri told a meeting in his office in early October that he was not happy with where the talks had gone. Teixeira admitted the team had 'overstepped our mandate—we were meant to explore issues'. The nature of the offer on the table was completely unacceptable to East Timor's political leadership. It would be political suicide for this two-year-old government to agree to sell out rights to its resources for a few billion dollars. Some advisers still talked about settling for cash. Antunes now thought that US$10 billion, if it were on the table, would have to be considered seriously. Another option, favoured by half the team, was simply to push for a bigger share of Greater Sunrise. Alkatiri wanted East Timor to raise broader issues of downstream benefits from the development of Greater Sunrise at the next meeting, namely onshore processing of Sunrise gas in East Timor. Galbraith and Daniel were to be absent from the next negotiating round in late October, and this changed considerably the tenor of East Timor's negotiating stance.

At the 11 August meeting in Canberra Downer had dismissed East Timor's push for a pipeline to be part of the agenda. He said it was a commercial decision. In reality the two governments, as joint regulators of developments in the JPDA, had the power to decide how any field was developed. The Australian government had already put the Sunrise project within its 'major project facilitation' scheme. This was ostensibly about cutting red tape for multi-billion dollar projects, but in some instances the projects extracted subsidies from Canberra. Woodside had already talked to Canberra about a subsidy in the order of $200 million to swing the decision to build a floating LNG plant, which would pay no tax in Australia, to building an onshore plant in Darwin that would pay tax. Woodside had dangled the prospect of a floating LNG plant in front of the Australian government in an effort to secure the subsidy for the Darwin option. The tax revenue from processing gas from the Bayu-Undan field was in the order of US$1 billion, indicating that the revenue from Sunrise would be about double this amount. East Timor wanted Australia, at the very least, to level the playing field by guaranteeing that it would not subsidise a pipeline to Darwin, and even better would be a deal that included a preference for a pipeline to an LNG plant in East Timor.

Evidence presented to the parliamentary hearings on the Timor Sea Treaty in 2002 revealed the enormous benefit to northern Australia of piping the Sunrise gas to Darwin. Modelling produced by Dr Peter Brain from the National Institute of Economic and Industry Research showed 'economic benefit' of $22 billion and 20 000 new jobs. The modelling, commissioned by the Northern Territory Chamber of Commerce and Industry and the Territory Construction Association, was presented to the JSCOT hearings in Darwin in 2002. For East Timor, this research underscored its determination to fight for the pipeline.[2]

It was evident that if East Timor raised these issues then the negotiations were likely to break down, for a while anyway. 'If it breaks down they will say we could not agree on a price. I would be certain that within two to three years they would come back and push for a solution,' said Einar Risa. Fellow Norwegian Geir Ytreland also pressed strongly for the pipeline to be put on the negotiating table. 'They will come back if things break down. The pipeline is the single most important tool for developing this country. It is better than money in the bank,' he said.

The impetus for raising the pipeline came from a Norwegian government technical assistance project. The Norwegian experience was instructive for East Timor because in the 1960s and 1970s the country had successfully pushed companies to locate their processing facilities for North Sea oil and gas in Norway rather than in the United Kingdom. While East Timor and Norway were very different countries, these advisers still believed that East Timor stood a fighting chance of securing these developments and would benefit from them.

The East Timor government had asked Woodside to produce a feasibility study on building a pipeline to East Timor and an LNG plant. The study produced the result expected by East Timor. Woodside said the project was not technically feasible. But Norwegian pipeline engineers had challenged Woodside's claims about the technical problems of putting a pipeline through the Timor Trough. Building pipelines at depths of more than 2000 metres was not a novel idea. At least two other pipelines, one in the Gulf of Mexico and another in the Black Sea, had been built to depths of around 2200 metres.

A review of the Woodside report by Norwegian engineering consultants Lucon A/S, who had engaged leading pipeline expert Dr Sverre Lund, was handed to the East Timor government in mid-October, ten days before the next negotiating round with Australia. The report said 'when seeing the results, the premises for the [Woodside] study appear to have been coloured by lack of incentives to demonstrate that the Timor-Leste alternative can be a realistic option'.[3]

Woodside had completed the study without surveying the seabed, and this increased their assessment of the cost and risks of the East Timor option. Woodside concluded that the likely depth would be 3000 to 3300 metres but Lucon said 2350 metres was a more reasonable estimate. Woodside had completed a 'desk-top' study which 'could in reality not allow a decision in favor of Timor-Leste, being in competition with a mature Darwin option'. And Woodside only looked at two options: a direct straight-line pipeline that maximised depth and an indirect route that maximised distance. It did not look for an 'optimum balance of distance and likely maximum depth'. These factors inflated the cost of the East Timor option. Lucon concluded that with some modifications the cost of the East Timor option could be brought into line with the Darwin option. A pipeline from the Sunrise field to East Timor was 'technically feasible'.

On the eve of the next meeting with Australia, due to commence on 25 October, Alkatiri instructed his negotiating team to push for the following:[4]

- An agreement which would state that the respective claims to maritime boundaries would be negotiated under a separate agreement at a later date.
- A minimum of 70 per cent of the revenue from Greater Sunrise and a deferral of boundary claims for 30 to 50 years or the life of the resources.
- Compensation for the loss of income from the BCL fields to be paid over a period of one year.

- No link between the agreement and the level of Australian aid. Alkatiri added curtly on this point, 'I saw some link with aid. I'm sure the aid will continue. We are looking for our own resources, not the aid.'
- And while Sunrise could involve a simple revenue split, he wanted a Timor Sea Treaty type arrangement for unknown resources, meaning that East Timor would be a partner with regulatory control. In other words he wanted a treaty arrangement for the disputed area.
- A pipeline in East Timor and the downstream benefits from Greater Sunrise.

As Galbraith and Daniel were unable to attend this next meeting, Alkatiri received a written submission from them. They urged him to accept the fixed dollar amount, arguing that the US$4.35 billion could be sweetened by linking the compensation to the rate of inflation, thereby making it a politically acceptable settlement for East Timor. Their arguments were strongly supported by a second written submission made to Alkatiri by Kathryn Khamsi, the Harvard-educated legal adviser and coordinator in the Timor Sea Office who, like many women who worked in East Timor appeared awe-struck by the Galbraith charm and swagger. Alkatiri ignored their advice.

13 THE BREAKDOWN

'Well, they get their country back, they get Indonesia off their back and they get 90 per cent of an absolute windfall and they're still not grateful. I am amazed.' Comment by Adelaide talkback radio host Jeremy Cordeaux in an interview with Alexander Downer, 26 October 2004

On the morning of 25 October, at around 11 a.m., just as José Teixeira began his opening address to the Australian side, a minor earthquake rumbled through Dili. Earthquakes are a common occurrence in this region, but it was an ominous sign of what was about to come. The two sides were back in the Hotel Timor's large conference room, almost six months to the day after Alkatiri made his memorable welcoming address in which he accused Australia of profiting from a crime. On this occasion the no-man's-land between them was a little narrower.

Teixeira said the discussions in Canberra and Darwin had 'explored only one possible approach to participation in the sharing of Timor Sea resources'. East Timor was not confident that a fair and equitable resolution could be achieved within these parameters, he said. It did not appear that the cash settlement would result in an outcome that East Timor deemed fair, that it 'could live with'. He noted the rise in oil prices over the course of 2004, and said the creative solution should reflect 'the full value of the resources'. He asked that this meeting explore resource-sharing arrangements and highlighted the Timor Sea Treaty as a model. A bigger share of Greater Sunrise for East Timor was another option. Teixeira was bringing the agenda back to exactly where it had been two years earlier when Alkatiri pressed Downer for the joint development of Sunrise. But he went further when he said that any creative solution should also address future discoveries in the disputed area and the benefits of onshore processing which so far had gone to Australia. He noted that this issue had been raised at the 11 August 2004 meeting with the Australian foreign minister.

Chester, the hard man sent in by Downer, said there appeared to be a 'slight disconnect' between the two sides and revealed why Downer had agreed to proceed with the talks. 'One reason why Downer agreed [to the talks] was to give Greater Sunrise a way forward,' he said. The negotiations were not about recognising the rights of Australia's newly independent neighbour, they were about Woodside's interests. 'Our main aim is to give Greater Sunrise a chance to be exploited,' he added. In making this point Chester subscribed to Woodside's arguments about a so-called 2010 marketing window and its Christmas deadline. 'The window is very, very short—time is running out if we are to reach a solution by the end of the year.' East Timor also needed to do some 'repair work on the bilateral relationship', he cautioned.

Australia persisted with its cash offer and, as predicted by Galbraith, Chester drove down the compensation figure. He offered just US$2.8 billion to be paid in instalments over the life of the project. This was the gross amount to be paid, whereas the real value in today's dollars was about half this amount at a 5 per cent interest rate. Chester claimed that East Timor had overstated the value of the disputed resources and argued that Sunrise was worth only US$9 billion in tax revenue, while Bayu-Undan was worth US$8 billion. These figures could not possibly be correct because Sunrise is roughly twice the

The breakdown

size of Bayu-Undan. Chester had deflated the amount of revenue in dispute, and boosted the amount that East Timor was already receiving.

When East Timor pressed the issue of compensation for the revenue collected from Australia's unilateral licensing of production at the BCL fields, Chester pointed to his back pocket and said: 'We have already spent it. It's paid my salary—I paid my mortgage with it. We are not giving it back. What was the value [oil price] to make out there was US$2.5 billion? It all went when oil was US$10 a barrel. You'd want it back at US$50 a barrel.' A cursory glance at an oil price graph shows that the US$10 a barrel Chester referred to only related to a period of less than one year when world oil prices briefly went down to that level in 1999. Analysis by Philip Daniel put the average price for the production from these fields at US$25 a barrel.

On the morning of the second day of negotiations a story appeared in the *Sydney Morning Herald* which said that East Timor had put the pipeline and LNG plant on the table.[1] The idea of putting this story out had come from Teixeira on the Sunday before the meeting as he drove back from the beach. It was like tossing a hand grenade into the room.

As Chester continued to press for the acceptance of cash, East Timor's team broke for private meetings in order to consult the prime minister. The team raced across Dili to the *Palácio das Cinzas* where the president and the prime minister were holding their regular weekly meeting. After a short briefing on the offer they firmly rejected it.

Downer's team in Dili informed him that the meeting was not proceeding as planned, and so he decided to go public in an interview with a supportive, home-town radio host, Jeremy Cordeaux. In the exchange they painted the Timorese as greedy, opportunistic and ungrateful.

Cordeaux: Could I ask you one question about East Timor, there seems to be—I don't know whether you'd call it greed or opportunism, what exactly do the East Timorese want? We went there and we gave them their country back and no government in this country had thought about that for 25 years or had the guts to do it for 25 years, and then there's the great wealth of the oil and gas that is there—what do they want? Do they want the lot, do they—I thought they had got out of the deal that was brokered a pretty good shake? So they want a 100 per cent do they?

Downer: They want not only that, they want a very substantial share . . . if not all of certainly the lion's share of the oil and gas resources outside of the joint development area because they claim that the boundaries should be drawn in a way that would give them still more of that oil and gas, and we don't agree with that.

Cordeaux: Well, they get their country back, they get Indonesia off their back and they get 90 per cent of an absolute windfall and they're still not grateful. I am amazed.

Downer: We're in the middle of the negotiations, so I have to be careful about what I say. I'm supposed to be the nation's leading diplomat so I had better live up to my title if not my reputation.[2]

On the morning of the third day of talks, Chester made Australia's final offer. The two countries would keep existing arrangements but Australia would pay an additional US$3 billion in instalments to East Timor for ratification of the Sunrise agreement. He said East Timor had to accept this offer by 5 p.m. that evening or it would lapse and negotiations would be terminated. At Chester's final meeting with Teixeira he made a direct threat about Australia's future course of action. 'This is the end of our attempt to find a creative solution,' he said, warning that Australia might look at measures to force East Timor to ratify the Sunrise agreement. He said these were his 'musings', diplomatic-speak for veiled threats.

It was all over by noon and the Australian delegation was heading back. There was only two months to go until the Christmas deadline set by Downer on 11 August, but the Australian negotiators cut the process short when their one and only solution was rejected.

It was the first meeting after the federal election and the 'brainstorming' days were over.

Members of the Australian negotiating team lingered in the foyer of the Hotel Timor and in parting conversations with some of East Timor's advisers they expressed their indignation at the country's refusal to accept the cash offer. Dean Bialek, the former law lecturer who was now very much a DFAT man, gave one of East Timor's advisers a tutorial on how the Australian negotiators had 'gone out on a limb' to get Cabinet to approve their offer. 'You need to understand how our Cabinet process works,' said DFAT's new recruit, pounding the counter of the hotel's cafe several times as he made his point.

Chester and Moraitis sauntered along next and enquired about the whereabouts of Peter Galbraith. 'We would have had a deal by now had he been here. He *understands* how these things work,' said Moraitis. In the space of three months Galbraith had been transformed from Downer's nemesis, the single biggest obstacle in the process, to the only individual on East Timor's team who had sufficient wisdom to conclude a deal. Moraitis was the tall, well-groomed and cultured diplomat who, like so many of his contemporaries, was agreeable, intelligent and engaging in conversation. This worldly bureaucrat who had enjoyed postings to European capitals had visited East Timor shortly after InterFET landed in 1999 and did not appear to relish the task at hand in these negotiations. He protested privately over the perception of DFAT officials as 'heartless bureaucrats', saying that he and his colleagues had worked around the clock to help secure the UN Security Council resolution in 1999 for East Timor. While he had a reputation as a tough manager within DFAT, Moraitis wasn't the punisher and straightener that Downer needed for these negotiations. Unlike Chester, he didn't have the mongrel in him. Remarkably, Moraitis recognised Manuel Mendonça, one of the Timorese civil servants waiting in the lobby whom he had met five years earlier when Mendonça was in a cantonment as a member of the FALINTIL resistance army.[3] Apropos of nothing, Chester then made a point about how he had demonstrated against the Vietnam War. He would accuse some during this campaign, particularly Ian Melrose, of being un-Australian for opposing their government on a single issue, and yet he had done the same thing.

Chester then pressed the East Timor advisers for an explanation about a paper on the Timor Sea Office website from a Timorese NGO that had called for postponing the development of Greater Sunrise.[4] He was told that the website also posted statements that supported Australia's position, including a letter from his minister to the *Wall Street Journal*, and another from his departmental secretary, Michael L'Estrange, to the *Guardian*. East Timor was practising full transparency and had nothing to hide, he was told. As Chester walked off he turned to the advisers and said that from now on the two countries were back to two meetings a year and that there would be 'no Sunrise'.

After the East Timor delegation had departed Chester then began to aggressively spin his version of events to the media. Aided by the Australian ambassador Margaret Twomey, who rounded up anyone waiting in the lobby who looked like a journalist, an exasperated Chester faced the informal press gathering.

> **Chester:** We had a good three rounds of discussions. Where we've got to today is that we sense there may not be a creative solution possible. We've put forward a number of ideas, we've put forward a number of proposals. All of those proposals have been rejected. We've suggested permanent boundaries. East Timor was not prepared to negotiate permanent boundaries, they rejected that idea, quite surprisingly I have to say, quite surprisingly. They suggested a Hong Kong-type solution; by that they meant to put aside permanent boundaries for a long time in return for a financial settlement. We were prepared to look at that; we made an offer of a substantial amount of money.
>
> **Q:** How much?

Chester: How much? Many billions of dollars to get them to ratify an agreement they'd already signed, that's what we are talking about—the IUA. We made that offer in Darwin, we were very close to getting an agreement in Darwin, we were optimistic we'd get an agreement here. The East Timorese changed their negotiating position, totally, they added all these new demands—that we would put forward a pipeline to East Timor rather than leaving it to the industry to determine, and many other quite significant demands, and rejected the significant monetary offer.

Q: They did not want to discuss a permanent boundary?

Chester: Did not. Did not. If you can explain that?

Q: Median line?

Chester: We were prepared to discuss all options for a permanent boundary. We did not discuss a permanent boundary because East Timor made it very clear they did not want to talk about a permanent boundary, why I have no idea.[5]

The Australian delegation had *not* been prepared to discuss all boundary options. A proposal for a median line boundary had never been put to a formal meeting of the team. Chester later told Teixeira that the offer had been put informally to Galbraith. Making such an important offer informally to just one member of the negotiating team seemed implausible. Galbraith later denied that the proposal had been put.

Chester then publicly declared that the absence of Galbraith had been a significant factor in the breakdown.

Q: East Timor changed its position?

Chester: And team.

Q: Yes I noticed that Peter Galbraith is not in the team. Do you prefer to have Peter Galbraith?

Chester: All I'd say . . . in Darwin we were very close to a deal. This week East Timor backed away.

Finally, he predicted the end of the world for East Timor.

Chester: My understanding is that there's plenty of other fields to develop. There are many fields exclusively in Australia's territory, off the coast of Australia, and I think they're in Mauritania, Middle East, Africa. Woodside, they've got alternatives. They [Woodside] won't come back. This means Sunrise won't be developed for the next 10–20–30 years. That's really what we are talking about.[6]

* * *

Back at the *Palácio*, Alkatiri was holding a meeting with his Council of Ministers but he broke away to give a press conference to the local and international media. Speaking in three languages—first Tetum, followed by Portuguese and then English—he explained that the two sides could not reach an agreement because Australia only wanted to talk about money. 'We were talking about Timor-Leste participation in the development of the disputed resources; they were talking about money. We were too far apart to reach agreement.' Alkatiri also released a statement that set out the issues in a deliberately measured, down-beat tone.

> The third in an intensive series of talks over the last month between the governments of Timor-Leste and Australia regarding disputed Timor Sea resources ended today without an accord.
>
> The talks were aimed at achieving a so-called 'creative solution' to the Timor Sea dispute—sharing Timor Sea resources and resolving competing Timor-Leste and Australian claims without setting a permanent maritime boundary. Under a permanent maritime boundary set according to international law, Timor-Leste would be entitled to three times the revenue to which it is entitled under current interim arrangements.
>
> Prime Minister Alkatiri said: 'During these exploratory sessions, we have put a number of possible means of resource

sharing on the table for purposes of discussion. We were willing to be flexible in terms of their implementation. Unfortunately, we were told categorically that none of these possible means of resource sharing could be contemplated.'[7]

The Timor Sea Office also worked on an opinion piece for the prime minister that set out East Timor's case for the pipeline and LNG plant to be part of a fair settlement. Published on the opinion page in the *Age*'s Melbourne Cup edition, it ran under the simple headline 'All East Timor seeks is a fair go'.[8] East Timor had taken a bruising, but many East Timorese, including leading academics and NGO representatives in East Timor, applauded the government for taking this principled stand.

A short time after the negotiations collapsed Margaret Twomey was at a private dinner in Dili where the board game *Diplomacy* was being played. Twomey drew France as her country, while an adviser from the Timor Sea Office drew Britain. Twomey, who had not played the game previously, was horrified at the prospect of having to enter into an alliance with this adversary. 'But can I trust you?' she asked the adviser repeatedly. Musing on how various politicians would play the game, Twomey said dismissively that Alkatiri would be 'banging on about sovereignty'.

In mid-2004, as Downer became increasingly exasperated with the dispute, he sent to Dili this slim-figured, coolly efficient and very tough diplomat who had previously held a pivotal intelligence-liaison post at Australia's High Commission in London. In this role she was seconded to the Office of National Assessments and met regularly with high-level intelligence officials from the UK Foreign Office and the US State Department. Twomey, in her early forties, had served as deputy high commissioner at the time of a military coup in Fiji, another troublesome neighbour in Australia's immediate orbit. Like Chester, Twomey was a heavy hitter, one of the punishers and straighteners in DFAT. During her term as ambassador a succession of embassy officials finished their assignments prematurely.

Raised in rural Victoria's Catholic heartland, Twomey was also an astute choice on another level—she regularly attended Sunday mass at the Portuguese-era Motael Catholic Church on the Dili waterfront, and she sang in a church choir.

But this seasoned diplomat came under enormous pressure throughout the negotiations. She was known to work extremely long hours, presumably while writing circuitous cables to Doug Chester on the negotiations. She was forced to defend at length Australia's position in a meeting with Timorese staff working for the embassy. When Twomey greeted a group of wealthy tourists from Australia who had arrived in Dili on the *Orion* cruise ship in 2005 she immediately had to field hostile questions about Australia's conduct in the dispute. For Twomey, the answer was simple. She firmly believed that a fair outcome involved closing the Timor Gap at the Timor Trough, 2/3 of the way towards East Timor. For her an acceptable outcome was just a case of 'joining the dots'.

* * *

Three weeks after the collapse of the talks, the Australian government revealed an ambitious agenda to claim the seabed beyond its 200-nautical-mile limit. Downer, together with Attorney-General Philip Ruddock and Industry Minister Ian Macfarlane, announced that Australia had lodged its submission with the United Nations to confirm the extent of its maritime jurisdiction over 'vast areas' of continental shelf beyond the 200-nautical-mile limit. This followed the requirement under UNCLOS for Australia to lodge its submission on the limits of its continental shelf by the tenth anniversary of the convention's entry into force.

The ministers' statement said that under UNCLOS a coastal state was entitled to areas of continental shelf beyond 200 nautical miles where it could be demonstrated that the shelf is part of the submerged landmass. Australia's submission would be examined by an international body of experts—the Commission on the Limits of the Continental Shelf (CLCS)—commencing in early 2005 and its decision would be 'final and binding'. The submission had the potential to add about 3.4 million square kilometres of continental shelf to Australia's maritime empire—an area equivalent to almost half the Australian continental landmass, as shown in Map 1. It was, potentially, the world's largest such entitlement, they said proudly.[9]

When it came to the Timor Sea the Australian submission referred only to the boundaries with Indonesia; it mentioned neither the existence of East Timor nor the ongoing negotiations. The submission made no reference to the Timor Sea Treaty area established in May 2002, although it could be seen on a map included in the submission which had the Indonesian boundaries locked in around it.

The submission explained the interaction between the 1972 seabed boundary and the 1997 Australia–Indonesia fisheries boundary, and in it Australia sought to claim sole jurisdiction over the areas claimed by both Australia and East Timor:

> There are two maritime boundary treaties between Australia and Indonesia within the Argo region—the 1997 Treaty . . . that establishes a seabed boundary and an EEZ boundary in the central part of that region and a 1972 treaty that establishes a seabed boundary in the eastern part of the region. The seabed boundaries and the EEZ boundary defined by the treaties diverge in a number of areas. In the areas between the divergent boundaries, Australia exercises seabed and subsoil jurisdiction and Indonesia exercised jurisdiction over the water column.[10]

Australia's submission was so voluminous that the CLCS had to establish a new subcommission and schedule special meetings to consider it. '. . . in view of the volume of work that the examination of the submission by Australia entailed, the Subcommission had scheduled six weeks of resumed meetings . . .' said the chairman of the Subcommission, Harald Brekke. The additional workload led to funding difficulties at the CLCS although, unlike the excuse of limited resources used by the DFAT officials in November 2003, the Commission did not go as far as saying that this constraint actually prevented it from doing its work. Three members of the commission from developing countries had received support from its Trust Fund to attend meetings on the Australian submission, costing around US$40 000 per meeting.[11]

East Timor challenged the Australian submission vigorously. 'This is a clear assertion of jurisdiction by Australia in relation to areas that include maritime areas which are in fact disputed between Timor-Leste and Australia,' East Timor's response said. Australia had relied on the 1997 fisheries boundary (which follows the median line) throughout, even though this boundary was yet to be ratified.[12]

East Timor urged the Commission to ensure that it did not prejudice its rights, asking it to 'expressly deny' any endorsement that Australia had an entitlement beyond 200 nautical miles in the Timor Sea, not to draw any inferences from the map included with the submission showing the Australia–Indonesia boundaries, and not to conclude that this map limited East Timor's maritime boundary claims.

In making this submission, Australia claimed the full extent of its seabed rights in relation to resources, while a year earlier it had dramatically shrunk the area of its jurisdiction that related to people—asylum seekers specifically. This is what James Ensor of Oxfam had called the Australian government's 'elastic borders'. In a column in the *Sydney Morning Herald* Ensor wrote:

> The supposed threat posed by 14 asylum seekers beaching on Melville Island—50 kilometres off our northern coast—triggered a frenzy of activity in Canberra designed to tighten our borders by excising Melville and thousands of other islands from the Australian migration zone. Towed back out of Australian waters, the asylum seekers face deportation from Indonesia, a country which has not ratified the 1951 Refugee Convention.

The breakdown

At the same time in Darwin, Australian Government negotiators were furiously stretching our elastic border to a point hundreds of kilometres off our northern coast in negotiations over a new maritime boundary with East Timor.[13]

The ambitious claim unveiled by the Australian government in its submission to the CLCS was ominous for the Timor Sea negotiations. If East Timor were to succeed in getting a fair share of the disputed resources, the submission foreshadowed that it would have to pay a very high price.

14 CALLING IN THE COMMANDOS

'Hope is not a strategy. It has to be based on a realistic assessment of the prospects. You have to have a hard-nosed assessment. I'll eat my shoe if they agree.' Peter Galbraith telling Marí Alkatiri and the East Timor negotiating team that Australia would not agree to anything other than a cash settlement

Immediately after the abrupt end of the talks in Dili, Australia's best friend in the East Timor government began plotting revenge. José Ramos-Horta was appalled by Australia's negotiating tactics, and especially its issuance of a take-it-or-leave-it ultimatum. The deal that Chester insisted East Timor accept was completely at odds with the understanding Ramos-Horta had reached with Downer on 11 August.

Ramos-Horta decided to embark on a deliberate strategy to publicly expose Chester's tactics and at the same time buy himself some credibility with his own government. He was well aware of the perception within the East Timor government of his close relationship with Australia. A month after the end of the talks Ramos-Horta gave a broad-ranging address to the Lowy Institute for International Policy in Sydney, and as he came to the end of his speech he took aim at the conduct of Chester.

Following the Dili meeting in October, Mr Doug Chester abruptly ended the talks and seemed in a hurry to return to Canberra. Said he: 'Take it or leave it by 5 p.m. of 27th October.' Mr Doug Chester wanted the East Timorese side to accept on Australia's terms a permanent maritime boundary with a US$3 billion compensation spread over 30 years. This figure was much less than a US$4.5 billion figure offered by the Australian side during the Darwin talks.

It was agreed in Dili that there would be no comments to the media by either side. However within minutes of this agreement, accepted by our side on the insistence of Mr Doug Chester, the same Mr Doug Chester was feeding to the media his spin on the talks, alleging that our side had changed its mind, that we had rejected Australia's many creative proposals.[1]

He repeated the same message for ABC Radio's influential *PM* program, in which he added, 'Of course, we cannot accept ultimatums. We cannot accept blackmail. We are poor but we have a sense of honour, of dignity, of our rights.'[2]

Ramos-Horta had the big picture politics absolutely right, but he had not been fully briefed on how Australia's final ultimatum had changed subtly at the latest Dili meeting. Australia had dropped its demand for the Timor Trough boundary, and had instead linked the payment to East Timor's ratification of the Sunrise agreement. This changed the nature of the negotiations fundamentally. They were no longer about recognising that two countries had valid claims over the disputed resources. As Chester put it at his media briefing, Australia was being forced to cough up this money in order to get East Timor to ratify an agreement that it had already signed. The subliminal message was that East Timor had ratted on an international agreement and had blackmailed Australia into paying US$3 billion.

At the end of 2004 Woodside followed through on its threat to pull the plug on the Sunrise project. All staff working on the project were transferred elsewhere. It was as Chester had promised: 'no Sunrise'.

In his broadside Ramos-Horta had deliberately avoided attacking the Australian politicians as he knew they were the key to getting a deal, especially John Howard, who had a very high regard for Ramos-Horta. In January 2005 Ramos-Horta and Howard crossed paths at a meeting of regional leaders in Jakarta following the tragedy of the 26 December tsunami. Howard warmly embraced East Timor's foreign minister and they briefly discussed the Timor Sea dispute. Ramos-Horta explained that his prime minister was preparing to write to Howard so that the negotiations could be restarted. With Alexander Downer looking on, Howard told Ramos-Horta, 'We've got to resolve it this year.'

Convinced that it was in East Timor's best interest to resolve the imbroglio with Australia because of the potential windfall in revenues, Ramos-Horta also wanted to eliminate what had become a serious irritant in bilateral relations between the two countries. In his view Australia was fundamentally important to East Timor's well-being and security. He told the Lowy Institute, 'Timor-Leste's vital strategic interests must be anchored in a close relationship with our two closest and giant neighbours—Australia and Indonesia.'

Upon returning to Dili, Ramos-Horta asked his policy adviser, Janelle Saffin, to draft a letter to Howard and said he wanted Galbraith to be involved. Ramos-Horta's perception of Galbraith had changed dramatically in recent months. Earlier in 2004 Ramos-Horta had been furious with his tactics, but now that Galbraith had gone from being a grenade thrower to a deal maker he had resurrected himself in the eyes of the foreign minister. Galbraith had begun staying at Ramos-Horta's retreat in the foothills of Dili when in town. Ramos-Horta wanted to ensure that the Australian prime minister would respond positively to this gesture, so he arranged for a draft to be sent to Chester and to Downer's office. They responded in the affirmative. Alkatiri signed the letter and it was dispatched via a diplomatic bag in late January. In the letter, which began 'Dear John', Alkatiri said he was disappointed that the negotiations had reached an impasse and he was writing in the hope that they could breathe new life into them. Alkatiri gave a 'personal assurance' that he was committed to an outcome that was in the interest of both countries. In settling the dispute Alkatiri said they should focus on an equitable sharing of the resources, security, and economic infrastructure, education, training and technical proficiency aimed at reducing the very high level of unemployment in East Timor. It used the words 'financial assistance' in relation to the type of settlement that East Timor was after—even though this had been expressly ruled out by Alkatiri in October. In a tacit endorsement of Downer's claim about having brought East Timor into being, Alkatiri concluded by saying he was cognisant of the 'decisive role' played by Australia in helping to secure the independence of East Timor.

Encouraged by this friendly gesture, the Australian government proposed in January that the two countries get off to an early start by scheduling a meeting for March. East Timor's overture meant that it had to curtail its public comments on the dispute in the lead-up to this meeting. DFAT continued to complain about East Timor's briefing of the media, however, while it was stepping up its own efforts to influence public opinion. But this did not restrict East Timor's supporters in Australia and elsewhere.

Just as a draft of the letter was bouncing back and forth between Canberra and Dili, so were the tennis balls at the Australian Open tournament in Melbourne. Ian Melrose's latest television advertisements were going to air. Over in Washington, ETAN began working the congressional offices on Capitol Hill. Congressman Barney Frank arranged for a second letter to be sent to John Howard. All the heavyweights who signed the 2004 letter signed this one (Nancy Pelosi, Republican Chris Smith, Tom Lantos and James Jeffords), but there was one new name—Senator Edward Kennedy.

In keeping with a new proactive stance on this issue, the Australian embassy in Washington dispatched a senior official to Capitol Hill to rebut the letter. Greg Wilcock, a first secretary, met with staff from the offices of nearly all the Congress members who had signed the letter. With staff from at least two offices he went over it paragraph by paragraph, spelling out the Australian government's concerns. Wilcock appeared to be acting on very strong instructions from Canberra.

Afterwards the staff gave an interesting account of what had transpired. In some of the recorded comments, the Capitol Hill staffers said:

First office: I did meet with him [Wilcock]. He needs to go to diplomacy school.
Second office: Rebut would be putting it nicely! I actually thought the guy I met with was very abrasive and unprofessional.
Third office: Yep, I met with Greg Wilcock from the embassy on Friday. The tone of the meeting was different than I expected it to be, to say the least.

Their problems were as follows:
- They are very upset with the tone of the letter, and wished that someone could have come to talk to them about the issue first before rebuking the Australian government in this very public way. It was an 'unnecessary offense', and he seemed quite insulted.
- They had a particular problem with the last paragraph, which said something about Australia's leadership in 1999 in helping free the people of Timor-Leste, as if that help has not been ongoing. They feel that Australia has done an enormous amount for East Timor in terms of development assistance and thought that the letter calls this assistance into question.
- They also wish to separate the issue of marine boundaries from the issue of preventative death—they feel that the marine boundary issue is a legal one that has nothing to do with socioeconomic issues.

- They are in the process of resolving this dispute and negotiations are currently ongoing. Australia has a historical claim to its continental shelf but they understand that there are overlapping claims of sovereignty and are working to resolve equitably.

I just told him that I appreciated him talking to me about it and that I would bring his concerns to my supervisor and the Congressman.

Fourth office: One staffer reported that the Aussie official, Greg Wilcock, was rude. Indeed, the staffer more or less kicked him out of the office.[3]

Some of Wilcock's rebuttals echoed what Chester had begun telling journalists in a series of private briefings, though Chester had gone much further in his rhetoric by arguing that East Timor was not in need of money. He told journalists how the country was having difficulty spending its proposed national budget and, while this was true, it partly reflected the elaborate array of anti-corruption procedures that were still being bedded down. In one briefing Chester said East Timor didn't need additional revenue because it was saving around half of its petroleum revenue in a new Petroleum Fund. In an effort to avoid becoming another victim of the resource curse—or a country that would have nothing left when its resources ran out—East Timor was saving around half its petroleum revenue in a permanent fund, yet in Australia's new propaganda war this exemplary policy, modelled on Norway, was used against it.

Chester began an intense round of background briefings for journalists ahead of the March talks after acknowledging that Australia had lost the 'media war' in 2004. Under his stewardship this would not be the case in 2005. 'We will not come second in the media war this time,' he warned Teixeira. He called a formal briefing and afterwards released the full transcript, which ran to fourteen pages, in an attempt to show that the Australian government was being fully transparent about its media campaign.[4] Not all of his briefings were made public in this way, and this transcript showed that a lot of what he was telling the media was simply not true. Basic factual errors included his claims that:

- 'Australia has never offered any money in these negotiations yet.' Chester's media briefing in Dili on 27 October, when he talked about the 'many billions' offered, contradicts this statement.
- Negotiations with New Zealand over a permanent boundary took 18 years. Downer said when announcing the agreement with New Zealand 'this is a treaty that's taken us four years to negotiate'.
- Bayu-Undan was worth US$8 billion in tax revenue and Greater Sunrise US$9 billion. Chester had almost doubled the value of Bayu-Undan based on East Timor's estimates which were prepared with the help of an Australian Treasury official, while he had halved the value of Sunrise as its reserves are about twice as big as Bayu-Undan.
- Australia's claim was based on its continental shelf. Geological opinion has affirmed since the late 1960s that the two countries sit on the same shelf.
- East Timor was putting nothing more than an ambit claim in the areas outside the JPDA. East Timor had said it was so confident of its legal position that it would agree to have the case heard at any international arbiter of Australia's choosing.

The Timor Sea Office compiled these errors in a two-page note and sent it to journalists and the support groups in Australia. The TSJC also included it in a press kit announcing the formation of a 'people's delegation' to negotiate on behalf of the Australian people with the East Timor government since it claimed that DFAT's team did not represent the will of the Australian people. The delegation joined a demonstration outside the DFAT head office and then attempted to enter the building. The delegation consisted of Bishop Hilton Deakin of Melbourne's Catholic Archdiocese, Senator Bob

Brown, Ian Melrose, 91-year-old Mavis Taylor (who had been made a 'National Living Treasure' by the National Trust and passed away in March 2007), former InterFET soldier Chip Henriss-Anderssen and Tom Clarke from the TSJC.

When DFAT learned of the demonstration and the formation of the people's delegation, it claimed that East Timor had orchestrated these activities. DFAT was trying to muzzle East Timor's public comments about the dispute and reacted firmly to the prospect of more public demonstrations. Teixeira was told angrily that the Australian government had evidence of 'communication' between the Timor Sea Office and support groups in Australia and that the government did not want any more of it. The complaint indicated that Australia's intelligence services were monitoring the telephone conversations of East Timor's advisers as the Timor Sea Office had told the Timor Sea Justice Campaign the time and location of the meeting. At a previous meeting Chester had hinted at Australia's monitoring of internet use by East Timor's advisers.[5]

* * *

On the eve of the next round of talks, scheduled for 7 March, Alkatiri chaired a meeting of the negotiating team in Dili, and began by saying that the team should avoid creating 'expectations that are not real'. Alkatiri managed to utter only a couple of sentences before Galbraith intervened and took over the meeting. Galbraith circulated a briefing note which again outlined why East Timor should accept the cash settlement offer that Alkatiri had firmly ruled out in October. On offer was a cash settlement for a suspension of claims for 99 years and a commitment not to reduce Australian aid. Galbraith argued forcefully that East Timor's leverage to secure a deal was diminishing because Woodside was moving on to other projects—just as Chester had said would happen in his 27 October media briefing— and Australia's demonstrated willingness to negotiate had reduced the leverage from East Timor's public campaign. He then seriously questioned the strength of East Timor's legal position. The 'special circumstances' pleaded by East Timor to widen the treaty area only applied when there was a tiny atoll whereas East Timor was seeking to apply them to significant Indonesian islands and landforms. He argued that it made no sense to trade off money in the bank against waiting a decade or more for justice through an uncertain legal avenue. In making this argument he used a very high and unrealistic 10 per cent discount (interest) rate. A high discount rate made having the money now seem more valuable, but this rate was double the US long-term bond rate of around 5 per cent. He constructed the presentation artfully. It was a brazen initiative by Galbraith.

Alkatiri challenged the argument. 'The strategy of Australia is to use Sunrise as a way of getting us to give up everything. They want to use it to discuss overlapping claims,' he said. The US$3 billion offered by Australia only equalled the lost revenue from the BCL fields, he added. Antunes also strongly challenged Galbraith's analysis of the law. He said any court would apply the principle found in UNCLOS of an 'equitable solution' when a large resource was situated in an area of overlap.

Something very strange was happening in that room, said Norwegian adviser Einar Risa. It appeared that some members of the team knew very well what the other side was willing to accept, he said. 'You have to step into their shoes,' Galbraith said. Teixeira shot back, 'That doesn't mean you have to become like them.'

Galbraith's standing among some group members may have been diminished when they learned of some unflattering comments that he had made about them. Galbraith had told a colleague of Einar Risa that East Timor's petroleum sector was being run by a 'hopeless' Norwegian and a 'crazy' Portuguese lawyer. The real issue for Galbraith was that he saw himself as 'The Negotiator' and he wanted a deal that reflected his views. He consistently argued that East Timor had to read the other side, that it had to realise when it had actually won, something he argued had happened back in October when Australia made its US$3 billion offer. There was a big element of intellectual hubris in all of this. Galbraith had come up with a solution he knew was acceptable to Australia and would help address the needs of a very poor country relying on volatile oil revenue for its main source of income. It protected East Timor by giving it a secure income stream. The Galbraith solution might have won support when the negotiations began and the oil price was around US$30 a barrel, but now in early 2005, with prices nudging US$60 a barrel, it was the wrong time to be talking about a deal that offered no upside.

Alkatiri did not want to agree to anything that could be construed as a sell-out. He said:

> The issue above all for me is domestic politics. If all kinds of settlements are without prejudice to [maritime boundary claims] we can settle. Not this 100 years wording, that in practice means to give up everything. If immediately after they find another resource it is the end of this government.[6]

The prime minister gave his instructions on how he wanted his negotiators to proceed. They were almost identical to the ones issued in late October. Galbraith's advice was rejected again. He remained unfazed and launched into the government for pursuing what he viewed as a naive strategy:

> The instructions are very clear—they will not lead to any agreement or progress. Hope is not a strategy, it has to be based on a realistic assessment of the prospects. You have to have a hard-nosed assessment. I'll eat my shoe if they agree. Do you want a low-key or a confrontational round?[7]

From Alkatiri's perspective, the 'creative solution' only came about because the Sunrise field had become entangled in the broader maritime boundary dispute, and he did not share Australia's desire to make it a final settlement of the overlapping claim. He cautioned that, 'Sunrise is not a final objective—if the creative solution is not really creative then we get back to maritime boundary discussions.'

* * *

When the meeting began in Canberra, the DFAT officials regained their composure after the demonstration outside their head office, and the negotiations quickly made progress. What soon emerged was a deal that might involve an increase in East Timor's share of Greater Sunrise but no compensation for the revenue collected from the BCL fields. At this meeting the Australian government turned on the charm. Downer met privately with Teixeira and expressed a strong desire to 'be rid' of the dispute. The East Timor delegation was invited to dine at one of Canberra's best restaurants, The Ottoman, in the parliamentary triangle, an offer that all but one delegation member accepted. This was a step up from the normal protocol for these negotiations, which had been limited to informal drinks. At the end of this meeting the process was back on track. East Timor was constructively trying to reach an agreement and a truce had been called in the media war. A follow-up meeting would be held the following month in Dili.

* * *

The next meeting was scheduled for 26 April, one day after ANZAC Day, Australia's official day of commemoration for all Australians who have served and died in war. The previous year Australian negotiators had chosen the 20 September anniversary of the InterFET landing in Dili to give them a slight propaganda edge. While the April date had been chosen at random, it would give maximum impact to the next phase of the public campaign being waged by businessman Ian Melrose.

Early in his media campaign East Timor's strategists had discussed with Melrose the role that could be played by Australia's

Second-World-War veterans who were deeply indebted to the East Timorese for their support. In 2004 Melrose had produced a short television advertisement showing a single veteran wearing his war medals:

> **Veteran:** Me and my mates risked our lives so Australia could be free and fair.
> **Voiceover:** In East Timor eight out of 100 children die before the age of five—a deplorable situation. When it comes to oil and gas, come on Australia, give East Timor the entitlements it is due under international law so it can feed its children. Let's be fair.

The veteran happened to be Alec Melrose, the father of Ian Melrose. After producing another set of advertisements with other Second-World-War veterans who had not served in East Timor, Melrose began working towards a version for ANZAC day featuring the Timor veterans who had for decades lobbied tirelessly on behalf of the people who saved their lives. Melrose rounded them up to fight one last time for East Timor.

* * *

Ten days after the bombing of Pearl Harbour in December 1941 a contingent of Australian and Dutch soldiers landed on the outskirts of Dili, in the vicinity of what is now Presidente Nicolau Lobato International Airport. The Portuguese governor, Manuel Ferreira de Carvalho, protested at the landing because it violated Portugal's neutrality. The landing of 'Sparrow Force', as the Allied presence on Timor was known, was completely speculative as there was no firm evidence that the Japanese were headed there. Germany had concerns about any violation of Portuguese sovereignty as this might open up the Azores Islands in the Atlantic Ocean as a strategic base for the Allies. A series of diplomatic exchanges between Germany and Japan ensued. Archival records of debates amongst Japan's prime minister, emperor and defence chiefs, unearthed by historian Henry Frei, confirm that invading East Timor was not part of Japan's original war plan but that the Allied landing forced Japan to make the decision to invade on 20 February 1942.[8]

Despite being uninvited, the Australian soldiers quickly gained the support of much of the local population. Australia initially landed 250 members of the 2/2 Independent Company, an elite commando force that was a forerunner to today's SAS. The Australians were joined by 140 troops from the 2/40th Battalion who had survived a Japanese encirclement in Dutch Timor, and about 200 Dutch soldiers.[9] The commandos quickly took the initiative and launched highly effective guerrilla warfare keeping the Japanese forces confined to the capital for almost six months. Attempts by the Japanese to establish outposts were aggressively challenged. Bernard Callinan, who was in the first landing and became the commanding officer in East Timor, wrote a remarkable account of the extraordinary bravery, goodwill and hospitality shown to the Australians by the Timorese, many of whom served alongside the Australians as *criados* (servants).[10] The Portuguese, most notably the district and *posto* (post) administrators, and the *deportados* (deported), including the father of José Ramos-Horta, also risked their lives to support the Australians. As a result, a force of no more than 700 men, many of them wracked by tropical illnesses, tied down around 20 000 Japanese soldiers and inflicted an estimated 1500 casualties during a twelve-month guerrilla campaign.[11]

But the Japanese hit back, launching a country-wide offensive in August 1942 in which it razed entire villages, crops and livestock as they sought to encircle the Allied force.[12] The following month 2/2 Independent Company was reinforced by the 2/4 Independent Company, and in November the battle weary 2/2 soldiers were withdrawn. The tempestuous Timor Sea proved to be problematic in supporting the troops from Australia. HMAS *Voyager* ran aground while landing the 2/4 and was destroyed by Japanese planes, while lifeboats were known to capsize when evacuating troops. The

Japanese extended their control over the half-island by removing most of the Portuguese administrators, and as reprisals mounted some Timorese informed on the Australians. By the end of the year a few hundred Australians from the 2/4 Independent Company were confined to a rugged area on the southern side of the island near the town of Samé. The commandos had their backs to the Timor Sea, and in January 1943 a decision was made to withdraw nearly all of the Australians, with strict orders to leave the *criados* behind.

More than 60 years later, Ralph Coyne recounted the immense sorrow he felt on that Timor Sea beach on 10 January 1943, and for many years to come, after leaving behind his *criado*:

> It was one of the most distressing experiences in life. One felt so disloyal that this youngster had helped us to survive, and now I saw myself as his killer—sending them back to hostile territory. It is one of the heartaches and sense of shame I have carried for many years.[13]

Callinan told the leader of the Portuguese evacuees, Dr Carlos Brandão, that he would attempt to evacuate 'all pure-blooded Portuguese', leaving behind the 'natives'.[14] The final evacuation took place exactly one month later, on 10 February 1943. Callinan wrote of the farewell which took place at the point where the Dilor River met the Timor Sea:

> On the beach there had been a repetition of the earlier farewells between the Australians and their ever-loyal *criados*, who had never faltered in their devotion and unselfishness. As the successive evacuations took place the ultimate separation had become more and more obvious to the natives, but they had not grumbled nor deserted; they were prepared to serve until the end.[15]

After the Australians left many of the *criados* were rounded up by the Japanese and executed. Small groups of commandos from 'Z' special unit continued to land in Timor, but their operations were compromised when the Japanese obtained their code book. Still the Australian government urged the local population to fight on. RAAF planes dropped leaflets that carried a picture of a group of smiling Australian soldiers standing in front of a traditional hut, with a Portuguese message in block letters: '*OS VOSSOS AMIGOS NÕA* [sic] *VOS ESQUECEM*'—your friends do not forget you. But in an ominous sign of what was to come decades later, the headline message had actually misspelt the word 'not'.

The RAAF continued to bomb the island from Darwin, at times killing many Timorese. An August 1945 intelligence report from the Services Reconnaissance Department revealed that 'the only results of air attacks heard was the killing of a large number of Ossu natives in the large Christmas attack'. The report also noted that in many areas hamlets had disappeared. At the end of the war the Timorese were close to starvation. There was virtually no commercial activity and most of the cash crops had been abandoned.[16] In 1930 the official estimate of the population was 472 221 and it was growing at 1 per cent. The 1947 estimate identified only 433 412 people, indicating that a minimum of 40 000 Timorese died as a result of the war, or nearly 10 per cent of the population. And while population censuses in developing countries are unreliable, the real loss is likely to have been significantly higher.[17] By comparison Australia lost 40 commandos.

The Second World War left a lasting impact on the people of East Timor. Visitors in the 1970s wrote that people talked about the war as if it had happened yesterday.[18] Despite the immense suffering, the Timorese forged a close kinship with their big, near neighbour. Cliff Morris, a former commando, returned in 1973 and discovered that the younger generation knew about the war in great detail—including individual actions—because village elders had retold this great history.

While Australia's epic engagement in Timor was documented by the legendary war cameraman Damien Parer, it was considered a sideshow when compared with New Guinea. Nonetheless the

Australian soldiers who served there never forgot the support that the Timorese afforded them, which in many instances saved their lives. The 2/2 and 2/4 veterans showed their gratitude to the Timorese by raising money among themselves in the early 1970s to build a monument high in the hills above Dili at Daré. They chose a typically Australian gift which might also be of practical use to the Timorese—an in-ground swimming pool made of 'pebble-crete', a mixture of pebbles and cement which was popular in Australia at the time of its construction. It was a solidly built and thoughtfully designed gift as it came with an adjacent concrete canopy to provide some respite from the scorching sun. Three decades later, when they were well into their eighties, some of the last surviving veterans would make an even more significant gesture to help secure East Timor's future.

* * *

When Ian Melrose proposed producing a television advertisement to coincide with ANZAC Day, East Timor veteran Paddy Kenneally—one of the most vocal advocates for the Timorese throughout the Indonesian years—helped to round up an enthusiastic group of former comrades who lived in Perth. Dressed in their best suits and ties for the ANZAC Day march, and all wearing a row of war service medals, they sat around a garden table with an Australian flag and swimming pool in the background. The statements made by the veterans were delivered in a dignified but firm manner, leaving no doubt that they were engaging in a life and death struggle on behalf of this vulnerable new nation. And while many of the men were typically conservative, older Australians who may have voted for the Coalition government, their statements were aimed directly at Prime Minister John Howard.

George Greenhaigh, wearing two gold and three silver war medals, opened up with this simple but arresting statement: 'Every man here owes his life to the Timorese.'

John Burridge, a commander in the 2/2 Independent Company, added, 'Thousands of Timorese died because of their assistance to us Australians.'

('Australia taken $2 billion' flashes onto a picture of Parliament House in Canberra and its mint green lawn.)

Ray Aitken, who has since passed away, said, 'John Howard shame on you.'

Bernie Langridge: 'The ANZAC spirit is all about a fair go.'

Greenhaigh: 'Children are dying in East Timor for lack of basic health care.'

Ray Parry: 'This is not the ANZAC spirit.'

Greenhaigh ended with: 'I never thought I could be ashamed to be an Australian.'

Another advertisement, which ended on a slightly more positive note, began with Mervin Wheatley saying, 'John Howard you are making me ashamed.'

('$2 billion taken' flashes onto a picture of Parliament House.)

Ray Parry: 'The Timorese need this money to build hospitals and schools.'

Ray Aitken: 'Everything was destroyed in Timor and children are dying for want of basic health care.'

('Australia is taking from one of the poorest countries in Asia' appears on the screen.)

Langridge: 'John Howard make me proud again—give East Timor a fair go.'

And to ensure that the message was not misinterpreted as being about need rather than rights, Ray Parry added in another version, 'They don't want our charity—they want justice.'

In these advertisements Kenneally was filmed sitting at the table with his comrades, but he didn't speak. He did a version on his own carrying similar messages and which concluded with him saying, 'John Howard, I'd rather you did not come to my ANZAC Day parade.'

Howard was asked about the veterans' damning statements while attending the ceremony to commemorate the ANZAC landing at

Gallipoli, and he gave a harried response: 'I am aware of the debt owed by many Australians from World War II to the people of Timor . . . but I'm also aware that we played a major role in the freeing of the country,' he said. Downer tried to dismiss them out of hand, claiming that the advertisements were 'both dishonest and irresponsible' and would not influence the negotiations. But the storm created by the advertisements made it more difficult for Melrose to get airtime. After ANZAC day he pitched another set of advertisements featuring the veterans but this was rejected by the Commercial Acceptance Division of Free TV Australia, the industry authority for commercial television, for legal reasons.[19]

* * *

The following day, 26 April, Chester opened the Dili meeting and began immediately to steer the negotiations towards a quick resolution. Australia would offer East Timor a bigger share of the Sunrise revenue, but he said the maximum he could agree to was an increase of 25 per cent of the disputed part of Sunrise (one-quarter of 80 per cent). Adding this to East Timor's existing share would take it to a total of 38 per cent. This was the absolute limit, he said. By the end of this meeting, however, Australia had agreed to a figure that many in the East Timor government believed to be a fair outcome—50 per cent of Sunrise. The veterans had delivered the knockout punch that East Timor had needed all along.

The ANZAC week meeting in Dili established the broad parameters of the deal but there were still many details to work through. A follow-up meeting would be held in Sydney from 9–12 May. The timing coincided with the federal Budget, an all-consuming event for the Australian public and media.

Like previous meetings, this one also kicked off with a bang, or at least the threat of one. During the talks DFAT revealed that it had been advised by the Australian Federal Police of a possible terrorist attack in Dili and warned Australians to defer non-essential travel to

East Timor and avoid government buildings in the capital. 'We have received new information of a possible attack or bombing against East Timor government buildings in Dili on May 11,' DFAT said. Other embassies in Dili, including that of the United States, did not upgrade their travel advisories. A US diplomat, who asked not to be named, said that after assessing the Australian warning a decision was taken not to change the existing security notification for Americans working in East Timor. 'We have seen what [the warning] is based on and have chosen not to change the guidelines we are giving to our people who are staying here,' said a US embassy official.[20]

While Dili was being panicked, the meeting steadily worked through a draft text of the new treaty in a conference room at the Intercontinental Hotel with panoramic views of Sydney Harbour. Doug Chester was confident that this meeting would put the 'finishing touches' on a draft. Under the broad terms of the deal, East Timor gained half of the revenue from Sunrise, but Australia secured control of the seabed and the fisheries (known as the water column) in the area around this field. It was business as usual for Australia in terms of its jurisdiction over the disputed area. This was a mammoth concession for East Timor to make because it meant that Australia would gain control of all of the fields in an area identified by East Timor's advisers as highly prospective. East Timor would only get a share of any future finds if, like Sunrise, they straddled the JPDA. Given that it knew of the existence of Sunrise Permian, East Timor was taking a huge gamble on this field also straddling the JPDA in the same way as the one above it. East Timor would also be granted control of the water column within the JPDA.

The agreement would say nothing, however, about the pipeline. East Timor had pushed for a clause that said the Australian government would use its 'good offices' to assist East Timor in landing the pipeline and refrain from subsidising one to Australia. This proved an impossible condition to secure.

Shortly after this meeting Downer told Parliament that all major elements of the deal had been agreed by both countries and there was now just some 'fine tuning of some minor aspects'.[21] All that was needed next was for the two cabinets to agree to the proposal, he said.

After a year of bad press from the dispute, the Australian government wanted to project a good image in its relationship with East Timor, and particularly with its resistance hero President Gusmão. A visit by Xanana Gusmão to support the work of eye surgeons in East Timor was transformed into a state visit during which he met John Howard at his harbourside residence in Sydney. Teixeira went as Alkatiri's representative. Gusmão presented Howard with a traditional *tais* made largely of maroon fabric. Howard joked that the present resembled the football jersey of the Queensland side the president was to see playing in a State-of-Origin match with New South Wales. During this visit, Alkatiri was the subject of more negative press that appeared to be timed to undermine his authority at a sensitive stage in the negotiations. A front-page lead story in the *Australian* said Alkatiri's younger brother had secured a monopoly contract to supply armaments, including tanks, attack helicopters and patrol boats, to the East Timor government.[22] The story produced a headline from hell—'Timor PM link to arms contract'.

Based on tender documents obtained from within the East Timor procurement department the story revealed that Bader Alkatiri's company, Caval Bravo, had a contract to supply ammunition to the police and armed forces. Alkatiri responded by saying that the contract had been won competitively, and it was only for ammunition. But in fact the original contract won by Caval Bravo in 2002 had been rolled over at a significantly higher price without going back to tender, a practice permitted under the tender guidelines. The rollover had been priced at exactly the second-best bid price in the original tender—or almost 50 per cent higher than the original tender price of US25c per bullet. At this time an increasing number of Alkatiri companies were gaining government contracts.

During President Gusmão's visit, the Australian government flew the entourage around in one of its new Royal Australian Air Force

VIP jets. While on board Teixeira was showing off a new fountain pen to colleagues and accidentally sprayed the cabin with ink. When asked by the crew about the ink marks, Teixeira said they had been there before. The visit coincided with an impasse in the negotiations and Teixeira was troubled by the agreement that his country was being forced to sign, especially the loss of resources which he believed rightfully belonged to East Timor. Some members of the delegation began to make an impression on an expensive bottle of scotch that was in the plane's liquor cabinet, and as they drank one of them said in a lamenting tone, 'This will make up for Buffalo, Laminaria and Corallina.' It became a US$2.7 billion bottle of scotch—quite possibly the most expensive drink in history.

15 INDEPENDENCE DAY MINUS 1

'Each of us will have to live with the consequences. It will be such a pity if we are not able to reach a compromise—a failure of our intellect.' José Ramos-Horta to Alexander Downer, Canberra, 4 November 2005

Doug Chester returned to Canberra in mid-May 2005 thinking that at last he had clinched the deal that would please his political masters and confirm his reputation as a fixer. He had reached this point previously—six months ago when he landed in Dili—but this time he felt safely home. On returning to Canberra, he advised his minister, and Prime Minister John Howard, that a deal was at last assured.

Chester had shown a burning determination to secure an agreement at the April and May meetings. It was his suggestion that they begin work on a draft treaty, which focused the attention of both sides, and throughout the negotiations he tried to avoid getting caught up in detail that might slow down proceedings. He kept his own side focused on securing an outcome, but he was so determined to secure a deal that he ran ahead of what had been established at the May meeting.

The line for public consumption agreed to verbally by the two sides at the end of the May meeting was that both had made 'further good progress at these talks; no agreement has been reached; we are now working through further details'. Alkatiri warned the following week that there remained important details to be resolved: 'I do believe that we are close to a deal. But we do not have a deal yet. We still have some details, some very important details that are going to guarantee our claims on maritime boundaries and Australia's also during the life of the project.'[1] Later that month, during a trip to Norway, he warned that the 'devil is in the detail'.

Ramos-Horta also wanted to put this heated issue to rest. He was so determined to be rid of it that he announced the outline of the agreement in an opinion article in the *Age*, an initiative that infuriated Alkatiri. He chose his words carefully, saying that the fifth round of talks had resulted in a 'draft document' to be discussed by respective cabinets. In East Timor the agreement would be presented to the president and his advisory body, the Council of State. Ramos-Horta revealed the key elements of the deal which until that time had been kept under wraps—a fifty-fifty split of the Sunrise field and a 50-year moratorium on maritime boundary claims. The issue of the pipeline which he believed should come to East Timor, was unresolved. He said experts from 'Saudi Arabia, Dubai, Kuwait and Germany all believe bringing the pipeline to Timor-Leste is technically feasible and makes sense commercially'. Ramos-Horta then heaped praise on Howard and Downer saying they were 'true friends of Timor-Leste'.[2]

Two months passed and Chester received from East Timor its latest draft of the treaty. He was furious when he saw that substantial changes had been made to the draft that he believed had been agreed to at the May meeting.

On 26 July 2005 he sent a letter to Teixeira, and made sure he copied it to Ramos-Horta. Chester wrote that he was 'absolutely taken aback' by the changes made to the draft agreement as Teixeira had said for many weeks that any changes required by East Timor would be of a technical nature only. He said that changes made to Article 4 (4) and (5), Articles 12 and 13, and to Annexe II, were clearly substantial changes which ran 'counter to the agreement' reached in the last round of negotiations. The changes related to issues which had been 'canvassed fully' at that meeting. Chester indicated that his own credibility was on the line because he had passed on to his Minister and the Office of the Prime Minister the 'assurance' of the East Timor government that any further changes would not go to the substance of the agreement.

After receiving this letter, Ramos-Horta started thinking that the obstacle to a deal was not the Australian side. He has a view that Anglo-Saxons are people who keep their word, and that when they make a commitment they honour it. He has described himself self-deprecatingly as an 'incorrigible naïf' who believes what people tell him. Ramos-Horta came to realise that the approach taken by East Timor in these negotiations was to focus too much on the 'detail' and not on the bigger picture. It was a case of not being able to see the forest for the trees. Or, as Galbraith might have put it, a case of not realising that you have won.

The months rolled on, and still no agreement was forthcoming. When Ramos-Horta attended the 60th anniversary of the United Nations General Assembly in September he spoke with Downer briefly and realised that Australia had lost patience and was preparing to dump the agreement. In early November Downer asked for a meeting with Ramos-Horta in Canberra. Downer was in a bad mood when they met in his Parliament House office, and he had no kind words about Teixeira. 'Your colleagues in government have no idea,' Downer told Ramos-Horta, insisting that the Australian government would not be moved by East Timor's public campaign or its support in Australia. 'Ian Melrose can spend every cent he has—we won by a bigger margin at the last election,' Downer roared. In fact Downer's margin had gone down by 2.5 percentage points as a result of the Brian Deegan challenge. And while the Coalition had won with a 3.4 per cent swing overall, it lost two seats in Adelaide—the target of the Melrose advertising blitz.

Ramos-Horta kept his cool. He knew that he had to be on good terms with Downer to secure an agreement. He told Downer that if they failed to reach an agreement then both countries would have to live with the consequences. 'It will be such a pity if we are not able to reach a compromise—a failure of our intellect,' he said.

Downer proposed that they should have one last meeting to try to secure a deal. Immediately after his meeting with Downer Ramos-Horta telephoned Alkatiri from what he knew was a 'secure line'. 'They're prepared to walk out—do not underestimate them. With the current deal if you pull at the rope it will break,' he said. This was no longer a legal issue, he explained, it was political. 'With due respect to lawyers this requires political leadership,' he told Alkatiri, the lawyer politician. Ramos-Horta then made comments to the media. As with many of his public statements, he told the journalists what he hoped would happen—there was a good prospect for concluding an agreement by the end of the year.

* * *

Throughout 2005, as work on the treaty hung in the balance, the Australian government refused to approve a new legal code for the JPDA drafted by officials from the two countries, thereby stalling plans for the development of a new oilfield, Jahal Kuda Tasi. Downer's office also exacted retribution against those who had been critical of the Australian government's stance in the negotiations in 2004.

In late 2004 thirteen of the leading NGOs in East Timor had signed two press statements that called on both governments to negotiate a maritime boundary, and also called on Australia to be fair. One of the signatories was Forum Tau Matan (FTM). In January 2005 FTM was awarded funding of $65 830 from AusAID for human rights training, monitoring and popular education on the development of East Timor's justice system. Five months later FTM was told by AusAID's Dili office that the funding would be withdrawn.

A letter dated 6 June from AusAID's Dili manager, Peter Ellis, to FTM explained the decision in vague, bureaucratic language:

In the past few months there have been a number of significant developments in the Australian development cooperation with Timor-Leste. Australia's Country Strategy for Timor-Leste is now nearly finalised. In this context, we have been reviewing the ways in which we engage with NGOs in different sectors.³

Ellis had in fact strongly opposed the decision to cut the funding but he was overruled. Ellis has since returned to Canberra and he has found that his role in Dili has affected his career negatively.

Later in 2005 all of the signatory organisations learned that they had been put on a 'black list' and would no longer receive funding. The Australian government had effectively decided not to fund the entire NGO sector in East Timor, even though the promotion of democratic governance is one of the important objectives of Australian aid policy.

Demetrio do Amaral de Carvalho, who in 2004 won the prestigious Goldman international award for environmental advocacy, said his organisation, Haburas Foundation, had been denied funding of US$15 000 for environmental education. At a meeting on 10 November 2005 Haburas was told:

> ... that because FTM was denied funding, AusAID must be consistent and not fund other organizations that signed the same press releases. We were told that unless Canberra changes its view, AusAID would not be funding the NGOs that signed the releases.⁴

Appearing before a Senate estimates committee, Murray Proctor, AusAID's deputy director-general, Asia Division, confirmed that the minister had made the decision after being informed by AusAID of the link between the statement and FTM. Proctor said when this information came to his division 'it was reviewed, and it was considered, in the end, that it was not appropriate to continue funding an organisation that was openly critical of Australia'.⁵ The final decision was made at the ministerial level. Proctor confirmed that after making this decision the bureaucrats sent the matter to the foreign minister's office. 'It was taken up to the ministerial level and the decision was taken,' Proctor said.

This evidence contradicts the explanation given to FTM by AusAID's Peter Ellis. The decision had nothing to do with a new 'Country Strategy' or any review of AusAID's NGO program in East Timor. It also contradicts comments by Australian ambassador Margaret Twomey that the money had been withdrawn because FTM had mismanaged it. FTM director, João Pequinho, disputes Twomey's assertion and says AusAID had only paid around $10 000 at the time the decision was made.

Proctor also told the committee:

> There were many statements about Australia not negotiating as an equal partner, about belittling East Timor and about interference in the nation's politics—the notion that there was a process of stealing natural resources belonging to the Timor-Leste people. As a whole it was a fairly strong statement.[6]

The press statement Proctor was referring to followed Doug Chester's ultimatum on 27 October 2004. It read:

> TIMOR-LESTE CIVIL SOCIETY DEMANDS A FAIR MARITIME BOUNDARY
> Civil Society Organizations in Timor-Leste have followed the negotiation process concerning Timor Sea oil, held in Canberra and Darwin, Australia, last month. It has come to our attention that Governments of both Timor-Leste and Australia do not want to further discuss the Maritime Boundary, but have opted instead to discuss only distribution of money from natural resources, which both governments euphemistically call a 'creative solution'. The signatories of this statement, civil society [groups] of Timor-Leste, would like to present our opinions, which we believe are important to express. While we feel it is important that both governments heed our opinions, they are directed especially towards the government of Timor-Leste.

Based on prior knowledge concerning negotiations, we strongly encourage the governments of Timor-Leste and Australia to:

1. urge the negotiators who, at this moment, are discussing the future of the people of Timor-Leste, to respect the national sovereignty of the Democratic Republic of Timor-Leste, and quickly set the maritime boundary between the two countries according to current international legal principles.

2. urge Australia, in connection with point 1, to return to the International Court of Justice and the International Tribunal of the Law of the Sea in order to solve international disputes of maritime boundaries.

3. Greater Sunrise should be East Timor's territory, development can not be started until a boundary or IUA is in place. We condemn pressure exerted by Woodside Oil Company to quickly begin exploitation in this area.

4. stop the exploitation of Laminaria-Corallina and other oil fields in disputed territory. This includes halting the issue of new licences. It would be sensible and fair to put revenues from such fields in an escrow fund to be divided fairly once a boundary agreement is reached.

We strongly urge the government of Timor-Leste to give priority to the Maritime Boundary discussions rather than negotiating the division of resources with a government that is stealing natural resources that rightfully belong to Timor-Leste.[7]

An earlier statement was very similar except that it called on Australia to negotiate 'with our government as an equal partner and not [belittle] us with offers of "Christmas presents" '. The groups that signed the statement were 'dismayed by Australia's support for Woodside's hunger to extract Sunrise gas as fast as possible . . . Our rights are based on international law and moral principles, not on Australian public opinion polls.'[8]

Contrary to Proctor's evidence to the Senate committee, the statement did not accuse Australia of 'stealing'. It asked that the revenues from the disputed fields be placed in escrow until a permanent boundary was agreed. The NGOs had in fact made exactly the same request as the US parliamentarians had made in their letters to Prime Minister John Howard in April 2004 and March 2005. Australian politicians and bureaucrats had not dared to publicly challenge the statements of this very powerful group. In any event, Proctor's evidence confirmed a policy of not funding any international group that publicly criticised the Australian government.

The funding cuts for NGOs in East Timor, which are ongoing, were very much at odds with the Australian government's stated policy of promoting democracy and good governance in the region. In 2004 AusAID asked Pam Thomas, director of the Australian National University's Development Studies Network (DSN), to evaluate the community-based small grants project in East Timor and the role of NGOs in the governance and democratic process. She demonstrated that there was very strong evidence that these groups played a vital role in East Timor's fledgling democracy and were worthy of ongoing support. The Australian government's decision to no longer support these NGOs seemed to undermine the main thrust of its policy agenda in working with countries in the region. Says Thomas, 'It was very disappointing that funding to selected NGOs has been cut. After all, it is their democratic right to demonstrate peacefully and to write letters and this seems to me an excellent example of democratic processes working effectively. I was under the impression that functioning democracies were what the Australian aid programme was trying to promote.'[9]

The funding cuts have not been limited to groups in East Timor. In late 2004 DSN had applied for funding of $145 000 to hold a conference on East Timor at Victoria University in July 2005. Thomas had received strong indications from AusAID that the conference, which would bring together development agencies and senior members of the East Timor government, would be funded. But in the wake of the demonstrations outside the head office of DFAT in March 2005, AusAID told Thomas that it could no longer fund the conference because of the 'delicate' Timor Sea dispute. Thomas was told that AusAID feared the conference could be used as a 'platform' to attack the Australian government on the Timor Sea dispute.

* * *

The prospect of reaching an agreement at the proposed November 2005 meeting did not look good at the outset—the two sides had great difficulty even agreeing to a date for staging one last negotiating round. Australia insisted that the meeting had to be held by the end of November, whereas East Timor wanted it in December. Late November was going to be a very busy time in East Timor, with the 30th anniversary of the unilateral declaration of independence falling on 28 November. A date was finally set for a meeting in Darwin on 27 November.

Ramos-Horta was pessimistic about the prospects for a deal because he thought the negotiating instructions given by Alkatiri were inflexible. Alkatiri did not want to give ground on the outstanding 'details' that had been left unresolved for six months. Ramos-Horta asked Alkatiri, 'Are you going to stand by to give instructions to secure a deal?'

The first 'detail' related to how the median line would be described in the agreement. Australia wanted it to end directly below A16 and A17. It wanted to completely nullify any suggestion that East Timor had a claim extending beyond the eastern and western borders of the JPDA.

A second, more substantive issue, related to how the 50-year moratorium on maritime boundary claims would work. Australia wanted to ensure that East Timor, or indeed any third party, would not be able to find any possible avenue to exercise its right to a maritime boundary at some point in the future, and so it insisted on significant changes to the wording of this section.

The Australian government wanted to extinguish any possibility, however remote, of a backdoor challenge by East Timor at some point in the future. The Australian advisers were concerned that the agreement would somehow unravel and they would find themselves involved in another maritime boundary dispute with East Timor down the track. As Chester had put it, this was to be the final settlement for the Timor Sea. In Article 4 (4) of the new treaty Australia insisted on adding a clause stating that the treaty would achieve a cessation of any proceedings 'that would result in, either *directly or indirectly*, issues or findings of relevance to maritime boundaries or delimitation in the Timor Sea' [*emphasis added*].

So great was Australia's concern that it insisted on a new paragraph in Article 4 that actually prevented third parties outside the agreement—any court, tribunal or other dispute settlement body—from hearing proceedings or making comments or findings on issues relating to maritime boundaries in the Timor Sea. It read:

> Any court, tribunal or other dispute settlement body hearing proceedings involving the parties shall not consider, make comment on, nor make findings that would raise or result in, either directly or indirectly, issues or findings of relevance to maritime boundaries or delimitation in the Timor Sea. Any such comment or finding shall be of no effect, and shall not be relied upon, or cited, by the Parties at any time.

Australia also secured some overall degree of control in the revenue sharing. The Australian government proposed that it would collect revenue as it would have done under the original Sunrise agreement and then distribute to East Timor the difference between what it would derive from the 20.1 per cent allocated to the JPDA and what it was owed under a 50 per cent carve-up. However the original division that allocated only 20.1 per cent of Sunrise to the JPDA would be reaffirmed in the new treaty. A pivotal requirement of the new deal was that the Sunrise agreement would be ratified by East Timor at the same time.

Independence day minus 1

The meeting in Darwin went for an entire day and broke down as both sides refused to give ground on the outstanding details. Teixeira was on the phone to Alkatiri throughout the long day, while Ramos-Horta's departmental secretary, Nelson Santos, was also on the phone to his boss. East Timor gave ground on both the extension of the median line and the wording of the moratorium. Finally, at around 11 p.m., the two sides reached an agreement.

At that final moment, Chester told Teixeira that East Timor would get 'many millions' of dollars from this agreement. Teixeira reminded him that Australia was not giving East Timor anything—the negotiations were the result of overlapping claims. Fearful that this final agreement could unravel yet again, Chester took the prudent though unusual step of insisting that the heads of both delegations sign the document.

At this final meeting East Timor's negotiating team had been reduced to just six members; all but one of them being Timorese nationals. Galbraith and other international hired guns were no longer required. The team included one new member, José Lobato-Gonçalves, the only child of East Timor's first prime minister who had recently been appointed executive director of the TSDA, the joint East Timor–Australia regulatory authority. Lobato, in his early thirties and a former FRETILIN member of parliament, is an unusually tall and well-built Timorese, having escaped the childhood deprivations experienced by those of his generation who remained behind. Lobato-Gonçalves was raised by relatives in Jakarta, where he also graduated in management. He is an impressive though unassuming individual who, with broad shoulders, a gentle nature and composed demeanour, is very likely to lead his country when the generation who rose to prominence before 1975 finally moves on.

It was José Lobato-Gonçalves who, as a two-year-old, was taken from the arms of his 25-year-old mother, Isobel, on the Dili docks moments before she was executed by the Indonesian military on the day of the December 1975 invasion. Lobato-Gonçalves's life was spared after some brave and tenacious negotiation by his uncle José Gonçalves, an economist, who then raised him in Jakarta. Three years later, on New Year's Eve 1978, his father, 32-year-old Nicolau dos Reis Lobato was killed in a battle with the Indonesian military as the 'campaign of encirclement' rounded up the fragmented FALINTIL which had fled to the top of the mountainous spine of East Timor near Turascai. Lobato-Gonçalves's presence at this last meeting added a poignant touch as East Timor restored some semblance of the sovereignty that, together with so much more, was taken away by Indonesia's 24-year occupation and the international conspiracy that allowed it to happen.

* * *

The formal signing of the *Treaty on Certain Maritime Arrangements in the Timor Sea* took place on 12 January 2006 in the Cabinet room at the Commonwealth Government Offices in Phillip Street, Sydney. It was signed not by the prime ministers but by the foreign ministers of both countries, 'in the presence of the prime ministers'. The Australian government's dislike of Alkatiri was so great that they did not want him to sign the new treaty and had suggested, though not insisted, that it be done by the foreign ministers. Alkatiri was happy to accede to this formality.

Together with the treaty, Ramos-Horta and Downer signed complementary letters that expanded on the moratorium on maritime boundary claims and had the effect of denying the existence of East Timor when it came to such claims. The letters say that the treaty does not prevent a party from 'continuing activities', including the regulation of existing and new activities, in areas authorised by legislation that existed on 19 May 2002. The letter from Downer to Ramos-Horta informs him that Australia does have such legislation in place—the *Petroleum (Submerged Lands) Act 1967* and the *Offshore Minerals Act 1994*—to regulate activities south of the Australian–Indonesia 1972 boundary. The letter from Ramos-Horta to Downer says that East Timor had no legislation in place as at 19 May 2002, and he notes Downer's letter. East Timor could not possibly have had legislation in place on 19 May 2002 because it did not come into being as a nation until the following day. These letters say that as far as the disputed area outside the JPDA is concerned, East Timor does not exist. Australia's airbrushing of East Timor's claim in its submission to the Commission on the Limits of the Continental Shelf was no oversight, and with this new agreement it had, as far as maritime rights are concerned, succeeded in going back to the time when Indonesia occupied East Timor.

After the signing, Alkatiri and Howard stood side by side at joint podiums, with their foreign ministers on either side, to take questions from the media. Alkatiri made it very clear that the negotiations had been an extremely hard slog for his new country but he said, 'finally two friendly countries succeeded to finally finalise this agreement'.[10]

Few of the questions asked by journalists related to the agreement. Six Australians had been killed overnight in an Egyptian bus crash and the Sydney media focused on this and other domestic issues. However, just before the press conference wound up, the journalist Angela MacDonald-Smith, who had been following the dispute throughout, asked about East Timor's bid to pipe the gas from Greater Sunrise to an LNG plant in East Timor. Alkatiri responded:

> Above all [the distance from] Timor-Leste and to Australia, [is] much closer. This is the one thing, so of course we keep, not hoping but fighting, to have this plant there and the pipe to Timor-Leste. We do believe that it is technically feasible, it is economically also feasible, and they have been trying to get that pipe line there and I hope that it will go there.[11]

As Alkatiri spoke, Howard turned to his side and began leaning further and further away from him, discomfort written all over his face, as though Alkatiri had no right to speak of aspirations which conflicted with Australia's interests. At the end of the press conference Howard and Downer promptly dismissed the East Timorese. While DFAT had entertained the Timorese during the talks, there was no champagne on offer now that the agreement was sealed. This was contrary to protocol at the signing of every other Timor Sea agreement, starting with Gareth Evans and Ali Alatas in 1989 as they flew over the Timor Sea. Alkatiri, Ramos-Horta and Teixeira were ushered out of the building minutes after the press conference had finished. Howard and Downer had to return to a meeting of the Asia–Pacific Partnership on Clean Development and Climate Change, the anti-Kyoto protocol group led by Australia and the United States that is committed to the continued expansion of fossil fuel use. It was highly apposite that Australia signed an agreement for the development of a huge fossil fuel resource at the time of this meeting.

The East Timor delegation returned to the nearby Wentworth Hotel, the place favoured by Howard for election-night celebrations, where they ordered champagne, and there Alkatiri recounted with some amusement the reaction of Howard to his comments on the pipeline. But he was not amused by Downer's statement about how Australia had been 'very generous' in its negotiations with East Timor. Alkatiri decided it was time for one last press statement on the Timor Sea dispute that emphasised the direct benefit to Australia of onshore processing of the gas in Darwin. The statement would not quote him; he delegated that task to Manuel de Lemos, director of the Timor Sea Office, who had been involved in the negotiations since 2000.

The statement, headed 'Australia also a winner in Timor Sea deal', said in part, 'It is inappropriate to characterise the result of these negotiations as a "very generous" gesture on the part of Australia. The resources at stake in these negotiations were claimed under international law, Mr. de Lemos concluded.'

Just after Alkatiri had finished giving his instructions about the statement Margaret Twomey appeared in the hotel lobby and the Timorese invited her to join them for a glass of champagne. As she picked up her glass someone in the group proposed a toast:

'To the pipeline!' The next day Alkatiri got an idea of the price he was to pay for having finally secured a fair settlement. DFAT failed to provide any diplomatic assistance at Sydney airport for his return to East Timor.

* * *

From that first meeting on the *Olympia* in January 2000, to the final conclusion of negotiations in January 2006, East Timor secured a three-fold increase in resource control and revenue from the Timor Sea. Its share of all the known Timor Sea resources north of the median line rose from 22 per cent in 2000, to around 41 per cent in 2002, and to 60 per cent in 2006. In dollar terms, Australia's opening offer of a fifty-fifty carve-up in line with the terms of the former Area A of the Timor Gap Treaty, which was confirmed in the February 2000 Exchange of Notes, would have delivered around US$6 billion over 20 years or more from Bayu-Undan, plus a further US$2.4 billion from Greater Sunrise spread over 40 years or more. The 2002 Timor Sea Treaty delivered US$16 billion over the same periods. The 2006 treaty has now increased the total to US$24 billion, divided equally between revenue from Sunrise and Bayu-Undan. This means East Timor secured a further US$8 billion in potential revenue to be earned over a period of several decades. While these results will depend on oil prices, estimates indicate that in the final phase of negotiations East Timor more than doubled the 'take it or leave it' offer of October 2004 by holding out for what it believed was a fair and just outcome. The results of six years of negotiations can be summarised in this table which uses the value of the resources[12] at the time of the January 2006 settlement:

THE OUTCOME	2000	2002	2006
Resource share to East Timor, %	22	41	60
Revenue to East Timor over resource lifetime, US$ billions	8.4	16	24

Securing a percentage rather than a flat dollar settlement for Greater Sunrise means there is potential for further upside should the amount of recoverable resources increase as the field is developed. The 25 per cent increase in the Bayu-Undan oil reserves in late 2006 indicates that there is a very strong likelihood of this happening.

Several lessons emerge from these six years of negotiations. East Timor's leaders had a clear understanding of their country's rights under international law and withstood pressure to forgo them. Despite the vast economic disparity between the two countries, East Timor, aside from a few minor lapses, resisted turning itself into a charity case during the dispute. There was a deliberate, disciplined strategy of keeping the focus on rights rather than needs. By raising the issue of economic disparity, East Timor would have found itself on a slippery slope, allowing Australia to switch the focus from entitlement to 'financial assistance'. East Timor developed and stuck to clear, simple and convincing messages, calling on Australia to do one of three reasonable things: enter into good faith negotiations; put the revenue from disputed resources into escrow; or to submit to any international arbiter of its choosing. With these messages, East Timor was appealing to the inherent sense of 'fair go' that is shared by most Australians.

While insisting that this was a rights issue, East Timor's leadership was still willing to be flexible when they were entering into a negotiation that required trade-offs. They did not try to get everything all at once as this was a sequenced negotiation. East Timor focused on what was achievable in each phase; in May 2002 it got 90 per cent ownership of the oil and gas resources in the JPDA as a first base and then moved on from there in the second phase. But it was also careful not to forfeit its negotiating leverage, and despite being pressured into signing the Sunrise agreement in 2003, East Timor maintained the upper hand by pressing Australia to enter into negotiations over a maritime boundary. When, as expected, Australia proved intransigent, East Timor was able to defend a high-risk tactic of holding off ratification of an international agreement.

Finally, East Timor's disciplined strategy meant that it got maximum leverage from its international support network. These networks remained independent of the East Timor government and produced very effective messages. It does not hurt to have friends with money to spend.

Could East Timor have done better? Some of the key players, most notably Ramos-Horta, did not see gaining 50 per cent as a great triumph, given that the country could possibly have secured 100 per cent of all the disputed fields and the area around Sunrise had the dispute gone to independent arbitration. He believed that it would only be a good outcome if East Timor also gets the pipeline and LNG plant. Alkatiri had said that 70 per cent of Sunrise was the bottom line in his view. Fifty per cent was probably the minimum that was politically acceptable in East Timor, and the maximum that Australia was prepared to offer. The figure was signalled publicly as an acceptable outcome by East Timor's maritime law expert, Antunes. In his book published in 2003 titled, *Towards the Conceptualisation of Maritime Delimitation*, he said that a likely fair settlement would 'result in a rough 50/50 division of Greater Sunrise', but this would be part of a deal that also attributed the BCL fields to East Timor.[13] When the 50 per cent result came through, Antunes seemed quite pleased at having presaged the outcome of the negotiations.

As for the BCL fields, East Timor gained nothing, although there was no certainty that it would be awarded them in the event that the dispute went to the International Court of Justice or the ITLOS Tribunal, as Professor Brownlie had indicated in his private advice. These fields were central to East Timor's rhetorical armoury because they sat squarely within the area overlap of the claims by both countries.

While the deal between the two governments had been signed and ratified by both parliaments, approval for the development of

Greater Sunrise by the joint East Timor–Australia authority is likely to be circuitous, involving a continued struggle between the two countries. East Timor has already attempted to interest a multinational much bigger than Woodside in order to leverage the economic benefits. Late in 2005 Alkatiri and Teixeira began secret negotiations over Greater Sunrise with the French multinational Total. Alkatiri met Total's senior vice president for *Asie-Extrême Orient*, Michel Seguin, in Singapore in September 2005, and Teixeira met him in London later that month. The government had begun work on a plan to give Total half of its 20 per cent entitlement to the entire project in exchange for building a pipeline and an onshore LNG plant in East Timor. Under East Timor's 2005 petroleum laws a State Participation clause allows the government to take a 20 per cent interest in any project. While Alkatiri had strongly endorsed the principles of British prime minister Tony Blair's Extractive Industries Transparency Initiative, a global program to improve governance in resource-rich developing countries, he began behind-closed-doors talks to award a pivotal stake in the development of a US$57 billion oil and gas field. The plan horrified some of East Timor's experienced international advisers, who eventually persuaded Alkatiri to abandon it. Advisers believed that the terms of the proposal with Total would have short-changed East Timor, which was why it was dropped. As well, it was difficult to see how such a plan could ever have gained Australia's support through the joint authority.

If the pipeline does not eventuate it may not be the end of the world. When the negotiations were in abeyance in mid-2005 the East Timor government received the results of the *Zephyr-1*'s seismic survey, which indicated the existence of several petroleum prospects, including one that was potentially many times the size of Greater Sunrise. The results led in early 2006 to the successful auctioning of six blocks in the area between East Timor's southern coastline and the northern border of the JPDA. This was quite a significant achievement for a new entrant to this global industry, although Australia had tried to thwart this initiative because two corners of the survey area fall under its 200-nautical-mile claim, as shown in Map 2. East Timor was following Australia's example and practising unilateral exploitation. The government believed that it could proceed because it had informed Australia of the seismic survey (but not about the auctioning of blocks). The Australian government fired off a formal diplomatic note in October 2005 protesting East Timor's auction. A year later, when East Timor held a ceremony in Dili for the signing of contracts with successful bidders, the Australian Ambassador Margaret Twomey turned down her invitation to attend. She was overheard saying that the blocks were located in an area that 'we claim' and as a result she could not be seen at the ceremony. The Australian embassy in Dili appeared poorly informed on the specific details of the auction. As late as November 2006 it requested from the East Timor government a map showing exactly where the new blocks were located.

Indonesia had overlooked this potential treasure trove on East Timor's doorstep; it had been completely sidetracked by the negotiations over the Timor Gap. During the 24 years of occupation it had been spellbound by the illusory Kelp Prospect.

* * *

Leaving aside the 'communications' devices housed in the roof cavity of the Australian embassy in Dili, the most sophisticated piece of technology in East Timor is a *Bloomberg* terminal which sits in the 'dealing room' of the *Banco Central de Timor-Leste*. The terminal is used to monitor East Timor's bid to beat the resource curse. An urbane, softly spoken Timorese, Abraão de Vasconselos, the general manager of the central bank, is responsible for investing nearly all of East Timor's petroleum revenue in US government bonds. With the *Bloomberg* terminal de Vasconselos can track the value of the US$1 billion (and rising) that this new country held in US Treasury bonds as at the end of 2006. With petroleum revenue of around US$700 million expected in 2006–07, followed by around US$1 billion in each of the three subsequent years, the assets of the Petroleum Fund, set up at the end of 2004, should grow exponentially under a policy of retaining one-half to two-thirds of gross revenue.

The fund is designed to safely invest the nation's petroleum revenue so that the government will be able to pay for services with a perpetual stream of interest earnings when the oil and gas resources are exhausted. Along the way, East Timor will hopefully avoid the resource curse by controlling the inflow rate of petrodollars into the economy.

Transforming non-renewable physical assets into financial assets that will last forever is the crux of East Timor's savings policy. The concept of 'inter-generational' equity is an inherent part of it; the moral imperative is that natural resources belong not only to the current generation but to those in the future as well. East Timor's fund is modelled on Norway's successful oil fund. Launched in 1996 it has US$250 billion in assets and is projected to reach US$450 billion by 2010.[14] East Timor's fund is designed to avoid the pitfalls of natural resource wealth by investing offshore in low-risk government bonds, and by spending only the sustainable income from petroleum wealth. In many resource-rich developing countries the inflow of revenue from exports of oil and other mineral resources has crippled their economic development by inflating their exchange rates and making other export sectors uncompetitive. These receipts financed inflationary spending on grandiose projects that turned into white elephants and the latest military hardware.

In East Timor currency appreciation is not a real danger because it has adopted the US dollar as its currency, but the objective of investing safely is of fundamental importance for a very poor country. For the first five years a minimum of 90 per cent of the fund's assets must be invested in US bonds. After that the fund may move into blue chip equities and other government bonds. Some NGOs in East Timor were critical of the decision to invest all the money in US bonds, as they argued that in effect East Timor was buying war bonds to finance the war in Iraq. They also cited the risk that the US dollar could devalue substantially, thereby creating inflation at home and reducing East Timor's purchasing power.

Under East Timor's Petroleum Fund law, all petroleum-related revenue flows directly into the fund—rather than first being paid into consolidated revenue—via an earmarked bank account held with the US Federal Reserve in New York. This not only includes royalties and company tax, but any petroleum-related tax payment such as sales tax. Monies can be withdrawn to fund Budget expenditure, but this requires approval from the national parliament and the money can only move from the fund to the Budget. A council of eminent persons, including community leaders from NGOs and the Church, oversees the operation of the fund and reports directly to parliament.

The government's policy of saving a significant proportion of its resource wealth is a challenging objective in a post-conflict country where people have seen a great deal of death in their immediate families and communities. The notion of saving for the future in these circumstances can be an alien concept.

The restraint adopted by the government involves spending only 3 per cent of the value of petroleum wealth in the ground that has been licensed for development, together with the value of financial assets, including accumulated interest, in the fund. This is the 'sustainable income' from petroleum wealth—the amount that can be spent in the current year, and in every year in the future, without prejudicing future generations. There is nothing in the law to prevent a future government spending above this level if it wants, but when proposals to withdraw funds are put to parliament the executive must also submit an estimate of the sustainable income at that time. Transparency is the only check in the system to prevent a future government from squandering the nation's resource wealth.

The government's fiscal conservatism largely reflected the influence of Alkatiri who was fully cognisant of the dangers of resource wealth and the need for a robust system to manage the country's oil revenue. So far the government has not been able to spend anywhere near the limit. East Timor's first government excelled at saving, but did less well when it came to spending, which should have been a more straightforward exercise.

16 FROM ASHES TO ASHES

'At the beginning there were some expectations. We are now free, we will start a new life, and the government promises to the people to improve the way of life, to reduce poverty. We have much oil so that people will get enough for their lives. It did not happen—waiting four years, people became poorer and poorer.

It seems they did not have enough experience, maybe. East Timor is quite small, only one million people, it is not so difficult to manage everything, but it did not happen.' Monsignor Ricardo da Silva, Bishop of Dili, July 2006

The year 2006 began in auspicious style for tiny impoverished East Timor. On New Year's Day, billionaire investor and 'open society' guru George Soros flew into Dili with an entourage on his private jet for a three-day visit as a guest of President Gusmão. During his time in Dili Soros heaped praise on the system introduced by Alkatiri for managing the nation's petroleum revenue, although he thought more could be done to monitor how the money was being spent. And then the following week Alkatiri and Ramos-Horta departed for Sydney for the signing of the new Greater Sunrise Treaty, where they camped at the Wentworth Hotel. Alkatiri had time to do some shopping in Sydney's department stores before heading home.

SHAKEDOWN

These moments of political glory would be fleeting. On the day Alkatiri departed Dili, 11 January, a group of around 159 soldiers from East Timor's army, many of them veterans, lodged a petition with the president about discrimination within the FALINTIL-*Força Defensa Timor-Leste* (F-FDTL), as East Timor's army is known. The defence force chief, Taur Matan Ruak, also received the petition, as did the defence minister Roque Rodrigues and a number of embassies. Gusmão wrote to Ruak on 16 January urging him to resolve the dispute promptly. The Alkatiri government had excelled at the complex, high-level work of government. International aid organisations, including the United Nations, had held up East Timor as a genuine success story in the difficult business of post-conflict reconstruction and development. But it was about to learn the cost of neglecting the simple things.

Hailing from the western region of East Timor, the soldiers claimed that the F-FDTL's top brass, who came from the eastern part of the country, had discriminated against them in terms of pay, conditions and promotions. Led by veteran resistance fighter Lieutenant Gastão Salsinha, who had been denied a promotion to the rank of captain because of his involvement in the smuggling of lucrative sandalwood timber, the 'petitioners', as they became known, asked the president to mediate in the dispute. One of the legacies of the independence struggle was that the surviving leaders of the resistance army were mainly easterners. Many of the westerners were assigned to the eastern-most base in Los Palos where they lived in makeshift huts that were far inferior to the conditions afforded to soldiers in other bases. Their assignment to the east also meant a long and expensive journey home during leave periods, which also resulted in a high rate of absenteeism.

At this time, after nearly four years of independence, East Timor was superficially peaceful and stable, but fault lines were deepening. Widespread discontent emerged in April 2005 when the Catholic Church staged three-week protest against the Government over a proposed school curriculum that made religious education optional.

In a highly organised operation, the church trucked people into Dili from around the country, where they camped outside the *Palácio*. The rally remained peaceful, although it took on a vitriolic tone as the demonstrators labelled Alkatiri a Marxist and called for his removal from office. East Timor's oldest and most revered institution had a deeper grievance. After playing a significant role in the independence struggle the FRETILIN government had sidelined it, and even one international aid agency believed the demonstration reflected legitimate grievances over the government's autocratic style. Some members of the church, however, are believed to have urged defence force chief Brigadier-General Taur Matan Ruak to stage a coup, although this is denied by the head of the Catholic Church in East Timor, Bishop Ricardo da Silva.[1]

The unpopular government was running against the odds in its bid to build a brighter future for the much-abused people of East Timor. One in two post-conflict countries lapses back into deadly conflict within five years, and East Timor was exhibiting some of the pre-cursors that have led to renewed conflict around the world. The government's divisive and increasingly authoritarian style was a warning sign that had been noted publicly by institutions such as the World Bank. A sharp economic contraction following the UN's downsizing from 2001, and the government's inability to spend its budget, was a second significant indicator. The post-independence afterglow was being overtaken by rising frustration caused by worsening poverty and mass unemployment. Human development indicators, such as child mortality, were going backwards. Too many people had seen nothing tangible from the new government, and increasingly, what they did see or perceive of it was corruption, nepotism and self-serving largesse. Rising oil prices created scope for the government to hit the spending pump, but an inexperienced and cumbersome administration was unable to deliver the benefit of this windfall to the people. Corruption had taken hold of the country, distracting the government from the formidable task of nation building. 'Especially in the last year, everybody could clearly find corruption,' said Bishop da Silva. The acronym KKN was on the lips of every cab driver in Dili; it stands for Korupsaun, Kolusaun and Nepotismu (Corruption, Collusion and Nepotism).

With increasing frequency, people heard about corruption and nepotism in relation to the Alkatiri family. The prime minister's brothers, Ahmed and Bader, had launched a Soeharto-style network of companies using different names to bid for government contracts, often handing them on to other businesses in return for a significant cut. An in-depth analysis of the construction sector—a sector of fundamental importance to the country's development—by a leading international aid agency found that contracts were consistently awarded to a network of Alkatiri companies. The confidential report, circulated in November 2005, said that reputable firms had ceased bidding for government contracts because genuine bids would not win tenders. A summary of the study said:

> We have little scope to address what we found to be the foremost constraint in the growth of the sub-sector: corruption. We found corruption to be widespread in public sector construction projects and especially in government procured projects. We found evidence of the lowest bid winning even when that bid is below the Government's own engineer [sic] estimate, also when it belongs to a politically powerful but unqualified firm.
>
> We found that 'lowest bid' does not mean 'best' or even the lowest cost bid, that firms that exist only on paper win contracts and sell their award for a percentage. Construction firms admitted their own use of bribery to the Tender Board and of course reported that other firms also participated. The pre-qualification process is widely reported to have been based more on influence than capacity of firms.[2]

The notorious contract for the sale of bullets to the security forces (at a price that was increased by 50 per cent without going to tender), created the saddest irony of all in the violence of April–June

2006; most of the bullets used to kill and maim the Timorese were sold to the government by Bader Alkatiri's company.

The divide between the *loro sa'e* (rising sun, or easterners) and the *loro monu* (setting sun, or westerners) had never previously been a major source of conflict. The violence of 2006 was a case of small differences in a small place. But there is an economic cleavage in the tiny country. The eastern region has more flat land and is generally more productive, and this brought traders into the capital from the east. While the west has the rich coffee growing mountains, most of the extreme poverty is found in this rugged region. This disparity may have worsened as the economy turned down after 2001. If there was discrimination in East Timor, it was also felt by the easterners. The capital is located in the western part of the country, and the official indigenous language originates from the west and is not spoken widely in the east. The eastern domination of the armed forces had a deeper significance, however, as some regions in the west of East Timor, close to the Indonesian border, had tended to support integration with Indonesia. This new east–west division—magnified by mismanagement—was layered on top of the existing split between the vast majority who supported independence, and the minority who in 1999 had wanted special autonomy with Jakarta. Added to this was the fact that the core of the 3000-strong national police force, the *Polícia Nacional de Timor-Leste* (PNTL), including the commissioner, had worked for the former Indonesian police force, thus tarring it as a pro-autonomy entity in competition with the F-FDTL.

But the complaints of the petitioners should have remained a minor, manageable problem that could have been easily resolved. Brigadier General Taur Matan Ruak, declined to attend a meeting with 418 petitioners called by Gusmão on 8 February to discuss the petitioners' complaints. Immediately after this meeting the unarmed petitioners went AWOL, refusing to obey orders to return to their barracks.

As the dispute dragged on the ranks of the petitioners swelled until 594 soldiers—almost half the army—joined the protest. About

200 of these were soldiers who had been chronically absent without leave for months or years.³ Alkatiri also refused to hear the soldiers' complaints, and concurred with his defence force chief's decision to sack them on 16 March, with retroactive effect to 1 March, after they defied his deadline to return to their barracks. With the stroke of a pen, a mob of muscular, angry rebels was born.

Surprisingly, Alkatiri did not believe that sacking almost half the army would create instability. 'The Government is in control of the situation. The party presently in charge is a big party and therefore has the power to go to the base to control the situation. While this party is in power there won't be any instability,' Alkatiri said following the sacking. The legalistic Prime Minister said the decision was 'the only legally and politically permissible solution' to the crisis.⁴

And, after having worked closely together throughout the Timor Sea negotiations, Alkatiri's handling of the dispute opened up a rift between himself and the president. One week after the sacking, in a national radio and TV broadcast, Gusmão lambasted the decision as 'unfair' and 'wrong'. 'I do not see the decision as correct,' he said.⁵ In an incendiary broadside lasting 27 minutes the president appeared to have sided with the westerners, and after these comments were broadcast the first houses were burnt.

A series of demonstrations in the capital followed, culminating in riots outside the *Palácio* on 28 April that erupted into violence after other malcontents, most notably the gang Colimau 2000, swelled the ranks of the petitioners.⁶ The crisis exposed the penchant for overseas travel found within the government: defence force chief Ruak and defence minister Rodrigues were on a tour of Malaysia and the United States inspecting military equipment on the eve of this last and fateful demonstration. At 11.30 a.m. the first stones were thrown.⁷ At around midday the demonstrators broke into the grounds of the *Palácio* and torched vehicles parked immediately outside Alkatiri's office—just 20 metres from the front entrance—while nearly all the building's ground floor windows were smashed with rocks. The mob knew exactly where the first-floor cabinet room was located; its windows were given special treatment. Interior Minister Lobato arrived on the scene wearing a flak jacket and told his officers to 'kill them all'. A fully automatic F2000 machine gun, and 2000 rounds of ammunition, were signed over to the minister by the PNTL General Commander.[8]

Alkatiri dispatched the F-FDTL to control the fracas, and in the process two people were shot dead and about 60 wounded. The incident prompted a group of the F-FDTL's military police, led by the high-ranking Major Alfredo Reinado, who during the Indonesian years had worked in shipyards in Perth, to defect on 4 May with guns and ammunition in protest at the government's use of the army to quell the riot.

Alkatiri was unfazed by the violence and continued to defend the decision to sack the soldiers, but others, most notably Ramos-Horta, seriously questioned his leadership. The violence erupted ahead of FRETILIN's party congress, which is held every five years, and this prompted a challenge for the position of secretary-general. José Luis Guterres, the urbane ambassador to the UN and the United States who lived in East Timor during the Indonesian years, campaigned for the position on the need for a more sensitive and transparent prime minister. The party secretary-general is a key position as the holder is in turn appointed as prime minister. But Alkatiri outfoxed Guterres by changing the voting procedure so that delegates had to show their hands, an intimidating procedural change given that many of them were government employees. Gangs of thugs loyal to Alkatiri circled around the gathering inside the national university gymnasium, intimidating the delegates throughout the meeting. Delegates were forced to vote district by district so that they could be closely monitored. Alkatiri won with support from 93.7 per cent of the 662 delegates, an overwhelming result that Guterres said was reminiscent of Communist Party elections: 'They have chosen an electoral method that is typically Leninist and used by the leaders of communist countries to maintain their power.'[9] The presence of representatives from the Communist Parties of China, Portugal, Mozambique and Cuba at the congress created the feeling that 'Little Cuba' had indeed come into being. Alkatiri remained optimistic after his win and in a vaudeville moment sang a stirring rendition of an independence song at a concert held at the conclusion of the congress.

But the victory would be short-lived. On 23 May, a few days after the Congress had concluded, Reinado's group provoked a clash with the remainder of the F-FDTL in the hills above Dili, while other clashes occurred outside Dili involving police officers, petitioners, and members of armed civilian hit squads broke out around the city. A pitched battle between the F-FDTL and PNTL at the PNTL headquarters culminated in the massacre on 25 May of eight PNTL officers as they surrendered in a poorly planned UN intervention. On the same day a mother and her young family who were related to interior minister Rogerio Lobato were incinerated by youths who attacked their home with petrol bombs. Six people, including four children below the age of 18, died in the blaze.

* * *

As East Timor spiralled out of control and to the brink of civil war, Australian ships were heading in the direction of the island. Prime Minister John Howard had on 12 May announced the deployment to East Timor of two transport ships, HMAS *Kanimbla* and HMAS *Manoora*, supported by the guided missile frigate HMAS *Adelaide*. It was a deliberate, pre-emptive intervention on Australia's part which had not been requested by East Timor and was at the time protested by Ramos-Horta. But as events transpired the Australian military reinforced its just-in-time reputation for arriving on the scene of regional flare-ups. Four Blackhawk Australian Army helicopters fitted with long-range fuel tanks swooped over the capital city on the evening of 25 May en route to secure the airport after being dispatched from Darwin. After the airport was secured an 'air bridge' of C130 Hercules aircraft brought in hundreds of Australian troops with a mandate to restore order.

From ashes to ashes

A total of 1300 Australian troops arrived in Dili as part of Operation Astute, but the forces were initially ill-equipped, indicating that an operation of this scale had not been envisaged. The Australian forces arrived with only a handful of vehicles—armoured personnel carriers and jeeps. In order to mobilise the troops the army had to hire all of the available 4WDs held by a local rental company, and also revive others which had been mothballed. They were later joined by forces from New Zealand, Malaysia and Portugal, taking numbers to more than 2000. President Gusmão stepped in and assumed the role of armed forces commander, defying the protest of Alkatiri who insisted that the move was unconstitutional. Alkatiri reluctantly agreed to the intervention on the condition that the Portuguese forces be included. Late on the afternoon of 25 May a convoy of seven 4WD vehicles crammed with defence and DFAT officials, and Australian soldiers, ventured into the epicentre of the main fire-fight as they went up the mountain overlooking Dili, driving around the road's numerous blind, hairpin bends, in order to secure the signature on the security agreement of the president, and then back down again for the prime minister's signature. On both trips the occupants could see tracer bullets—which also meant real bullets—flying over the convoy.

The decision by Australia to dispatch its armed forces appeared to save the day. But this deployment may have actually served to destabilise East Timor. In the opinion of a senior defence attaché based in Dili, the rebel groups provoked clashes with the F-FDTL in order to bring about foreign intervention. The provocative attacks on the F-FDTL by Reinado only came about *because* armed intervention by Australia had been set in motion. Reinado said from his mountain hideout that he would only surrender to an international force, and that he was looking forward to having a Victoria Bitter with his mates from the Australian Defence Force.

The government of East Timor had for all intents and purposes ceased to exist. Ramos-Horta, Gusmão, church leaders and at least half the country, called on Alkatiri to accept responsibility for East Timor's descent into chaos and violence, but he refused to go.

He remained defiant even when Gusmão threatened to resign if Alkatiri did not stand down, and when Ramos-Horta resigned as foreign minister. Alkatiri regained his composure and conceded only one mistake throughout the entire episode—he admitted that he should have sacked each of the soldiers individually, rather than as an entire group.

Alkatiri clung onto power for another four weeks, but then on 19 June the ABC's *Four Corners* program aired sensational allegations about his involvement in the distribution of guns to civilian hit squads.[10] The most credible allegations were made by the commissioner of police, Paulino Martins, who revealed a letter he had written to Alkatiri informing him of the distribution of the guns. Martins alleged that Alkatiri told him to keep quiet about it. The program also quoted claims from Vincente 'Rai Los' da Conceicão, a little-known resistance army veteran who had been sacked from the F-FDTL in 2003 for his involvement in smuggling sandalwood. Rai Los claimed he had been instructed by the prime minister and the interior minister to establish civilian hit squads to kill FRETILIN opponents. He produced SMS messages sent from Lobato's telephone suggesting that he burn the trucks of demonstrators: 'Opposition will come from Ermera intending to demonstrate in Dili to put down the government. Why not stop them at the coffee plantation in Rai Laku and burn all 26 trucks?' Another SMS from Alkatiri was less incriminating; it simply asked where he was going. (It is possible to send SMS messages from a fabricated telephone number in East Timor, and the telephone numbers of Alkatiri and Lobato are widely known.) But it is a fact, however, that Rai Los met with Lobato and Alkatiri at the residence of the prime minister on 8 May. He claims that Alkatiri told him to 'eliminate' petitioners, a statement disputed by Alkatiri,[11] but the UN Commission of Inquiry established that Lobato gave ten machine guns and 6000 rounds of ammunition to the Rai Los group.[12] On 24 May, the F-FDTL also began arming civilians, establishing the pretext for a civil war.[13]

Lobato was detained at Dili airport on 20 June, the morning after the program was screened, and was then reported to have implicated Alkatiri in his statements to the prosecutor general, Longuinhos Monteiro. It was at this point that Alkatiri's position became untenable. He resigned on 26 June and then faced questioning by the prosecutor general. Alkatiri, however, remained secretary-general of FRETILIN, and continued to effectively run the government. He regularly summoned senior ministers to meet at his residence which was guarded by Australian security. He then assembled a formidable legal team of five international lawyers which included Miguel Galvão-Teles, the lawyer who advised on the Timor Sea negotiations and confronted Australia's attempt to have East Timor accept the Timor Gap Treaty. The UN Commission of Inquiry concluded there was 'reasonable suspicion' that Alkatiri 'at least' had knowledge of the distribution of weapons to the civilian groups.[14] It said there was evidence that he knew of the distribution on 21 May, and he failed to use his authority to denounce this practice.[15] It recommended that he be investigated to determine whether he 'bears any criminal offences for weapons offences', and it said the armed forces chief and defence minister should be prosecuted for illegal weapons transfers.

Alkatiri blamed outsiders for orchestrating the violence. Prior to stepping down as prime minister he accused pro-Indonesia militias and 'a third party' of fomenting unrest in the country. These comments earned him a stinging rebuke from the Indonesian president Susilo Bambang Yudhoyono. After resigning he said the Australian government, with help from the Australian media, had brought him down because of his tough stand on the oil negotiations. He threatened to use his influence in the FRETILIN party to block ratification of the new treaty. 'I have no doubt that some ministers and officers in Australia don't like me because I was known to them as a tough negotiator,' he said.[16]

The UN concluded that the April–May violence led to the deaths of 38 people and at least 69 suffered injuries. More than

150 000 people were living in camps and about 2000 homes destroyed. With more than 250 weapons issued to PNTL and F-FDTL unaccounted for there remained the potential for further conflict. Deadly violence in East Timor became a routine occurrence even after the arrival of international forces.

The UN inquiry did not examine the possible involvement of outsiders in the unrest, which was a significant omission in view of Australia's unilateral deployment of its forces and the destabilising effect this may have had. Alkatiri's inept handling of the dispute alone was sufficient justification to call for his resignation, but he would not have resigned without the well-documented hit squad allegations. Yet there are some elements of the pivotal hit squad story that just don't stack up. Rai Los abandoned his involvement in the hit squads after four members of his group were killed in a clash on 24 May by the loyalist remnants of the F-FDTL, who were meant to be on the same side. But it was clear that Rai Los, like Reinado, provoked the attack, as his group was patrolling in the foothills above the F-FDTL base outside Dili where they ran into an F-FDTL patrol. Lengthy correspondence from Rai Los to Lobato and President Gusmão obtained by *Four Corners* looked far too sophisticated to have come from someone who grew up in the districts of East Timor and spent most of his adult years in the resistance army in the mountains. This supposedly secret group, *Equipa Segurança Secreto Fretilin (ESSF) Groupo Rai Los* (Rai Los Group) the FRETILIN Secret Service Team, produced correspondence featuring a letterhead with a unique logo, together with text boxes containing full details on the distribution of each gun. It seems implausible that a so-called secret civilian hit squad would produce such documentation in the first place. The sophisticated nature of the paperwork indicates that Rai Los could not have acted alone. The *Australian* newspaper, which had run an aggressive anti-Alkatiri agenda during the crisis, cited 'inconsistencies' in the story and thought Rai Los behaved oddly. After making the allegations on *Four Corners*, and with Alkatiri and Lobato still in power, he was seen sipping coffee on the lawn of the president's home. 'Conceicão didn't look anything like a man in fear for his life'.[17]

The Rai Los group had been taken into the president's fold by Bendito Freitas, a well-educated and respected Timorese who had a long career working for international organisations, including the United Nations. Freitas was camped out in his mountain home near where the Rai Los group was based, and after clashing with the F-FDTL they turned up at his residence, fully armed, and told him in strident terms that they wanted him to take them to the president. On 29 May Freitas arranged for an escort by a special police unit and, together with a priest and two nuns, made the 90-minute journey to Dili with the Rai Los group, where they told the president their extraordinary claims about the meetings with the interior minister and prime minister, and how they came to receive the weapons and the lethal instructions. Gusmão was aware that the *Four Corners* crew was in Dili and he asked Freitas to assist Rai Los in documenting the evidence and in communicating with the media. Freitas created the letterhead and logo and wrote letters backdated to the 20th and 28th of May from Rai Los to the interior minister and the president. The letters were featured as 'Confidential Documents' on the program's website.[18] Freitas also translated the interview between the reporter Liz Jackson and Rai Los. The program later won Australia's highest media award. When Gusmão called for Alkatiri to step down he sent him a copy of the *Four Corners* documentary.

East Timor's Prosecutor-General, however, notified Alkatiri on 5 February 2007 that he and international advisers had found no evidence against him and that the investigation was now closed. Alkatiri declared he would sue the ABC for the allegations made in the *Four Corners* program. 'The ABC damaged my image, my family and my party,' said Alkatiri.[19] One month later Rogerio Lobato, after withdrawing his statement implicating Alkatiri, was found guilty by a panel of three international judges of four counts of manslaughter and one of unlawfully using firearms to disturb public order. He was sentenced to seven-and-a-half years' gaol. Alkatiri showed public loyalty to Lobato, attending the court hearing of the man who remains his party vice-president. Lobato's lawyer declared that he would appeal the decision.

The possible involvement of outsiders in East Timor's turmoil had been raised by Alkatiri, who made vague claims of foreign interests having urged the East Timor military to overthrow his government. 'I still have no clear information from the command if they were Australian or American, but surely they were English speaking.' Asked if he had any evidence of Australian involvement in the coup attempt, he answered, 'Evidence? No. But the only prime minister in the world that was really "advising me"—quote, unquote—to step down was the Prime Minister of Australia during these, say, these difficult days,' Alkatiri said.[20] Howard had made an extraordinary intervention in East Timor's internal affairs when on 26 May he publicly castigated the country's leadership. 'There is no point beating around the bush. The country has not been well-governed and I do hope that the sobering experience for those in elected positions of having to call for outside help will induce the appropriate behaviours inside the country.'[21]

While there is no definitive evidence of direct involvement in these events by the Australian government, it had since independence followed a pattern of making East Timor feel vulnerable, as Bruce Haigh has put it. From the very beginning of East Timor's independence, when the country was taking a defiant stand in the oil negotiations, Australia pushed for an early and sharp reduction in UN security. In 2002 a substantial UN peacekeeping force of around 5000 soldiers and 1250 police officers was in place, but the Australian government took an increasingly tough approach at the United Nations as relations with Dili soured. The following year, 2003, Australia began pushing the UN for a sharp reduction in peacekeeping numbers at the UN Security Council, and then in 2004 lobbied for an end of UN peacekeeping in East Timor. In advance of the UN Security Council meeting in May 2004 the

Australian government had lobbied the United States and Britain to back a complete withdrawal of the military component.[22]

Influential political commentator Laurie Oakes, a 30-year veteran of the Canberra press gallery, outlined Canberra's deliberate 'desertion of Dili' after East Timor gained independence:

> It is pretty clear that things started to go off the rails in early 2004, when the UN Security Council was considering an extension of the mandate of UNMISET (the UN Mission in Support of East Timor). The East Timorese government wanted the presence of peace-keeping troops to continue.
>
> UN Secretary-General Kofi Annan produced a report calling for a reduced peace-keeping operation, but one that would still see 350 soldiers remain.
>
> Australia opposed leaving any troops in East Timor, asserting that a UN police presence would be enough.
>
> Downer argued that because Indonesia had accepted East Timor's independence and armed militias were no longer coming over the border, all that was left was an internal security problem which police could handle. The US and Britain, because they tend to accept that Australia has expertise and clout in its own region, were inclined to accept the Downer view. On ABC radio at the time, Downer played down Annan's recommendation as simply the result of East Timorese lobbying. The East Timorese government, he said, wanted 'some peace-keeping force there for another year just as a security blanket'. Their wishes 'have been very much at the top of the secretariat's mind'.
>
> Why weren't East Timor's wishes also at the top of Australia's mind? It is a valid question.
>
> Downer's attitude was astonishingly dismissive and contemptuous, especially given his stance in the current crisis that Australia has to respect the wishes of the East Timorese government.[23]

Downer's claim that East Timor just wanted a 'security blanket' was reminiscent of what former DFAT secretary Ashton Calvert had said in 1999 to his US counterpart, Assistant Secretary of State Stanley Roth, when he dismissed the need for peacekeepers for the 1999 ballot. Labor's foreign affairs spokesman Kevin Rudd, who became the Opposition leader in December 2006, said Australia 'cut and run' from East Timor by pushing for a withdrawal of its troops shortly after independence.[24]

Ramos-Horta was also dismayed by the refusal of these influential countries to listen to East Timor's views: 'We are all quite puzzled as to why Canberra, London and Washington want to differ from everybody else on this issue. We, the Timorese, maintain a very close working relationship with the UN and they listen to us. Certain countries do not seem to think that our views are very relevant.'[25] Australia's position failed to convince the Security Council in its review of East Timor that year, but the size of the force was greatly reduced to less than 650 police and soldiers.

The following year Australia, again with the backing of the United States, finally succeeded in pressing the UN for a complete withdrawal of peacekeepers. Australia had asserted its special role in providing security to East Timor through a significant police training program—the largest component of its modest aid program in East Timor—and the Australian Defence Force had a training program for the F-FDTL, but there were no boots on the ground. Like every other facet of foreign policy, Australia's strategy in East Timor was aimed at serving the interests of Australia. The motivation of Australia and the United States in pressing for this withdrawal has also been linked to the demands of the Iraq war.

The renewed need for substantial Australian security assistance in independent East Timor is something that would not make the Australian government and its foreign policy practitioners at all unhappy. The eagerness with which Australia dispatched its ships underscores this point. One month after the troops landed the Australian Defence Department called for a tender to build a permanent military base for up to 3000 personnel at the former heliport near the centre of Dili, just across the road from the Australian embassy. It was also the location chosen for the proposed presidential palace complex. After the crisis subsided the military complex had to be rearranged to allow the Chinese construction firm to start work on the president's palace.

A truly independent East Timor, both politically and economically, could well have meant that Australia ended up with Little Cuba on its doorstep, as was feared three decades earlier. The presence of 300 Cuban doctors in East Timor, and the training of up to 600 Timorese medical students in Cuba, had not gone unnoticed. The US ambassador Joseph Rees, who had worked as a legislative aid to conservative Republican Chris Smith, was known to be highly agitated by the presence of the Cuban doctors, and believed that many of them were operating as spies in East Timor. Nor had Alkatiri's visit to Cuba in December 2005 gone unnoticed, during which he met with President Fidel Castro for six hours and returned full of praise for the country. Cuba does have excellent doctors and medical training, but the cooperation program may have sent the wrong signal to regional and global powers.

The interest in East Timor of a much bigger communist country, China, may also have raised more serious concerns. While China still has considerable poverty it has been exceedingly forthcoming in offering development assistance to East Timor for the benefit of the elite, who have in turn recognised its generosity. After agreeing to build the new foreign ministry on the Dili waterfront, renovating Alkatiri's office and committing to build a massive presidential complex, China was awarded an expansive stretch of the Dili waterfront for its embassy which is rivalled only by the grounds of the US embassy. The resource-hungry country has a keen interest in East Timor's resource wealth. In 2004 the Chinese government was granted the exclusive right to conduct a 'magnetic' survey of onshore oil and gas resources. Later that year a subsidiary of the state oil company Petrochina, BGP (Bureau of Geophysical Prospecting), partnered with a Norwegian seismic firm, GGS, to bid for rights to conduct East Timor's first seismic survey. The BGP–GGS consortium won the tender and this led to the *Zephyr-1*'s survey of a 30 000 square kilometre area in January 2005. Chinese petroleum companies, however, did not bid for exploration rights in the maritime area, though they appear to have other interests in East Timor. Teixeira had talked openly about granting China an extensive concession after being feted by the Chinese government during a visit there in May 2004. During the visit Teixeira became ill with dengue fever, a potentially fatal tropical illness, and later told how the Chinese had taken him to their best hospital and virtually saved his life. Other senior government members had also beaten a steady path to Beijing. Alkatiri visited in September 2003 and met Premier Wen Jiabao at the Great Hall of the People. Gusmão visited in January 2000 as president of CNRT and was invited there again in May 2006. He did not cancel the visit scheduled for 29 May–3 June until 25 May, the day the Australian military arrived as gun battles raged in and around Dili.

A section in East Timor's *Petroleum Law 2005* gives the government the absolute discretion to award an authorisation to anyone it likes, without going to tender. Teixeira had discussed using this discretion to grant China an extensive area of the country near the southern coastline in the oil-rich Cova Lima district for onshore development in return for building an oil refinery.

In late 2006 the Australian treasurer Peter Costello declared Australia's strong opposition to the locking up of natural resources by such opaque, bilateral deals. He put market-based access to natural resources at the top of the agenda of the G20 meeting he hosted in Melbourne. The G20 brings together ten of the top industrialised countries and ten of the significant emerging economies, including China. Costello warned that the practice of locking up natural resources, as opposed to the G20's principle of 'market production', could lead to conflict: 'If we don't have market production in a way which can guarantee emerging giant economies access to the energy and minerals that they need, the differences between countries, the friction and the dislocation could be quite severe. Not just to the economy but beyond that.'²⁶

Bruce Haigh wrote that John Howard, after learning about the company that Alkatiri was keeping, came to believe that an Alkatiri-run East Timor might also harbour terrorists:

> Howard was concerned with [Alkatiri's] links to Cuba and got himself into a state of mind where he believed an Alkatiri government would have been prepared to harbour terrorists. This line of thought was supported by the US administration. This might seem a bit hysterical but that is the prevailing intellectual atmosphere in the offices of Howard and Bush.²⁷

* * *

Ten days after the deployment of the Australian soldiers Alexander Downer flew to Dili where he encountered a very different President Gusmão. As Downer entered Gusmão's new office behind the *Palácio das Cinzas*, the president was overcome by the humiliation of his nation's collapse. He broke down and wept openly in Downer's arms. The hero of East Timor's resistance struggle, who had railed against Australia's theft of Timor oil and bullying tactics, was now in a complete state of submission.²⁸

Ramos-Horta remained composed during the crisis, and he is seen by foreign governments and oil companies as accessible and reasonable. In his first press conference after becoming prime minister on 10 July Ramos-Horta pledged to ratify the new treaty. Less than a week after he became prime minister Gary Gray, Woodside's chief lobbyist, slipped into Dili and met with him, as well as with Teixeira and other figures in the government. During his time there Gray could barely conceal his approval of the regime change. This indicates that Woodside believes it will have much less difficulty getting its preferred development plan for Sunrise approved by Dili; that is, piping the gas all the way to Darwin and processing it there. The unrest of 2006, though limited entirely to the capital, makes it all the more difficult for East Timor to push for onshore processing.

But Woodside's political antenna has misread the signals before; both Ramos-Horta and Gusmão remain resolutely convinced of the viability of piping the Sunrise gas to an LNG plant in East Timor, and the creation of a state oil company, the hallmarks of Alkatiri's nationalist economic agenda. Ramos-Horta flew to Kuwait in late July to meet a wealthy oil magnate, Sheikh Mubarak al Jabir al Sabah, and signed a Memorandum of Understanding for another study into the feasibility of building an LNG plant in East Timor. While in Kuwait Ramos-Horta stayed in Sheikh Mubarak's palace and slept in the same room as the one previously reserved for US President George W. Bush.

Upon his return Ramos-Horta received a visit from another oilman even more familiar with East Timor. Peter Cockcroft, the former BHP Petroleum executive who met with Gusmão in prison in 1998, spent two days talking to Ramos-Horta about the viability of building an LNG plant in East Timor as part of an 'energy hub' linked to other nearby gas fields. Cockcroft briefed Ramos-Horta as they travelled on windy roads to the eastern-most centre of Los Palos. Later Ramos-Horta signed him on as a well-remunerated petroleum adviser.

Cockcroft told Ramos-Horta that there was at least a 50 per cent chance of making a pipeline to an LNG plant to East Timor commercially and technically viable, and he said the country's proximity to Asian markets and other gas deposits (the Evans Shoal and Abadi fields) could help build a case for onshore development in East Timor. After independence Cockcroft worked as a pro bono adviser on petroleum issues to the president, who asked him to visit and speak to Ramos-Horta. In 2005 Cockcroft had briefed the president's advisory group, the Council of State, on these issues and he used one simple example to highlight the 'huge prize' of onshore development: had East Timor secured 100 per cent of Sunrise, Australia would still have come out in front in terms of the total economic benefit with onshore processing of the gas in Darwin. While Alkatiri had been speaking to France's Total about developing an LNG plant, Cockcroft told Ramos-Horta that East Timor was more likely to succeed if it could convince one of the potential buyers of the gas, such as a large Japanese power company, to join the project as part of a deal that involved buying Timor gas. With the buyers of the gas on board, the government could sell the concept of an East Timor LNG plant to the other joint venture partners.

* * *

Prime Minister John Howard also arrived in East Timor shortly after Ramos-Horta was sworn in as prime minister. 'I wish you well, and know you have a very good friend in Australia,' Howard told Ramos-Horta as they met on the airport tarmac. During the visit Ramos-Horta demonstrated the intimacy of their relationship when in a quiet moment he told Howard that he needed a media adviser and asked if he could help find him one. Naturally, Howard was delighted to accede to this very unexpected request. He contacted the former Liberal Party president, Shane Stone, who lived in Darwin, and asked him if he could recommend a suitable journalist. Stone suggested one of his neighbours, Julian Swinstead, a former tabloid journalist and senior Murdoch executive who was now semi-retired. The Liberal Party's international fund paid for Swinstead's salary while he worked in Ramos-Horta's office in late 2006. After accepting this generous offer Ramos-Horta appeared to be a compliant prime minister when it came to supporting Australia's interests, most notably the controversial proposal to operate independently of the UN command. But when it came to oil and gas he remained a steadfast advocate of East Timor's interests.

It was Howard's first visit to the city—now called 'Little Mogadishu' by Australian police—in more than four years, his last being for the Independence Day celebrations on 20 May 2002, when the first act of East Timor's new government was to table legislation that exercised the country's right to a 200-nautical-mile claim. During his previous visits in 1999 and 2002 Howard saw first hand the charred ruins left behind after the UN ballot, but these ruins were now joined by the results of a fresh wave of destruction.[29] Together they stand as a silent witness to the traumatic past of this new country, the unbearably slow pace of development since independence, the dearth of economic opportunities for a young, fast-growing population, the proliferation of KKN and the deep divisions after a generation of violence that were never mended. All of these factors combined to throttle the development of the world's newest nation, earning it the dubious distinction of becoming both the first nation and first failed nation of the twenty-first century. The great paradox is that this latest deadly wave of destruction and destabilisation took place immediately *after* Prime Minister Alkatiri settled the Timor Sea dispute by signing what he described as a 'win-win' for both countries.

* * *

On 20 February 2007 Woodside and the Australian government finally secured the 'title' they had been pursuing since 2002 for the development of the Greater Sunrise oil and gas field. The East Timor parliament approved on that day both the 2003 International Unitisation Agreement and the 2006 Treaty on Certain Maritime Arrangements in the Timor Sea (CMATS) with a vote of 48 in favour, five against and three abstentions in a parliament of 88 MPs. The vote indicated that some FRETILIN MPs supported the treaties, notwithstanding Alkatiri's threat to block approval. The two governments then brought the new treaty into force by an Exchange of Notes in Dili on 23 February. At this time Foreign Minister Alexander Downer wrote that he would invoke the national interest exemption and bypass the lengthy process of having the new treaty reviewed by parliament's treaties committee, the Joint Standing Committee on Treaties (JSCOT). Downer told the committee chair that East Timor had called on Australia to 'move ahead expeditiously' to bring the new treaty into force as it now had an 'opportunity to do this prior to presidential and parliamentary elections which will occur over the next few months'. Downer explained that the situation in East Timor was likely to be even more unpredictable after the 2007 elections. 'It is uncertain when an opportunity would arise after the East Timorese elections period,' he wrote.[30]

In late February public servants from DFAT, the departments of Attorney-General's and Industry made a brief appearance before the JSCOT. Kim Wilkie, the Labor MP for Swan who had grilled DFAT's deputy secretary David Ritchie in 2003 on his strategy to block, if necessary, the Bayu-Undan development, asked Bill Campbell QC to spell out what officials had really achieved in the negotiations over CMATS. Campbell appeared more than happy to explain in precise terms how the treaty meant there was no possibility of East Timor exercising any rights outside the JPDA, even in the event that a substantial resource was found in the area near Sunrise where Australia had tacitly acknowledged East Timor's rights by granting a 50 per cent share. 'You've done very well there,' Wilkie said with irony.[31]

As the agreement entered into force Australia lifted its security alert to Phase-5, its highest level, and East Timor was once again burning after the Australian military shot five of Alfredo Reinado's men in a botched raid on his base in the south coast district centre of Samé. The Australian army also shot dead two youths at Dili airport on 23 February, the same day that the treaty entered into force and the UN Security Council extended its peacekeeping mission for another twelve months. Reinado had become a popular hero after walking out of prison with 55 other escapees and surviving on the run for six months. He was a symbol of anti-government and anti-Australian sentiment in a broken country that was now pervaded by violence and hopelessness. After being warmly embraced as saviours in 1999, the raid on 4 March by elite SAS troops triggered a wave of anti-Australian sentiment, forcing the government to evacuate its non-essential personnel and urge other citizens to leave the country. The principal of Dili International School, Lyndal Barrett, said Australians were now being targeted. 'It hit home last night. My local cafe where I go for pizzas was stoned last night with all East Timorese standing out the front throwing rocks through the doors saying "Aussies go home we hate you",' Ms Barrett said.[32]

In the debate in the Australian parliament over the legislation to ratify the new treaty independent Peter Andren, the Member for Calare, touched on how the current violence was connected to the abusive foreign policy practised and perfected by Australia in its dealings with East Timor over the Timor Sea resources since 2000. Andren was possibly the parliament's most authoritative voice on East Timor, having followed events closely since October 1975. As a former television journalist with the Nine and Seven networks he had known well two of the newsmen killed at Balibo.

Political and social priorities seem to be sadly askew in East Timor and this economic rip-off adds to the cynicism among the poor.

With this treaty and this bill, we have pushed a poor developing nation into giving up half of its rightful claim to revenue from the natural resources that will ensure its future development for decades to come. Indeed, it is not too long a bow to draw to say that the deal that has been struck is instrumental in fomenting the current situation in Timor-Leste—the feeling of mistrust and of having been let down, and the feeling that they are being overlorded by a new colonial master in this whole process. Much of the blame for the unrest in Timor can be sheeted home to the feeling of complete abandonment felt by many of the people of Timor-Leste.[33]

Andren's comments echoed some of the more perceptive observations made at the height of the Timor Sea dispute, observations which were remarkably prescient. In March 2004 Senator Bob Brown told the Australian Senate's economics committee that Australia's conduct risked turning East Timor from a good friend into a 'hostile neighbour'. The following month President Gusmão warned that 'without money, democracy can fail'. Then there was the speech in the basement of St Canice's Church, Kings Cross, when Richard Woolcott intimated that Australia's treatment of East Timor in the Timor Sea dispute risked perpetuating a breakdown of governance, leading the country to become a 'failing, or a failed state'. He added: 'Australia must cooperate therefore with East Timor and Indonesia to consolidate Timor-Leste's independence and nurture its fragile institutions.'[34]

The building up of those institutions—the fabric to hold together this traumatised new nation so that it could develop and prosper—was badly neglected in the first four years after independence because the new government was forced to fight Australia's grab for Timor oil. It cannot be denied that the new government made mistakes. It visited *Animal Farm* upon the long-suffering Timorese,[35] it failed to spend the money it had available, and it mismanaged the armed forces dispute. But any new government faced with the task of building a new nation from rubble would be expected to make mistakes, especially when it did not have the support of its neighbours. East Timor only had a 50 per cent chance of survival when it became independent,[36] and the pressure applied by Australia meant that the new country really didn't stand a fighting chance. A large part of the responsibility for the mess that East Timor became rests with the Howard government, its Foreign Minister Alexander Downer and his well-groomed public service advisers.

ENDNOTES

Prologue
1. T. Mo, *The Redundancy of Courage*, Chatto and Windus, London, 1991. Timothy Mo's fictionalised documentary of idyllic pre-invasion life in Timor, political awakening and desperate struggle in the mountains begins with this paragraph: 'I don't want them forgotten: Rosa, Osvaldo, Raoul, Maria, Martinho, Arsenio. It would be easy to say in the glib way of those who can lead uninterrupted lives in placid places that such oblivion would be a fate worse than death. No fate is worse than death.'
2. Commission for Reception, Truth and Reconciliation (CAVR), *Chega! The report of the Commission for Reception, Truth, and Reconciliation Timor-Leste*, CAVR, Dili, 2005.
3. United Nations Development Programme, *Human Development Report 2004*, UNDP, New York, 2004.

Chapter 1: The great divide
1. United Nations Development Programme, *Human Development Report 2006*, UNDP, New York, 2006. Poverty line estimate from United Nations Development Programme, *Timor-Leste Human Development Report 2006*, Dili, 2006. East Timor's per capita GDP will undoubtedly increase significantly in subsequent years now that oil revenues are flowing. This will artificially inflate per capita GDP because most of it will remain in the Petroleum Fund so that the country will have a perpetual stream of income when the oil money runs out.
2. Michael Audley-Charles identified more than 30 oil and gas seeps during 28 months of fieldwork in East Timor in the 1960s. This work culminated in a PhD at London University and the book *The geology of Portuguese Timor*, Geological Society of London, London, 1968. See pp. 67–9 for a list and discussion of the seeps. A map showing the location of known seeps was produced by T. Charlton, 'The Petroleum Potential of East Timor—an oil industry consultancy report', 2002, www.manson.demon.co.uk/etreport.html.

3. F. Brennan, *The Timor Sea's Oil and Gas: What's Fair?*, Catholic Social Justice Series, Australian Catholic Social Justice Council, Sydney, 2004, p. 14.
4. 'Convention on the Continental Shelf, Done at Geneva, on 29 April 1958, Entry into Force: 10 June 1964', UNTS, No. 7302, Vol. 499, pp. 312–21.
5. R. Balint, *Troubled Waters: Borders, Boundaries and Possession in the Timor Sea*, Allen & Unwin, Sydney, 2005, p. 41.
6. 'Convention on the Continental Shelf, Done at Geneva, on 29 April 1958, Entry into Force: 10 June 1964', pp. 312–21.
7. N. Antunes, *Towards the Conceptualisation of Maritime Delimitation*, Brill, Leiden, 2003, p. 355.
8. Brennan, *The Timor Sea's Oil and Gas*, p. 16.
9. Antunes, *Towards the Conceptualisation of Maritime Delimitation*, p. 355.
10. W. McMahon, 'Ministerial Statement—Australian Practice in International Law', *Australian Yearbook of International Law*, Vol. 5, 1970–73, pp. 145–6.
11. Brennan, *The Timor Sea's Oil and Gas*, p. 16.
12. Department of Foreign Affairs, *Agreement between the Government of the Commonwealth of Australia and the Government of the Republic of Indonesia establishing Certain Seabed Boundaries in the Area of the Timor and Arafura Seas, supplementary to the Agreement of 18 May 1971 (Jakarta, 9 October 1972)*, Australian Treaty Series, 1973, No. 32, Australian Government Publishing Service, Canberra, 1995.
13. Brennan, *The Timor Sea's Oil and Gas*, p. 17.
14. Antunes, *Towards the Conceptualisation of Maritime Delimitation*, p. 57.
15. Brennan, *The Timor Sea's Oil and Gas*, p. 17.
16. M. Audley-Charles, *The geology of Portuguese Timor*, Memoir to the Geological Society of London, London, 1968, pp. 17–20.
17. C.S. Hutchison, *Geological Evolution of South-east Asia*, Clarendon Press, Oxford, 1989, p. 34.
18. Geir Ytreland, personal communication with the author, 20 February 2006. Ytreland further explained: 'The island of Timor represents the collision front between the Australian Plate and the so-called Banda Arc (basically, the Indonesian islands). This collision front (the island of Timor) sits on the northern terminus of the Australian Plate, or in this case, the North Australian Shelf. The deep water Timor Trench

[Trough] is created by the crustal shortening between Australia and Timor, approximately 3 cm per year, and the loading of a more than 3000 meter thick package of Pliocene erosional material from the uplifting Timor island during the last 3 million years. Timor Trench as such is a "continental sag", not a "subduction zone", and it does not represent any material change in geology when travelling from the JPDA northwards.

19. N. Shute, introduction to B. Callinan, *Independent Company*, William Heinemann, Melbourne, 1984, p. xxii.
20. R.R. Churchill and A.V. Lowe, *The Law of the Sea*, Manchester University Press, Yonkers, New York, Juris Publications, 1999, p. 190.
21. Interview with Dr Hasjim Djalal, 'Rich Man, Poor Man', *Four Corners*, ABC Television, 10 May 2004.
22. J.R.V. Prescott compilation, 'Australia–Indonesia (Timor and Arafura Seas)', Report Number 6–2 (2), *International Maritime Boundaries*, 1207–18, American Society of International Law, The Netherlands, 1993, pp. 1212–13.
23. Department of Foreign Affairs, *Agreement between the Government of the Commonwealth of Australia and the Government of the Republic of Indonesia establishing Certain Seabed Boundaries in the Area of the Timor and Arafura Seas, supplementary to the Agreement of 18 May 1971 (Jakarta, 9 October 1972)*, Australian Treaty Series, 1973, No. 32, Australian Government Publishing Service, Canberra, 1995.
24. J.R.V. Prescott, 'East Timor's Potential Maritime Boundaries', *The Maritime Dimensions of Independent Timor-Leste*, eds D. Rothwell and M. Tsamenyi, University of Wollongong, Wollongong, 2002, p. 89.
25. 'Boundary threat to seabed leases', *Sydney Morning Herald*, 21 December 1978, news.

Chapter 2: The spoils of conquest

1. Department of Foreign Affairs and Trade (DFAT), *Documents on Australian Foreign Policy—Australia and the Indonesian Incorporation of Portuguese Timor 1974–1976*, ed. Wendy Way, Melbourne University Press, Melbourne 2000, p. 52.
2. ibid., p. 58.
3. Interview with Alexander Downer, 'Rich Man, Poor Man', *Four Corners*, ABC Television, 10 May 2004.

4. Woolcott had already been made an Officer in the Order of Australia (AO) for services to diplomatic relations. In the Australian honours an AO is the equivalent of a knighthood and it is ranked below the AC.
5. 'Brief For Whitlam', 2 September 1974, Department of Foreign Affairs and Trade, *Documents on Australian Foreign Policy—Australia and the Indonesian Incorporation of Portuguese Timor 1974–1976*, ed. Wendy Way, Melbourne University Press, Melbourne, 2000, p. 90.
6. R. Furlonger, 'Cable to Whitlam', *DFAT 2000*, p. 94.
7. 'Record of meeting between Whitlam and Soeharto, State Guest House, Yogyakarta, 6 September 1974, 10 a.m.', *DFAT 2000*, p. 95.
8. A. Renouf, *The Frightened Country*, Macmillan, Melbourne, 1979, p. 442.
9. R. Woolcott, 'Letter from Woolcott to Whitlam', 6 September 1974, *DFAT 2000*, p. 241.
10. R. Woolcott, 'Cablegram to Canberra', 17 August 1975, *DFAT 2000*, p. 314.
11. ibid.
12. Malcolm Dan maintains that the embassy remained opposed to the use of force, and denies the charge that it became compromised by these briefings. In a letter to Gough Whitlam on 17 December 2000, in response to the release of the DFAT documents and to claims made by Desmond Ball and Hamish McDonald (see Endnote 14) he wrote: 'The Australian government's position was unequivocal. The written record makes it clear that while Australia's preferred outcome was that Portuguese Timor should eventually form part of Indonesia, this should be the result of an act of self-determination by the people of Portuguese Timor. The use of force was to be opposed'.

On the charge of having become compromised, he said: 'At no stage was the Embassy—or the Australian Government—compromised. One of our prime responsibilities as a mission was to keep the Australian Government informed well in advance of major developments. We fulfilled that task'.

M. Dan, 'Letter from Malcolm Dan', Whitlam Institute, www.whitlam.org/collection/2000/20001227_letterfrommalcolm dan/20001227_letterfrom_malcolmdan.rtf, [12 February 2006].
13. Allan Taylor's position in the Jakarta embassy was one designated for intelligence gathering. In 1998 he began a five-year term as director-general of Australia's covert spy agency, the Australian Secret Intelligence

Service, retiring from that position in February 2003. He is credited with having put ASIS on a statutory footing with the introduction of its own legislation in 2001. ASIS now has its own website: www.asis.gov.au

14. D. Ball and H. McDonald, *Death in Balibo, Lies in Canberra: Blood on Whose Hands?*, Allen & Unwin, Sydney, 2000, p. 12.
15. ibid., p. xi and p. 73.
16. See J. Jolliffe, 'Were the Balibo five nearly saved?', *Age*, 8 December 2001; and J. Fyfe-Yeomans, 'SAS Balibo '75 plan was aborted', *Daily Telegraph*, 21 December 2006.
17. A. Renouf, 'Submission to Peacock', 22 December 1975, *DFAT 2000*, p. 644.
18. 'Developments in the UN General Assembly after the invasion', *DFAT 2000*, p. 625.
19. A. Renouf, 'Submission to Fraser', 8 December 1975, *DFAT 2000*, p. 607. Renouf wrote that he understood Fraser's preference was for UN peacekeepers. Prior to the invasion Fraser had told President Soeharto in a letter delivered by Woolcott that he recognised 'the need for Indonesia to have an appropriate solution for the problem of East Timor'. These ambiguous words could have been interpreted by Indonesia as an endorsement of their invasion plans, although from Fraser's perspective they could equally have meant a proper act of self-determination.
20. R. Woolcott, 'Cablegram to Canberra', 5 January 1976, *DFAT 2000*, p. 657.
21. Record of Policy Discussion, 11 December 1974, *DFAT 2000*, p. 145.
22. Numerous cables on US policy formulation and the Soeharto meeting have now become publicly available. This record is reconstructed from a series of documents made public since 2001, including: National Security Archive, 'Ford and Kissinger gave "green light" to Indonesia of East Timor, 1975', 6 December 2001, Washington; National Security Council memo from W.R. Smyser to Henry Kissinger, 'Policy Regarding Possible Indonesian Military Action against Portuguese Timor,' 4 March 1975, Gerald Ford Library. For a good summary of the US position see D. Scott, *Last Flight out of Dili*, Pluto, North Melbourne, 2005, pp. 111–12.
23. 'Paper by Cdr R.B.M. Long', 30 May 1952, *DFAT 2000*, p. 18.
24. 'Department of Foreign Affairs News Release', 20 January 1978, *DFAT 2000*, p. 838.

25. R.J. Smith, 'Submission to Peacock', 26 April 1978, *DFAT 2000*, p. 840.
26. ibid.
27. ibid., p. 840, footnote.
28. X. Gusmão, *To Resist is to Win*, Aurora, Melbourne, 2000, p. 52, footnote.
29. ibid., p. 55.
30. The Indonesian military used Second-World-War code that could be easily intercepted by Australian signal intelligence in Shoal Bay. This began with the border incursions in October 1975 and continued throughout the Indonesian occupation.
31. Haigh had an outstanding career in the foreign ministry, where he served in Pakistan, Afghanistan, Iran, Saudi Arabia, South Africa and Sri Lanka. He was posted to South Africa in the mid-1970s during an intense period in the anti-apartheid struggle. At this time he befriended the anti-apartheid leader Steve Biko and the journalist and editor Donald Wood. Woods was 'banned' as a journalist by the South African authorities because of his writings and he escaped from South Africa. When Woods wrote about the life of Biko, who died in custody, and of his own persecution he said that an Australian correspondent had helped him escape from South Africa. The correspondent was played superbly by the gifted Australian actor Colin Hargreaves in the film *Cry Freedom*. There was just one problem—the journalist did not exist. Woods had created a cover for a diplomat who had helped him escape to Lesotho. That diplomat was Bruce Haigh who at the time of the film's release was serving at a desk in the Australian foreign ministry. See P. Daley, 'The Man Who Knew Too Much', *Age*, 3 February 1999, p. 13.
32. Bruce Haigh, personal communication with the author, 29 August 2006.
33. ibid.
34. R. Woolcott, 'Speech by Richard Woolcott at the launch of *The Timor Sea's Oil and Gas: What's Fair?*', 3 September 2004, www.uniya.org/talks/woolcott_3sep04.html.
35. Brennan, *The Timor Sea's Oil and Gas*.
36. R. Woolcott, *The Hot Seat: Reflections on Diplomacy from Stalin's Death to the Bali Bombings*, HarperCollins, Sydney, 2003.
37. R. Woolcott, 'Speech', 3 September 2004.

Chapter 3: The kelp in the coffin

1. B. Toohey and W. Pinwill, *Oyster: The Story of the Australian Secret Intelligence Service*, William Heinemann, Melbourne, 1989, p. 249; and personal communication with the author, September 2006. The Australian Security Intelligence Service is Australia's main spy agency. Equivalent to Britain's MI6 or the United States' CIA it places agents within Australian embassies around the world who have a mandate to bribe officials from the governments of their host country for information of strategic importance to Australia. The agency's base is on the fifth floor of DFAT's head office in Canberra.
2. E. Willheim, 'Australia–Indonesia Sea-Bed Boundary Negotiations: Proposals for a Joint Development Area in the "Timor Gap"', *Natural Resources Journal*, Vol. 29, 1989, p. 831.
3. P. Galbraith, 'East Timor's rights in the Timor Sea', *Maritime Studies*, Issue 118, May/June 2001, pp. 3–4.
4. Ernst Willheim, personal communication with the author, 8 March 2006.
5. *United Nations Convention on the Law of the Sea*, done at Montego Bay, Jamaica, 6–10 December 1982, p. 52. See later discussion and Endnote 25 in relation to J. Crawford who contends that the International Court of Justice (ICJ) in the case of Portugal *v.* Australia could not decide that Indonesia's presence in East Timor was unlawful. Article 74 (1) states: 'The delimitation of the exclusive economic area between States with opposite or adjacent coasts shall be effected by the agreement on the basis of international law, as referred to in Article 38 of the Statute of the International Court of Justice, in order to achieve an equitable solution.'
6. Ernst Willheim, personal communication with the author, 8 March 2006.
7. Submission cited by Brian Toohey and William Pinwill, 'Rough passage to accord on disputed sea', *Sydney Morning Herald*, 9 September 1988, p. 4.
8. *Australian*, 10 September 1988, p. 1.
9. The judgement said further: 'The Court however considers that since the development of the law enables a State to claim that the continental shelf appertaining to it extends up to as far as 200 [nautical] miles from its coast, whatever the geological characteristics of the corresponding seabed and subsoil, there is no reason to ascribe any role to geological

or geophysical factors within that distance either in verifying the legal title of the states concerned or in proceeding to a delimitation as between their claims.' ICJ Reports, *Case Concerning the Continental Shelf (Libyan Arab Jamahiriya/Malta Case)*, International Court of Justice Year 1985, 3 June 1985, p. 13, para. 39.

10. 'Timor Gap Treaty between Australia and the Republic of Indonesia on the Zone of cooperation in an area between the Indonesian Province of East Timor and Northern Australia (11 December 1989), www.atns.net.au/biogs/A002026b.htm.
11. 'Australia, Indonesia plan Timor oil search', *Sydney Morning Herald*, 28 October 1989, business section.
12. P. Keating, *Engagement: Australia faces the Asia-Pacific*, Macmillan, Melbourne 2000, pp. 129–31.
13. In R.S. Clark, 'Legality of the Timor Gap', *East Timor at the Crossroads: The Forging of a Nation*, eds Peter Carey and G. Carter Bentley, Cassell, London, 1995, p. 76.
14. J. Pilger, 'John Pilger reveals Australia's role by Bush's Sheriff', *New Statesman*, 5 April 2004, www.newstatesman.com/200404050005.
15. Clark, 'Legality of the Timor Gap', p. 76.
16. G. Evans, 1 November 1989, in Clark, p. 77.
17. J. Pilger, 'Bush's Sheriff'.
18. K. Scott, *Gareth Evans*, Allen & Unwin, Sydney, 1999, p. 260.
19. These are the forward prices used for this calculation. After 2030 the forward price is indexed at 2.5 per cent annually.

	2006	2010	2020	2030
West Texas Intermediate in 2006 derived from IEA forecast	55	40	42	44

These estimates from the US Department of Energy are conservative. They are used to derive the revenue estimates for the East Timor Budget. The oil price is linked to the liquified natural gas (LNG) in the LNG Sale and Purchase Agreement with Tokyo Electric and Tokyo Gas. This agreement sets out a formula for LNG relative to JCC, the weighted average price of all oil imported into Japan—an index quoted by the Japanese Ministry of Finance.

20. Crawford has refused to comment on the case, but in a recent article on self-determination he touched on it, saying that the ICJ's decision reflected its 'strictly bilateral' approach in contentious cases. He

criticised Portugal's reliance on the infringement of East Timor's right to self-determination because it called on the ICJ to find that the right had been violated. In fact, the 'Court could not decide that Indonesia's presence was unlawful'. He suggested that Australia's right to negotiate the treaty might have been challenged by the Court had Portugal focused on 'the obligation of states not to recognise a change in territorial sovereignty procured by the use of force'. This underscores Roger Clark's argument about the Treaty being the result of aggression that was inherently unlawful. See J. Crawford, 'Right of Self-Determination in International Law', *People's Rights*, ed. P. Alston, Oxford University Press, Oxford, 2001, pp. 33–5, and footnote 72.
21. Antunes, *Towards the Conceptualisation of Maritime Delimitation*, p. 359.
22. ICJ Reports, 'Case Concerning East Timor (Portugal *v.* Australia)', International Court of Justice, 30 June 1995, www.icj-cij.org/icjwww/icases/ipa/ipa_ijudgments/ipa_ijudgment_19950630.pdf.
23. D. Lague, 'Bid to cancel Timor Gap Treaty fails', *Sydney Morning Herald*, 1 July 1995, p. 2.
24. J. Cockcroft, *Indonesia and Portuguese Timor*, Angus and Robertson, Sydney, 1999.
25. D. Jenkins, 'BHP talks to jailed E Timor leader', *Sydney Morning Herald*, 20 August 1998, Sydney, p. 28.
26. I. Howarth, 'BHP makes $110m on Timor', *Australian Financial Review*, 14 April 1999, p. 19.
27. G. Earl, 'Gusmão assures Gap treaty is safe', *Australian Financial Review*, 27 February 1999, p. 6.
28. C. Fernandes, *Reluctant Saviour*, Scribe, Melbourne, 2004, pp. 58–9. Major Clinton Fernandes served in the army's intelligence core in the late 1990s. He was part of a group of officials, including former Lieutenant Colonel Lance Collins, investigated for the alleged leaking of information about East Timor. The then captain Fernandes was suspended. When he was eventually re-instated he was moved into personnel, where he's remained ever since. Major Fernandes' book is the result of a PhD. It is an insightful and controversial analysis of the strategy behind Australia's involvement in the events of 1999. He complained to the Inspector General of the Defence Force that the army had used intimidation and harassment to try to stop him turning his army-approved PhD into a book because it was critical of the

government. Professor Tony Coady supplied a letter as part of Major Fernandes' successful move to overturn the censure stating that the claims of possible breaches of national security laws amounted to nothing.
29. ibid., p. 64.
30. Andrew Caddy, managing director, finance, Timor Sea Designated Authority (TSDA), personal communication with the author, 14 February 2006. Caddy began working for the joint authority in 2000 at the time when the UN took over from Indonesia.
31. Nick Kyranis, managing director, technical, TSDA, personal communication with the author, 26–9 January 2006. Kyranis is the only former executive of the former Australia–Indonesia Timor Gap Authority now working for the East Timor–Australia joint authority—the TSDA. He has an encyclopaedic knowledge of the history of Timor Sea oil and gas.

Chapter 4: The get-out-of-gaol card

1. In 1996 the US Senate Select Committee on Intelligence held an inquiry into 'US actions regarding Iranian and other Arms Transfers to the Bosnian Army, 1994–95'. This followed a report on 5 April 1996 in the *Los Angeles Times* which said: 'President Clinton secretly gave a green light to covert Iranian arms shipments into Bosnia in 1994 despite a United Nations arms embargo that the United States was pledged to uphold and the administration's own policy of isolating Tehran globally as a supporter of terrorism.' Galbraith earned a special mention in the committee report for having indicated that Croatia should not block the shipment. 'The interchange between the United States Ambassador to Croatia and the President of Croatia in April 1994 did not constitute traditional diplomatic activity, at least as that term is understood by most Americans.' Senate Select Committee on Intelligence, 'Special Report', 4 January 1995–October 3, 1996.
2. Obituary, 'John Kenneth Galbraith', *The Economist*, 6 May 2006, p. 82.
3. During his stay in East Timor Galbraith's style became legendary. He once walked in on a meeting of advisers who were trying to fix a badly drafted defence law, and the complaints put him on the defensive. Galbraith argued that the law would not be ready in time if there were changes. He told the group that he had been working in the US Senate for 20 years and in his view the draft was fine, and he finished with this

compelling argument: 'Why do you worry so much if the law is well written or not? Once the US budget was published with the contents of a notebook and a list of phone numbers which were left with the draft by mistake. You can always change it later!'

4. P. Galbraith, *The end of Iraq: How American incompetence created a war without end*, Simon and Schuster, New York, 2006.
5. J. Morrow and R. White, 'The United Nations in Transitional East Timor: International Standards and the Reality of Governance', *Australian Yearbook of International Law*, Vol. 22, p. 26. They added: 'The clear expectation within the Australian Government was that the UN ought not be partisan as against one of its member states, Australia.'
6. D. Lague, 'Timor plea to revise oil treaty', *Sydney Morning Herald*, 8 May 2000, p. 7.
7. Speech to APEA Conference, Hobart. Published as P. Galbraith, 'East Timor's rights in the Timor Sea', *Maritime Studies*, No. 118, May/June 2001.
8. Jonathan Morrow, personal communication with the author, January 2006.
9. G. Barker, 'Bubbly and baby Gusmão celebrate Timor agreement', *Financial Review*, 6 July 2001, p. 8.
10. The International Court of Justice is the principal judicial organ of the United Nations, and its seat is at the Peace Palace in The Hague, The Netherlands. It is also known as the World Court. ITLOS is based in Hamburg, Germany.
11. International Tribunal for the Law of the Sea, *Order of 27 August 1999: Southern Bluefin Tuna Cases*, Hamburg, 1999.
12. T. Clifton, 'Fields of Dreams', *The Monthly*, July 2005, p. 37.
13. A. Downer, 'Changes to International Dispute Resolution', Media Release, Canberra, 25 March 2002.
14. A. Downer, 'Declaration', Canberra, 21 March 2002.
15. H. McDonald, 'Timor gas billions at sea', *Sydney Morning Herald*, 27 March 2003, p. 1.
16. V. Lowe, C. Carleton and C. Ward, 'Opinion In the Matter of East Timor's Maritime Boundaries', unpublished, 11 April 2002, para. 38–42.
17. A. Harding, 'E. Timor Struggles to Find its Feet', BBC, 20 May 2004, http://news.bbc.co.uk/2/hi/asia-pacific/3731475.stm [18 March 2007].

18. D. Greenlees, 'Leaders hint at Legal Push for Bigger Share of Seabed Riches', *Australian*, 21 May 2002, Sydney, p. 6.
19. ibid.

Chapter 5: Animal farm
1. Gusmão, *To Resist is to Win*, p. 47, Gusmão notes that FRETILIN turned to Marxism when they were on the run from the Indonesians in the mountains. He records a meeting of the Central Committee in May 1977 when 'Marxism was acclaimed'. Prior to the invasion there were some prominent anti-communists in FRETILIN.
2. H. Hill, *Stirrings of Nationalism in East Timor: FRETILIN 1974–76*, Otford Press, Sydney, 2002, p. 172.
3. Report of the United Nations Special Commission of Inquiry for Timor-Leste, Geneva, 2006, p. 18.
4. Morgan Mellish inspired this description of the president's pink palace in a column he wrote after a visit to Dili in July 2006. 'UN Efforts Amount to Castles in the Air', *Financial Review*, 26 July 2006, p. 20. Mellish, the *Financial Review*'s Jakarta correspondent, was killed in the crash of Garuda flight 200 in Yogyakarta on 7 March 2007. The author had worked with Mellish and also met him during his visit to Dili. The author briefed him on the Timor Sea dispute and other petroleum issues over dinner at the Esplanada Hotel. Mellish, a keen surfer, was unexpectedly impressed with what he saw of East Timor, the beaches, sunshine and fresh air, especially coming from his base in Jakarta. The author wasn't completely forthcoming, however, as some information had to be kept for this book. One fact withheld was that the Woodside lobbyist Gary Gray was in Dili on a secret visit to meet with senior members of the government. But this wasn't to be missed by Mellish, who called the next morning to say he knew Gray was in town. Before leaving he called to say goodbye and said emphatically that East Timor's oil revenue was like a giant 'honey pot' that was destined to be siphoned off by the elite, and that he would uncover this story.
5. Noam Chomsky, 'Forward', in *Masters of Terror*, Indonesia's military and violence in East Timor, R. Tanter, G. van Klinken, and D. Ball (eds), Rowman & Littlefield, Lanham, 2006, p. ix.
6. One Australian-educated minister, when discussing a proposed aid project in the sub-district of Natabora on the remote south coast, said he knew the locals well and described them as a 'lazy bunch of shits'.

Some months later the author travelled to Natabora for a petroleum sector briefing and found that several village chiefs and other community leaders had walked for three hours or more to attend the briefing. At some briefings around East Timor village chiefs walked for up to five hours, which meant a five-hour walk home. One village chief in the south coast sub-district of Uato Karabau walked for four hours on crutches to attend a briefing, but was offered a lift home in a vehicle afterwards.
7. For a gripping account of this history see R. Kapuscinski, *The Shadow of the Sun*, Knopf, New York, 1998. Kapuscinski reported on Africa for over four decades after first being posted there in 1957.
8. J. Joliffe, 'Businessman in Dili jail despite illegal arrest win', *Age*, 31 May 2003, p. 21.

Chapter 6: Tutorials in politics
1. 'Agreement between the Government of the Democratic Republic of Timor-Leste and the Government of Australia relating to the unitisation of the Sunrise and Troubadour fields', 6 March 2003, www.timorseaoffice.gov.tp/iua.htm.
2. M. Clark, *The Quest for Grace*, Penguin, Melbourne, 1990, p. 15.
3. P. Keating, 'A Time for Reflection: Political Values in The Age of Distraction', Manning Clark Lecture, National Library of Australia, Canberra, 3 March 2002, http://www.keating.org.au/main.cfm [18 March 2007].
4. G. Raby, 'Hearings on the Timor Sea Treaty', Joint Standing Committee on Treaties, Parliament House, Canberra, 14 October 2002.
5. Downer has released two white papers with the words 'national interest' in the title. The first was 'In the National Interest—Australia's foreign and trade policy: white paper', Commonwealth of Australia, 1997; and more recently 'Advancing the National Interest: Australia's foreign and trade policy white paper,' Commonwealth of Australia, 2003.
6. M. Baker, 'East Timor bows to PM on gas', *Age*, 6 March 2003, p. 2.
7. R. Brown, 'Consideration of Legislation', *Debates*, Senate, 6 March 2003, p. 9371.
8. J. Howard, 'Personal Explanation', *Debates*, House of Representatives, 6 March 2003, p. 12437. The comments by Brown were in fact made on the same day as this statement, not the previous day as stated by Howard.

9. The defendants made oral pleadings in February 2005 for the court to dismiss the claims, and in March and April filed motions to dismiss it.
10. Oceanic Exploration Co., 'Form 10QSB for OCEANIC EXPLORATION CO', Securities and Exchange Commission, 13 March 2006.
11. Platts Commodity News, 'US court lets stand Timor Sea "RICO" case against ConocoPhillips', September 26, 2006. A spokeperson for ConocoPhillips said: 'At the outset, ConocoPhillips would like to set the record straight by making it absolutely clear that it categorically denies the allegations of wrong-doing made by Oceanic/Petrotimor. Currently, ConocoPhillips is defending against the third incarnation of Oceanic/Petrotimor's specious claims. Oceanic/Petrotimor lost its first case in the Australian federal court system. After striking out there, Oceanic/Petrotimor filed its second complaint in the U.S. court system. This complaint was rejected by the U.S. court, which noted that there was a disturbing inconsistency between what Petrotimor claimed in the complaint and what it argued to the court. The court therefore directed Oceanic/Petrotimor to attempt to correct its defective pleading. Oceanic/Petrotimor's attempt to correct its defective pleading is its third try at suing ConocoPhillips or its affiliates'. Robin Antrobus, personal communication with the author, 19 September 2006.
12. See estimates from ABARE (the Australian government's commodity analyst) at www.abare.gov.au; and D. Ryan (from the WA Department of Industry and Resources) 'Stranded Gas—Western Australian Energy for the Future', address to 19th World Energy Conference, Sydney, 5–9 September 2004, www.worldenergy.org/wec-geis/congress/papers/ryand0904.pdf#search='goodwyn%20and%20north%20rankin%20and%20tcf'.
13. K. Schneider, presentation to the SEAAOC 2004 conference, 9 June 2004.
14. S. Lewis and N. Wilson, 'Christmas Deadline on gas deal', *Australian*, 29 July 2004, p. 1.

Chapter 7: The creative solution

1. Sighted by the author in December 2005. The bags were kept behind a temporary office in the backyard of the embassy compound.
2. Nuno Antunes' PhD was published as *Towards the Conceptualisation of Maritime Delimitation*.

3. I. Brownlie, 'Email to Ambassador Peter W. Galbraith', 30 April 2001, Blackstone Chambers, Temple, London.
4. J. Dowd, 'Whose oil is it anyway? Sovereign rights and international law in the Timor Gap dispute', address to the Lowy Institute for International Affairs, 20 July, Sydney.
5. Lowe, Carleton and Ward, 'Opinion In the Matter of East Timor's Maritime Boundaries', para. 40–41.
6. Antunes, *Towards the Conceptualisation of Maritime Delimitation*, p. 399.
7. Brennan, *The Timor Sea's Oil and Gas*, p. 31.
8. A. Downer, 'Australia's Sovereign Rights', letter to *Wall Street Journal*, 25 June 2004, opinion page.
9. The author led this discussion and outlined a campaign strategy with a strong international focus.
10. N. Wilson, 'No timetable for E Timor boundary', *Australian*, 11 November 2003, p. 18.
11. M. Alkatiri, 'Letter to Prime Minister Howard', 27 November 2003.

Chapter 8: The reluctant president
1. Australian Embassy Dili, 'Letter to Timor-Leste Foreign Ministry', No. 259/2003, DL003/00064, 8 December 2003.
2. V. da Costa Pinto, 'Letter to Angelo Mustica, Joint Venture Co-ordinator, BHP Billiton Petroleum', 16 January 2004, Ministry of Development and Environment, Department of Mineral Resources and Energy Policy, Dili, Timor-Leste. The same letter was sent to other joint venture partners.
3. The Greater Sunrise Unitisation Agreement Implementation Bill 2004, The Customs Tariff Amendment (Greater Sunrise) Bill 2004, Parliament House, Canberra, 2004.
4. M. Alkatiri, 'Australia is Undermining Sunrise Agreement', press release, Timor Sea Office, Dili, 21 March 2004.
5. M. Alkatiri, 'Timor-Leste Protests Unlawful Exploitation of its Resources', press release, Timor Sea Office, Dili, 30 March 2004.
6. N. Wilson, 'Release Taunts E Timor', *Australian*, 30 March 2004, p. 27.
7. G. Triggs and D. Bialek, 'The new Timor Sea Treaty and Interim Arrangements for the Joint Development of Petroleum Resources in the Timor Gap', *Melbourne Journal of International Law*, 3, 2002, p. 349.

8. This came out of a strategy discussion with the author, Dili, November 2003.
9. Helen Hill wrote in *Stirrings of Nationalism in East Timor*, pp. xii–xiii, 'Although Xanana was present in 1975 he was not among the well-known leaders observed by outsiders.'
10. *Maubere* is a Timorese word for the ordinary people, the Australian equivalent of 'battlers'.
11. Gusmão, *To Resist is to Win*, pp. 31–2.
12. J. Steele, 'Anger in East Timor as Australia plays tough over gas reserves', *Guardian*, 14 October 2003, www.guardian.co.uk.
13. M. L'Estrange, 'Oil deal is a winner for East Timor', *Guardian*, 20 October 2003, www.guardian.co.uk.
14. M. Davis, 'The Timor Gap', *Dateline*, SBS, 21 April 2004.
15. A. Roberts, 'E Timor slams Australian attitude', BBC News, 23 April 2004, news.bbc.co.uk/2/hi/asia-pacific/3651837.stm [18 March 2007].
16. Associated Press, 'East Timor president rebukes Australia over oil dispute', 27 April 2004.
17. P. Hartcher, 'Gusmão lashes out over oil rights', *Sydney Morning Herald*, 25 May 2004, p. 1.
18. R. Brown, Senate Economics Legislation Committee, *Official Hansard*, Parliament House, Canberra, 22 March 2004, p. E10.

Chapter 9: The secret envoy
1. Congress of the United States, 'Letter to Prime Minister John Howard', 5 March 2004, www.etan.org/news/2004/03houseltr.htm#letter.
2. Interview with G. Triggs, 'Rich Man, Poor Man', *Four Corners*, ABC Television, 10 May 2004.
3. Statement by S. Marks, International Commission of Jurists—Australian section, 'Timor Gap Dispute', 22 April 2004.
4. B. Campbell and C. Moraitis, 'Memorandum of Advice to the Commonwealth Government on the Use of Force Against Iraq, *Melbourne Journal of International Law*, Vol. 4, pp. 178–82.
5. D. Bialek, 'Submission to the Joint Standing Committee on Treaties—Review of Treaties, Timor Sea Treaties,' Parliament House, Canberra, 2002, p. 4.
6. ibid., p. 5.
7. ibid., pp. 5–6.

8. T. Dusevic, 'Hands off my petroleum!', Time, 10 May 2004, pp. 42–5.
9. T. Mapes and P. Barta, 'Deep Division—For East Timor, Energy Riches Lie Just Out of Reach', *Wall Street Journal*, 25 June 2004, p. 1.
10. J. Ramos-Horta, 'Letters to the Editor—Creating Myths About East Timor', the Asian Wall St Journal, 5 July 2004, p. A9.
11. J. Holmes and M. Ramsay, 'Rich Man, Poor Man', *Four Corners*, ABC Television, 10 May 2004.
12. Bruce Haigh, personal communication with the author, 29 August 2006. These sentiments came through in the internet chat session that followed the *Four Corners* program. One viewer made the point that Australia was now practising American-style foreign policy by seeking to create dependencies. The contribution from 'OzzieJak', called 'Have we sunk this low?', expressed the extremes of pride and disappointment felt by many Australians about their government's intervention in 1999 and subsequent dealings over the Timor Sea. 'OzzieJak' wrote: 'Some time ago a friend of mine described the difference between Australian and American foreign relations. He said that Australia would assist another country in trouble and help them until they were back on their feet and then get out. The Americans, on the other hand, would help a country out in the same way. The difference was that the Americans would tie up the financial structures and impose trade deals that benefited American businesses and disadvantaged the country they were assisting. I felt proud that Australia assisted East Timor. I am appalled by the actions of the Australian Govt in relation to the East Timor Sea Treaty. I am now ashamed to be an Australian in relation to this matter.'
13. Editorial, 'Don't leave Timor before job is done', *Australian*, 6 January 2004, p. 8. The Australian government has since pledged to 'double' Australia's aid program, but this is in nominal terms. As a share of national income it will still be around half the UN target, and this follows 15 years of continuous economic growth. It usually follows that when the economy turns down, one of the first programs to be cut is foreign aid.
14. Interview with Alexander Downer, 'Rich Man, Poor Man'.
15. R. Ackland, 'Ungrateful Timor gets the Downer treatment', *Sydney Morning Herald*, 28 May 2004, p. 15.
16. N. Wilson, 'Bedevilled in the Timor Sea', *Australian*, 29 May 2004, Inquirer section.
17. ibid.

18. D. Shanahan, 'Tough stance pushes the boundaries of goodwill with Dili', *Australian*, 28 May 2004, p. 13.
19. C. Pearson, 'How to strike political crude,' *Australian*, 31 July 2004, Inquirer section.
20. 'Estimates (Additional Budget Estimates)', *Senate Standing Committee on Foreign Affairs, Defence and Trade*, Canberra, 15 February 2007, pp. 58–60.
21. Federal Australian Labor Party, 'National Platform and Constitution 2004, As Adopted at the 43rd National Conference, Sydney 29 January–31 January 2004', p. 229, www.alp.org.au/download/now/platform_2004.pdf [13 January 2007].
22. M. Latham, radio interview with Neil Marks, 2LM, 22 July 2004.
23. D. Shanahan and N. Wilson, 'Latham "threat" to East Timor', *Australian*, 28 July 2004, p. 1.
24. Editorial, 'Latham throws oil on troubled Timor talks,' *Australian*, 28 July 2004, opinion page.
25. Oxfam/Community Aid Abroad, 'Two years on . . . What future for an independent East Timor?' Melbourne, 20 May 2004, www.oxfam.org.au/campaigns/submissions/easttimortwoyearson.pdf.
26. The author was present at this meeting.
27. P. Hartcher, 'Gusmão lashes out over oil rights', *Sydney Morning Herald*, 25 May 2004, p. 1.

Chapter 10: The consummate diplomat

1. Office of the Secretary of Department of Parliamentary Services, and the Parliament House Pass Office, February 2006.
2. A. Downer, 'Doorstop, Mayo Electorate Office', 27 April 2004.
3. A. de Jesus Soares, 'Listen to the Voices of East Timor's Victims', the *International Herald Tribune*, 10 August 2005, opinion page.
4. J. Ramos-Horta, 'Address to the Lowy Institute for International Policy', 29 November 2004.
5. R. Holbrooke, 'The Next S-G', *Washington Post*, 3 February 2006, p. A19.
6. J. Dunn, *Timor: A People Betrayed*, first published by Jacaranda, Brisbane, 1982; re-released after 1999 as *East Timor: A Rough Passage to Independence*, Longueville, 2003. Dunn was sidelined in DFA as a result of his support for East Timor independence. He spent the rest of his career working in the parliamentary library. His contribution

was recognised, however, by Australia and Portugal. In 2001 he was invested as a member in the Order of Australia and in 2002 the President of Portugal, Jorge Sampaio, conferred the honour of Grand Official of the Order of Prince Henry the Navigator.
7. Hill, *Stirrings of Nationalism*, p. 64.
8. Fernandes, *Reluctant Saviour*, p. 29. Pead had been counsellor in the Australian embassy in Jakarta—the same position held by Allan Taylor in 1975—at the time of the Santa Cruz massacre in 1991. She had tried to produce evidence of Timorese 'provocation' in an attempt to deflect international condemnation of Indonesia. Back in Canberra she headed the Southeast Asia branch of DFAT and led a delegation to the newly launched satellite service of the ABC, a public broadcaster, where she advised against focusing on East Timor.
9. S. Powell, 'E Timor sniping "damaging"', *Australian*, 22 May 2004, p. 14.
10. The author was the adviser.
11. The author was with Teixeira when he took the call.
12. Teixeira's record of the 11 August meeting.
13. ibid.
14. Brereton called the author, who was also rattled by these approaches.
15. P. Galbraith, 'Iraq: Bush's Islamic Republic', *New York Review of Books*, Vol. 52, No. 13, 11 August 2005, www.nybooks.com.
16. Gusmão, *To Resist it to Win*, p. 22, footnotes 31, 68. Gusmão says the executions reportedly took place on Christmas day and were carried out without the consent of President Lobato. Gusmão also indicates that Fernandes executed UDT prisoners during the August–September civil war, see p. 32: 'Alarico Fernandes and, later, Hermenegildo Alves were real executioners with a frenzied thirst for vengeance.'
17. ibid., p. 23.
18. G. Richardson, *Whatever It Takes*, Bantam, Sydney, 1994.

Chapter 11: People power
1. R. Mutton, 'Girl, 12, Chokes to Death on Worms', *Age*, 8 May 2004, p. 19.
2. D. Greenlees and P. Garran, *Deliverance: The inside story of East Timor's fight for freedom*, Allen & Unwin, Sydney, 2002. p. 245.
3. Fernandes, *Reluctant Saviour*, p. 95.

Endnotes

4. The origins of this lobby in Australia go back to the time of Indonesia's invasion of East Timor. Labor MP John Kerin, who later became Minister for Primary Industries and then Treasurer in the Hawke Government, had visited Dili as part of a parliamentary delegation in March 1975 and opposed Whitlam's policy. He had been feuding with Graham Feakes, the head of DFA's Southeast Asia branch, whom he labelled a leading member of the 'Indonesia lobby'. At the time when the newsmen were known to be missing in East Timor Kerin met Feakes at a cocktail reception and asked 'if everything was going according to plan'. The comment led to a heated altercation. See Ball and Mc Donald, *Death in Balibo*, p. 126.
5. 'Suharto tops corruption rankings', BBC News, 25 March 2004, news.bbc.co.uk/2/hi/business/3567745.stm. Transparency International said in its *Global Corruption Report*, that Soeharto's alleged haul was US$15–US$35 billion during 31 years of rule.
6. K. Scott, *Gareth Evans*, p. 252.
7. The author was awarded an AII fellowship in 2001.
8. There were two bills, the first the Customs Tariff Amendment Bill (2004), and the second the Sunrise Unitisation Agreement Implementation Bill (2004).
9. D. Nicholson, Senate Economics Legislation Committee, *Official Committee Hansard*, 22 March 2004, p. E5.
10. Bugalski later wrote an excellent legal paper on the dispute: N. Bugalski, 'Beneath the sea: Determining a maritime boundary for Australia and East Timor,' *Alternative Law Journal*, 29, 6, December 2004, pp. 289–98.
11. Carr had meant to refer to resources spokesman Joel Fitzgibbon. *Hansard* may have made an error although Carr's office failed to correct it.
12. K. Carr, 'Consideration of Legislation', *Debates*, Senate, 24 March 2004, p. 21777.
13. Written communication with the author, March 2007.

Chapter 12: The brainstorming trap
1. This figure was based on actual oil prices at the time, with the West Texas Intermediate forward curve indexed for inflation at 2.5 per cent from 2010. It valued the 81.91 per cent share of Sunrise at US$14 billion, plus Australia's 10 per cent share in the JPDA at US$2.7 billion for the BCL fields and US$2.9 billion for unknown prospects.

2. Evidence presented to Joint Standing Committee on Treaties, 'Hearings on the Timor Sea Treaty', Parliament House, Canberra, 3 October 2002.
3. Lucon A/S (Tanager, Norway), 'Pipeline Crossing of Timor Trench—Review of "Timor-Leste Gas Export Pipeline Feasibility Study", prepared for the Ministry of Development and Environment', Timor-Leste, 15 October 2004.
4. Author's record of meeting.

Chapter 13: The breakdown

1. T. Allard, 'Gas Plant Must be on Our Soil: Timor', *Sydney Morning Herald*, 26 October 2004, p. 4. Teixeira called the author on the Sunday afternoon and said we should float the pipeline idea in the media. This was consistent with what Alkatiri had said in his instructions for the meeting, although the strategy had not been discussed with the group as a whole.
2. A. Downer, radio interview with Jeremy Cordeaux, 5DN, 26 October 2004.
3. Mendonça was one of the few surviving child soldiers of the intensive years of fighting from 1975–79. He fled to the mountains at the age of nine with his parents and 14 brothers and sisters. His father, a Timorese veteran of Portugal's colonial wars in Africa, was one of the FALINTIL's hardcore who had shown the Timorese how to fight against overwhelming odds. His father went missing in action in July 1978 and throughout the course of this war Mendonça lost 12 brothers and sisters. He and his 16-year-old brother were part of a major surrender instigated by Gusmão in 1980. His brother was taken away by the Indonesian military and never seen again. Mendonça, who was small for his age, was considered too young to have been a combatant. But not all of his extended family who died in the war was killed by the Indonesian military. A photograph in the book by James Dunn, *Timor: A People Betrayed*, ABC Books, shows a headstone over the grave of 14 people from his extended family. All but one was killed on the same day—17 June 1977. The caption reads, 'The grave a family wiped out within the space of three years.' The book infers that the family was killed by Indonesians; on the opposite page are photographs of Indonesian soldiers. When asked about the photograph Mendonça explained that his relatives were executed by the FRETILIN leadership because they

had wanted to surrender. Schooled in the Indonesian system throughout the 1980s, he returned to the mountains after taking a bullet in his leg in the Santa Cruz massacre in 1991. Later he was captured, tortured and beaten, which left most of his ribs broken. There was a silver lining to these events—he met his wife while recovering from his wounds. Moraitis, who had travelled to East Timor in 1999, remembered meeting Mendonça when he came out of the cantonment after the landing of InterFET and greeted him warmly. Mendonça's job in the Timor Sea Office involved travelling all over East Timor to give briefings to village chiefs and other community leaders on the Timor Sea Treaty, the current negotiations and the government's plans to develop the nation's petroleum resources. During his years in the mountains he'd played a similar role mobilising support for the resistance. Timothy Mo's *The Redundancy of Courage* gives an excellent account of the contribution to the struggle in the mountains made by the Timorese veterans from Portugal's colonial wars in Africa and the FALINTIL's military campaign generally in the mountains.

4. C. Scheiner, 'The Case for Saving Sunrise', paper submitted to the Timor-Leste government, 28 July 2004, www.etan.org/lh/misc/04 sunrise.html [13 March 2006]. Chester asked the author and Mendonça about this publication.
5. Recording of the Chester briefing obtained by the author.
6. ibid.
7. M. Alkatiri, 'Statement by Timor-Leste Prime Minister on Timor Sea talks', Dili, 27 October 2004.
8. M. Alkatiri, 'All East Timor seeks is a fair go', *Age*, 3 November 2004, p. 17.
9. A. Downer, I. Macfarlane, D. Williams, Joint Statement, 'Australia lodges continental shelf submission', Canberra, 16 November 2004.
10. Commonwealth of Australia, 'Submission by Australia', Oceans and Law of the Sea, Commission on the Limits of the Continental Shelf (CLCS), New York, 15 November 2004, www.un.org/Depts/los/clcs_new/submissions_files/submission_aus.htm [3 March 2006].
11. Commission on the Limits of the Continental Shelf, 'Statement by the Chairman of the Commission on the Limits of the Continental Shelf on the progress of work in the Commission', 7 October 2005, New York, pp. 6 and 16.

12. Government of Timor-Leste, 'Timor-Leste Position Paper on the Australian Submission to the CLCS', Oceans and Law of Sea, Commission on the Limits of the Continental Shelf, New York, 11 February 2005.
13. J. Ensor, 'Coalition stretches credibility with Australia's elastic borders', *Sydney Morning Herald*, 27 November 2003, opinion page.

Chapter 14: Calling in the commandos

1. Ramos-Horta, 'Address to the Lowy Institute'.
2. Mark Colvin, 'Australia, East Timor relations at historic low: Horta', *PM*, ABC Radio, 29 November 2004.
3. Confidential summary obtained by the author.
4. Department of Foreign Affairs and Trade, 'Background briefing by DFAT senior officials on Timor Sea Issues', Canberra, 24 February 2005.
5. As Chester complained bitterly about East Timor's briefing of the media and NGOs on the negotiations it was agreed that the author should stay out of meetings in order to placate him and allow the negotiations to move forward. This was the second time that DFAT signalled that they were intercepting East Timor's communications. At the opening of the talks in Dili on 25 October 2004 Chester said words to the effect, 'I hope you all enjoyed the federal election and that some of you made money on it'. This seemed a very odd point to include in an opening statement, and it could only be linked to the fact that, during the election campaign, one member of the East Timor delegation had logged onto a betting website with the intention of putting a bet on the election outcome, although the bet was not made. The intercepting of the communications of Australian citizens is not restricted to cases where national security is at risk. Rules for intelligence monitoring approved by Downer on 25 October 2001 permit such interception under the *Intelligence Services Act 2001* for the purpose of 'maintaining Australia's economic well-being'. See A. Downer, 'Rules to Protect the Privacy of Australians', Parliament House, Canberra, 25 October 2001, which can be found on the ASIS website, www.asis.gov.au.
6. Author's record of the meeting.
7. ibid.

8. H. Frei, 'Japan's Reluctant Decision to Occupy Portuguese Timor, 1 January 1942–20 February 1942', *Australian Historical Studies*, Number 107, October 1996, p. 281.
9. 'Fighting in Timor', *Australians at War*, Australian War Memorial, Canberra, http://www.awm.gov.au/atwar/timor.htm [14 March 2007].
10. B. Callinan, *Independent Company*, William Heinemann, Melbourne, 1984, first published 1953.
11. J. Dunn, *Timor: A people betrayed*, p. 19. These figures should be considered as rough estimates provided by individuals who served in East Timor. They have not been repeated in the Australian War Memorial's official history of the East Timor campaign.
12. By wiping out livestock, particularly buffalo, the Japanese were in effect destroying the life savings of families and villages, a devastating setback for these people that took a generation to reverse. The Indonesian army also wantonly destroyed livestock when they departed East Timor in 1999.
13. R. Coyne in *Debt of Honour*, Let's Play Productions and Australian Film Commission, 2005.
14. Callinan, *Independent Company*, p. 216.
15. ibid., p. 227.
16. Report quoted in Dunn, *Timor: A people betrayed*, pp. 21–23.
17. ibid., p. 22.
18. Hill, *Stirrings of Nationalism*, p. ix.
19. Written communication with the author, March 2007.
20. M. Dodd, 'Americans unmoved by E Timor bomb alert', *Australian*, 12 May 2005, p. 2.
21. 'Cabinet to consider East Timor gas deal', www.smh.com.au, 30 May 2005.
22. M. Dodd, 'Timor PM Link to Arms Contract', *Australian*, 7 July 2005, p. 1.

Chapter 15: Independence day minus 1

1. S. Donnan and L. Colquhon, 'East Timor says no energy deal with Australia yet', *Financial Times*, 17 May 2005, www.ft.com.
2. J. Ramos-Horta, 'The shape of a fair deal for East Timor', *Age*, 30 May 2005, p. 19.
3. P. Ellis, 'Letter to Mr Joao Pequinho, director, Forum Tau Matan', 7 June 2005, Australian Embassy, Dili.

4. Statement by the 13 NGOs, 'AusAID "Blacklists" East Timor NGOs over Timor Sea Comments', Dili, 14 November 2005.
5. Senate Foreign Affairs, Defence and Trade Legislation Committee, *Official Committee Hansard*, Parliament House, Canberra, 3 November 2005, p. 85.
6. ibid.
7. Statement issued by NGO Forum, 27 October 2004.
8. Statement issued by NGO Forum, 29 September 2004.
9. Pam Thomas, personal communication with the author, 13 February 2006.
10. M. Alkatiri, 'Joint Press Conference', Commonwealth Government Offices, Sydney, 12 January 2006.
11. ibid.
12. These conservative estimates are based on the same oil price assumptions as those used earlier, with the 2006 price of US$55 a barrel and a forward price after 2030 of US$44 a barrel, indexed at 2.5 per cent per annum.
13. Antunes, *Towards the Conceptualisation of Maritime Delimitation*, p. 399.
14. These estimates from the Norwegian central bank have been converted from krone at 0.157 to one US dollar. In early 2006 the Norwegian government converted the assets of the Petroleum Fund into the Government Pension Fund. See www.norges-bank.noenglish.

Chapter 16: From ashes to ashes
1. Interview with the author, July 2006. Taur Matan Ruak says that he was approached to stage a coup, though he has declined to name who made the approach. See J. Martinkus, 'Of Coup Plots and Shadowy Figures, *New Zealand Herald*, 22 June 2006. This claim is corroborated by Australian military advisers working on the defence cooperation program in East Timor.
2. September 2005 study of the construction sector by an international aid agency. Obtained by the author on a confidential basis.
3. Report of the United Nations Special Commission of Inquiry for Timor Leste, Geneva, 2006.
4. United Nations Office Timor-Leste media summary, March 18–20, 2006.
5. 'Sacking of nearly 600 troops "unfair and wrong"—President Gusmão', LUSA news agency, 23 March 2006.
6. Report of the United Nations, p. 23.
7. ibid., p. 24.

8. ibid., p. 26.
9. Briefing to journalists at Hotel Timor, 18 May 2006.
10. 'Stoking the Fires', *Four Corners*, ABC Television, 19 June 2006.
11. Report of the United Nations, p. 38.
12. ibid., p. 39.
13. ibid., p. 7.
14. ibid., p. 40.
15. ibid., p. 63.
16. L. Murdoch, 'Alkatiri Lashes Australia Over Bias', *Sydney Morning Herald*, 6 July 2006, p. 12.
17. M. Dodd and S. Fitzpatrick, 'Conspiracy theory haunts East Timor', *Australian*, 15 July 2006, p. 28.
18. Interview with the author, Dili, 26 November 2006.
19. L. Murdoch, 'Alkatiri to sue ABC for role in his downfall', *Age*, 7 February 2007, p. 12.
20. Interview with M. Alkatiri, *Dateline*, SBS Television, 30 August 2006.
21. M. Dodd and P. Walters, 'Aussies Take Control in Dili', *Australian*, 27 May 2006.
22. R. Dalton and S. Powell, 'UN, Dili fight Canberra push to replace peacekeepers with police', *Australian*, 20 February 2004, p. 2.
23. L. Oakes, 'The Desertion of Dili', *Bulletin*, 13 June 2006, p. 16.
24. K. Rudd, 'Canberra withdrew too early', *Australian*, 15 June 2006, p. 12.
25. R. Dalton and S. Powell, 'UN, Dili fight Canberra push to replace peacekeepers with police', *Australian*, 20 February 2004, p. 2.
26. P. Costello, 'Joint Press Conference with the Hon. Trevor Manuel MP South African Finance Minister, Grand Hyatt Hotel, Melbourne,' 19 November 2006.
27. B. Haigh, 'Who benefits from the turmoil in East Timor', *Canberra Times*, 8 July 2006, p. B7.
28. P. Hartcher, 'Why Xanana Gusmao wept in Alexander Downer's arms', *Age*, 5 June 2006, p. 1.
29. ibid. After witnessing the latest wave of destruction in Dili last year Hartcher wrote: 'Now the blackened ruins of 2006 dot Dili, side by side with the unreconstructed ruins of the 1999 mayhem, each wave of destruction posing the same question with fresh urgency: can the 900 000 long-abused people of East Timor, only half of them able to read and three-quarters of them living with earth floors, build a future for themselves?'

30. Alexander Downer, letter to Dr Andrew Southcott, Parliament House, Canberra, 22 February 2007.
31. K. Wilkie and B. Campbell, 'Hearings on the Treaty between the Government of Australia and the Democratic Republic of Timor Leste on Certain Maritime Arrangements in the Timor Sea', Joint Standing Committee on Treaties, Parliament House Canberra, 26 February 2007, pp. 36–7.
32. ABC online, 'Australians arrive home from "volatile" E. Timor,' 6 March 2007, http://www.abc.net.au/news/newsitems/200703/s1864636.htm [10 March 2007].
33. P. Andren, 'Consideration of Legislation', *Debates*, House of Representatives, 28 February 2007, pp. 108–9.
34. R. Woolcott, 'Speech by Richard Woolcott at the launch of the Timor Sea's Oil and Gas: What's Fair?', http://www.uniya.org/talks/woolcott_3sep04.html [3 September 2004].
35. The FRETILIN-dominated parliament confirmed that despite the enormous suffering and hardship being experienced by the wider population, *Animal Farm* was alive and well in East Timor. In late 2006 it passed legislation granting every former minister a lifetime pension equal to his official salary, a government house, car, private staff, diplomatic passports, free international travel and other benefits. President Gusmão has since vetoed the bill, sending it back to parliament. Under the constitution, he will have to approve the bill if it is passed a second time by two-thirds of the parliament, where FRETILIN holds 55 of the 88 seats. The bill was followed by separate legislation covering pensions for former MPs. See T. Hyland, 'Poor nation, rich MPs: Timor's perks', *Sunday Age*, 4 February 2007, p. 11.
36. Research by former World Bank economists Paul Collier and Anke Hoeffler has established this as one of the more robust statistics in development economics. Jean-Paul Azam, Paul Collier & Anke Hoeffler, 'International Policies on Civil Conflict: An Economic Perspective' (14 December 2001), http://users.ox.ac.uk/~ball0144/azam_coll_hoe.pdf [14 March 2007].

INDEX

2/2 Independent Company 10, 212, 215, 216
2/4 Independent Company 212–13, 215
2/40th Battalion 212

7.30 Report 140, 150

ABARE (Australian Bureau of Agricultural and Resource Economics) 95
ABC Radio 201, 257
Ackland, Richard 130
advertising campaign 119, 151, 162, 163, 167, 169–74, 203, 211, 215–17, 223
Age, The 131, 161, 166, 222
Aitken, Ray 216
Alatas, Ali 38, 117, 165, 234
Albrechtsen, Janet 133
Alkatiri, Ahmed 91, 246
Alkatiri, Bader 219, 246, 247
Alkatiri, Marí Bin Amude xiii–xvi, 51, 53, 54, 56–9, 63–6, 68–78, 79, 81–2, 86–91, 94, 95–6, 100, 109, 120, 123, 127, 128, 130, 136, 138, 139, 147, 148, 154–6, 158–9, 168, 177, 180, 182–3, 185–6, 187–8, 194–5, 200, 202–3, 207–9, 219, 222, 224, 229, 231, 232–5, 237, 238, 241, 243–5, 248–56, 259–64

Alola Foundation 162
Andren, Peter 266
Annan, Kofi xiii, 47, 146, 257
Antunes, Nuno 101–2, 105, 122, 124, 154, 179, 182, 208, 237
ANZ Bank 90–1, 174
ANZAC Day xv, 210, 211, 215–17
Arafura Sea 8
Arrows Against the Wind 162
ASDT (*Associação Social Democráta de Timor*) xi, 69
Asian Development Bank 78
Asia-Pacific Economic Co-operation (APEC) 48, 137
Audley-Charles, Michael 9
AusAID 86, 138, 224–6, 228–9
Australia East Timor Association 172
Australia–Indonesia Institute (AII) 165
Australia–Indonesia Joint Authority 42, 90, 91
Australian 40, 98, 106, 108, 129, 132, 135–6, 219, 254
Australian Broadcasting Corporation (ABC) 121, 123, 128, 129, 140, 150, 165–6, 252, 255
Australian Bureau of Agricultural and Resource Economics (ABARE) 95
Australian Democrats 87, 169
Australian Greens 87, 119, 134, 169

Australian Labor Party 24, 34, 35, 41, 46–7, 87–8, 93–4, 134–6, 152, 158, 167, 168–9, 258
Australian Secret Intelligence Service (ASIS) 24, 35, 44, 158, 165

Babo, Julmira 160, 166
Balibo xi, 23–4, 177, 266
Ball, Desmond 23, 24
Banda Arc 9
Barker, Caroline 161
Barrett, Lyndal 266
Bayu-Undan field 42, 44, 45, 55, 60, 65, 77, 80, 84, 87, 89–90, 106, 115, 183, 188–9, 206, 235–6, 165
BBC 118, 128
BCL fields 13, 56, 58, 63, 99, 103–5, 109, 111, 112, 126, 154, 156, 169, 178, 185, 189, 208, 210, 237
Belo, Carlos Ximenes xii, 144
Belo, José 117
BGP (Bureau of Geophysical Prospecting) 259
BGP-GGS consortium 259–60
BHP Billiton 111
BHP Ltd 42, 45, 111
BHP Petroleum Ltd 44, 262
Bialek, Dean 113, 125–6, 191
Blue, Linden 92
Blue, Neil 92
BP Migas 90
Brain, Dr Peter 183
Brandão, Dr Carlos 213
Brekke, Harald 198
Brennan, Frank 32, 33, 105
Brereton, Laurie 47, 134, 135, 152
Brown, Bob 87–8, 119, 128, 171, 206–7, 266

Brownlie, Ian 64–5, 101–2, 104, 105, 237
Buffalo field xiv–xv, 13, 81
Bugalski, Natalie 166–7, 168
Burmah Oil xi, 6
Burridge, John 216

Callinan, Bernard 212, 213
Calvert, Ashton 47, 94, 257
Campbell, Bill 124, 177, 178, 179, 265
Carnation Revolution xi, 16, 69
Carr, Kim 168
Catholic Church 244–5
Caval Bravo 219
Centre for Strategic and International Studies (CSIS) 23
Chester, Doug 136–9, 145, 148, 151, 154–5, 174, 176, 177–8, 181, 182, 188–96, 200–2, 205–7, 217, 218, 221, 222–3, 226, 230, 231
Chevron 92
Chomsky, Noam 75, 120
Clark, Keryn 138
Clark, Manning 83
Clark, Roger 41
Clarke, Tom 207
Clinton, Bill 48, 52, 163, 164
CMATS *see Treaty on Certain Maritime Arrangements in the Timor Sea 2006* (CMATS)
Cockcroft, John 44
Cockcroft, Peter 44–5, 262–3
Cold Blood: The Massacre of East Timor 162
Commission on the Limits of the Continental Shelf (CLCS) 197–8, 199, 233
Conoco Inc 55

Index

ConocoPhillips (CoP) 55, 90, 92, 93
Conselho Nacional Resisténcia Timorese (CNRT) 51, 55, 57, 70, 115, 260
Conselho Nacional Resistência Maubere (CNRM) 43, 70, 115, 143
continental shelf 4–7, 9, 36–7, 38, 64, 65, 125, 196–7, 205, 206
Corallina field xv, 13, 81, 111, 227
Cordeaux, Jeremy 187, 189–90
Costello, Peter 57, 163, 260
Costello, Reverend Tim 163
Cottew, Zoe 82
Coyne, Ralph 213
Crawford, James 42
Cunningham, Gary 23

da Conceicão, Vincente 252, 255
da Silva, Ricardo 243, 245–6
da Silva da Freitas, Maria 60
Dan, Malcolm 22–3, 24
Daniel, Philip 85, 87, 100, 176, 178, 182, 183, 186, 189
Dateline 118, 121, 128
Davis, Mark 118
de Lemos, Manuel 135, 172, 234
de Jesus Soares, Aderito 145
de Vasconselos, Abraão 239
Day, Millissa 54
Deakin, Bishop Hilton 206
Death in Balibo, Lies in Canberra – Blood on Whose Hands? 23
Declaration on Principles of International Law Concerning Friendly Relations and Co-operation among States (1970) 40–1

Deegan, Brian 142, 223
Denton, Andrew 163
Department of Foreign Affairs (DFA) 16, 18, 19, 23, 24, 27, 29, 31, 37–8, 143
Department of Foreign Affairs and Trade (DFAT) 31, 32, 44, 47, 51, 66, 83, 84, 85, 94, 98, 105, 107, 113, 116, 124, 125, 129, 133, 134, 136–7, 148, 165, 177, 179, 191, 195, 198, 203, 206–7, 210, 217–18, 228, 234, 235, 251, 257, 265
Development Studies Network (DSN) 228
Djalal, Dr Hasjim 11
do Amaral de Carvalho, Demetrio 225
Dom Henrique 68
Dowd, John 102
Downer, Alexander xv, 17–18, 19, 46, 49, 50, 54, 57, 58–60, 62, 63, 64, 79, 81–4, 85, 86–7, 91, 105, 106, 119, 128, 129, 130–3, 134, 135, 136, 137, 138, 139, 140, 141–3, 148–52, 163, 164, 165, 169, 170–1, 174, 181, 183, 187, 188, 189–90, 191, 195, 196, 200, 202–3, 206, 210, 217, 218, 221, 222, 223–4, 232–3, 234, 257, 261, 264–5, 267
Downer, Sir John 82
Dusevic, Tom 177

East China Sea 92
East Timor Action Network (ETAN) 120, 203
East Timor Development Agency (ETDA) 55
Elang Kakatua field 42, 44, 45, 49

Elf Aquitaine 38
Ellis, Peter 224–5, 226
Ensor, James 138, 162, 198–9
equidistance lines xvii, 11, 12, 13, 36, 37, 105, 125
Equipa Segurança Secreto Fretilin (ESSF) Groupo Rai Los 254
Erdut Agreement 52
Evans, Gareth 34, 40, 41–2, 43, 103, 117, 165, 234
Exchange of Notes xvi, 54–5, 66, 235, 264
Exclusive Economic Zone (EEZ) 36, 105, 197
Extractive Industries Transparency Initiative 238

FALINTIL (*Forças Armadas de Liberação Nacional de Timor-Leste*) 29, 30–1, 39, 70, 157, 191, 232, 244
FALINTIL-*Força Defensa Timor-Leste* (F-FDTL) 244, 247, 249, 250, 251, 252, 254, 255, 258
Far Eastern Economic Review 128
Faulkner, John 168
Female Sea *(Tasi Feto)* 1
Fernandes, Alarico 157
Ferreira de Carvalho, Manuel 211
Fitzgibbon, Joel 134, 169
Flood, Phillip 165
Foley, Paul 84–6, 113, 138–9
Ford, President Gerald xi, 27
Foreign Affairs Council 133
Forum Tau Matan (FTM) 224–6
Four Corners 11, 121, 128, 129, 130, 252, 254–5
Frank, Barney 120, 121, 203
Fraser, Malcolm 25, 26, 35, 83
Frei, Henry 212

Freitas, Bendito 255
FRETILIN (*Frente Revolucionária do Timor-Leste Independente*) xi, xiii, 21, 55, 69, 70, 71, 72, 73, 75, 114–15, 143, 145, 147, 157, 158, 231, 245, 249, 252, 253, 254, 264
Fundacão Oriente 127
Furlonger, Robert 19

Galbraith, John Kenneth 52
Galbraith, Peter 36, 52–3, 55, 56, 57, 58, 59, 63, 65, 100, 101–2, 103, 107, 114, 122, 123, 124–5, 128, 140–1, 153–4, 156, 176–7, 178, 179, 180, 181–2, 183, 186, 188, 191, 193, 200, 202, 207–9, 223, 231
Galvão-Teles, Miguel 51, 65, 253
Garrett, Peter 158
General Atomics 92
GGS 259
Gray, Alsitair 155–6
Gray, Gary 93–4, 111, 168, 261
Greater Sunrise field xi, xiv, xv, xvi, xviii, 13, 56, 58, 60, 64, 79–80, 87, 97, 112, 126, 152, 155–6, 178, 180, 183, 186, 188, 192, 206, 210, 227, 233, 235, 236, 237–8, 243, 264
Greenhaigh, George 215–16
Guardian 115–16, 192
Gusmão, José Alexandre 44, 59–60
Gusmão, Kay Rala Xanana xiii, xv, 30, 44–6, 57, 59–60, 70, 71, 72, 74, 87, 110, 114–17, 118, 119, 128, 130, 138, 139, 143, 144, 157, 219, 243–4, 247, 248, 251–2, 254, 255, 260, 261, 262, 267

Index

Gusmão, Kirsty Sword 114, 116–17, 162–3
Guterres, Francisco 'Lu Olo' 87
Guterres, José Luis 249

Habibie, President B.J. xii, 46, 47
Haburas Foundation 225
Haigh, Bruce 31, 129, 256, 261
Hartcher, Peter 139
Hawke, Bob 34, 35, 158
Hayden, Bill 34, 37, 38
Henriss-Anderssen, Chip 207
HMAS *Voyager* 212
Holbrooke, Richard 146
Holmes, Jonathan 130
Howard, Janette 116
Howard, John xii, xiii, xv, 32, 46–8, 53, 57, 66, 81, 83, 86–8, 100, 106, 107, 109, 120, 124, 129, 131, 133, 134, 146, 147, 164, 166, 169, 170, 173, 179, 202, 203, 215–16, 219, 221, 222, 228, 233–4, 250, 256, 261, 263–4, 267
Human Development Index (HDI) 2, 86, 245
Human Development Report 2006 3
human rights 20, 40, 42, 77, 86, 121, 145, 224
Hutchison, Charles 9
Huybens, Elisabeth 66

Indonesia–Australia Timor Gap Joint Authority 90
Indonesian Communist Party 10, 27
InterFET xiii, 48, 58, 70, 104, 107, 164, 191, 207, 210, 289
International Court of Justice (ICJ) 11, 36, 38, 42, 61, 104, 105, 170, 171, 174, 227, 237

International Crisis Group 41
International Tribunal for the Law of the Sea (ITLOS) 61, 237
International Unitisation Agreement 2003 (IUA) xiv, xvi, 80, 81, 86, 88, 97, 112, 193, 227, 264
invasion x, xi, xxviii–xxix, 13, 14, 15, 17, 22–3, 24, 25–6, 27, 28–9, 31, 69–70, 99, 124, 145, 147, 157, 231
Islam, Dr Nurul 160

Jaco 12
Jahal Kuda Tasi field 224
Japan x, 28, 61, 84, 116, 211–14, 263
Jeffords, James 121, 203
Jockel, Gordon 26
joint development area 38, 64, 190
joint development zone (JDZ) 37
Joint Intelligence Organisation 26
Joint Petroleum Development Area (JPDA) xiv, xv, xviii, 58–9, 64, 65, 81, 103, 108, 109, 110, 112, 121, 125, 149, 154, 156, 179, 180, 181, 183, 206, 218, 224, 229, 230, 233, 236, 238, 265
Joint Standing Committee on Treaties (JSCOT) 84, 125, 184, 264–5

Keating, Paul 18, 40, 83, 93, 137, 158
Kelly, Paul 133
Kelp Prospect (also known as Kelp High) 37–8, 49, 155, 239
Kenneally, Paddy 215, 216
Kennedy, Edward 203
Kernaghan, James 93, 94, 95

Kerry, John 153
Khamsi, Kathryn 186
Kissinger, Henry xi, 27
Kitson, Paul 93, 94, 95, 97
KKN 246, 264
Koch, David 175

Lakor 13
Laminaria field xv, 13, 62, 81, 111, 113, 227
Langridge, Bernie 216
Lantos, Tom 121, 203
Latham, Mark 134–6
Law of the Sea 5–6, 7, 10, 19, 36, 61, 134
L'Estrange, Michael 116, 192
Leti 13, 104, 105, 126
Libya 38, 104, 105–6, 139
liquefied natural gas (LNG) 95, 183, 184, 189, 195, 233, 237, 238, 262–3
Lisbon 6, 16, 69, 118
Lobato, Isobel xi, 231
Lobato, Nicolau 68, 69, 211, 232
Lobato, Rogerio 69, 71, 73, 249, 250, 252–3, 254, 255, 256
Lobato-Gonçalves, José 231–2
Lowe, Vaughan 63, 64–5, 90, 104, 105
Lowry, Bob 73
Lucon A/S 185
Lund, Dr Sverre 185

McCredie, John 17
McDonald, Hamish 23, 24, 63
MacDonald-Smith, Angela 233
Macfarlane, Ian 113, 196
McMahon, William 7
Maher, Michael 166
Mahkota 127

Male Sea (*Tasi Mane*) 1
Malta 38, 105
Mapes, Timothy 128
Marcal, Arlindo 140
maritime boundaries xiv, xvi, xxvi, 7, 8, 11, 34, 36, 38, 61–5, 79–81, 89, 90, 92, 98–100, 101–4, 108–9, 118, 119, 120, 126, 136, 149, 151, 154–6, 169, 176, 179–80, 185, 194, 197–9, 201, 209–10, 222, 224, 226–7, 229–30, 232, 237
maritime law 11, 12, 63, 100, 102, 125, 154, 237
Maritime Zones Act (MZA) xiv, 66
Martins, Paulino 252
Matignon Accords 47
Meatij Miarang 13
Mellish, Morgan 279
Melrose, Alec 211
Melrose, Ian 119, 160, 161–2, 164, 169–70, 171–5, 192, 203, 207, 210–11, 215, 217, 223
Melrose, Margaret 162, 169–70
Mendelawitz, Dr Barry 174
Mendonça, Manuel 191
Minchin, Nick 57
Mitchell, Harold 163
Moa 13
Mobil 49, 95
Mochtar Kusumaatmadja 13, 30, 38
Moir, Alan 131
Moraitis, Chris 123, 124, 177, 178, 179, 180, 191
Morrow, Jonathan 53, 54, 57–8, 85, 101, 102, 123, 126
Mozambique 51, 70, 72, 78, 147, 158, 249

Index

Murtopo, Lieutenant General Ali 23
Mutton, Richelle 161, 166, 169

'National Living Treasure' 32, 207
National Trust of Australia 32
New York Review of Books 122, 153
New York Times 153
Newsnight 128
Nicholson, Dan 160, 166–8, 169
Nicholson, Peter 132
Nixon, Richard 136
Nobel Peace Prize xii, 144, 147
North Aegean Sea 92
North Rankin field 93
North Sea Continental Shelf cases 11
Norway 54, 86, 100, 184, 205, 222, 240

Oakes, Laurie 257
Oceanic Exploration 6, 8, 64, 79, 89–90, 91–2
Offshore Minerals Act 1994 232
Oliver, Dale 91, 92
Olympia 50, 51, 235
One Nation Party 169
Operation Flamboyant xi, 23
Operation Spitfire 48, 164
Operation Warden 164–5
Oquist, Ben 171
Osaka Gas 93
Oxfam Australia 69, 125, 138, 162, 172, 198

Palácio das Cinzas (Palace of Ashes) xxv, 189, 194, 245, 248, 261
Palácio do Governador (Governor's Palace) 68
Palácio do Governo (Palace of Government) 54, 67, 68, 70–1, 89, 127, 136
Paladin Resources plc 111
Parer, Damien 214
Parry, Ray 216
Paxman, Jeremy 128
Peacock, Andrew xii, 19, 24, 29–30, 31
Pead, Judith 147
Pearson, Christopher 133
Pelosi, Nancy 121, 203
'people's delegation' 206–7
Pequinho, João 226
Pertamina 44, 90
Pessoa, Ana 88
Peters, Brian 23
Petroleum Fund 78, 154, 205, 240, 241
Petroleum Law 2005 238, 260
Petroleum (Submerged Lands) Act 1967 6, 232
Petrotimor Companhia de Petroleos 8, 13, 79, 89–90
Petty, Bruce 131
Phillips Petroleum 45, 55, 57
pipelines 56, 183–6, 189, 193, 195, 218, 222, 234, 235, 237, 238, 262
'ploughshare women' 144
Polícia Nasional de Timor-Leste (PNTL) 247, 249, 250, 254
Portugal x–xi, xiii, 4, 7, 8, 12, 13–14, 15, 16, 21, 22, 26, 28, 42–3, 46, 47, 69, 89, 90, 100, 101, 102, 118, 137–8, 211, 249, 251
Potts, Michael 50, 51, 61, 62
Prentice, Jonathan 62–3
Prescott, Victor 11

Proctor, Murray 225–8
Puthucheary, Dominic 52, 177

Qatar 62
Quinn Emanuel 91, 92

Raby, Dr Geoff 84
Racketeer-Influenced and Corrupt Organization Act (RICO) 89, 91, 92
Rai Los group 252, 254–5
Ramos-Horta, Francisco 146
Ramos-Horta, José xii, xv, 43, 51, 55, 57, 58–9, 68, 69–70, 82, 87, 91, 94, 114, 129, 140, 141, 143–8, 150, 152, 155, 159, 171, 173, 200–1, 202, 212, 221, 222–4, 229, 231, 232, 234, 237, 243, 249, 250, 251–2, 258, 261, 262–3
Ramsay, Morag 284
Rees, Joseph 259
Refugee Review Tribunal 31
Reinado, Alfredo 249, 250, 251, 254, 265
Rennie, Malcolm 23–4
Renouf, Alan 20, 21
Resolution on Definition of Aggression (1974) 40–1
Rinnan, Arne 86
Risa, Einar 85–6, 96, 97, 100, 180–1, 184, 208
Rodriguez, Roque 244
Roth, Stanley 47, 258
Royal Dutch Shell 93
Ruak, Taur Matan 244, 245, 247, 248
Rudd, Kevin 134, 152, 168, 258

Saffin, Janelle 152, 202

Salsinha, Gastão 244
Santa Cruz massacre xii, 42, 100, 120, 162, 165
Santos, Nelson 140, 141, 148, 231
Schultz, Dennis 166
Schumann, John 142
Scott, David 69
seabed boundary treaty x, 8, 16–18, 29, 124, 197
Second World War xv, 10, 28, 40, 44, 164, 211–14, 217
Seguin, Michel 238
Senate Economics Committee 167–8
Serious Crimes Unit 160–1
Services Reconnaissance Department 214
Shackleton, Greg 24
Shanahan, Dennis 131, 133, 138
Shute, Nevil 10
Sing, Alan 92
Skylight Offensive 31
Smith, Chris 121, 203, 259
Soeharto, President xi, xii, 10, 16, 18, 19, 20, 23, 27, 31, 32, 43, 47, 165, 246
Soros, George 243
Special Operation Service (OPSUS) 23
Spence, Keith 96
Stahl, Max xii, 42
Statoil 86
Stewart, Paul 177
Stewart, Tony 24, 177
Stone, Shane 263
Sunrise agreement 60, 65, 81, 82, 84–5, 87, 88, 89, 93, 94, 95–6, 99, 112, 116, 167–8, 190, 201, 230, 236

Index

Sunrise field xi, xvii, 13, 62, 63, 64–5, 80, 81–2, 84–5, 87, 88, 91, 93–6, 99, 102–3, 104–5, 109, 112, 116–17, 135, 154, 169, 183, 185–6, 188, 194, 201–2, 206, 208, 209–10, 217–18, 222, 227, 230, 235, 237, 262–3, 265
Swinstead, Julian 263
Sydney Morning Herald 128, 130, 131, 139, 162, 166, 189, 198

Tampa 86, 124
Tanjong We Toh 13, 104
Taplin, Bruce 138–9
Tasi Feto (Female Sea) 1
Tasi Mane (Male Sea) 1
Taylor, Allan 22–3, 24, 165
Taylor, Mavis 207
Teixeira, José Fernandes 63, 100, 122, 148–9, 151, 152, 156–9, 176, 178, 180, 182, 187–8, 189, 190, 193, 205, 207, 208, 210, 219, 220, 222–3, 231, 234, 238, 260, 261
television advertising campaign 119, 151, 162, 163, 167, 169–74, 203, 211, 215–17, 223
Tetum 72, 194
Thawley, Michael 53
Thomas, Pam 228–9
Thompson, Jeremy 150
Time 128, 177
Timor Gap Treaty xii, xvii, 19, 40, 41, 42, 43, 44, 46, 49, 50–1, 54–5, 56, 57, 58, 60, 63, 64, 90, 103, 235, 253
Timor Sea Arrangement 59

Timor Sea Designated Authority (TSDA) 86, 90, 92, 159, 231
Timor Sea Justice Campaign (TSJC) 166, 167, 169, 172, 174, 206–7
Timor Sea Office 54, 82, 84, 114, 115, 116, 117, 139, 149, 151, 152, 186, 192, 195, 206–7, 234
Timor Sea Treaty xiii, xiv, xviii, 59, 63, 79–80, 82, 84, 85, 87, 89, 90, 91, 99, 101, 102, 104, 109, 116, 124, 125, 155, 183, 186, 188, 197, 235
Timor Trough x, xii, 4, 6–9, 11, 16, 30, 34, 35, 37, 39, 64, 65, 126, 151–2, 155, 176, 177, 184, 196, 201
Timorese Social Democratic Association xi, 69
Timor-Leste xiv, 33, 55, 80, 81, 109, 111–13, 155, 168–9, 178, 185, 194, 198, 202, 204, 222, 225, 226–7, 233, 266–7
Tjan, Harry 23
Toohey, Brian 34
Total 159, 238, 263
Towards the Conceptualisation of Maritime Delimitation 237
Treaty on Certain Maritime Arrangements in the Timor Sea 2006 (CMATS) xvi, 232, 264, 265
Triggs, Gillian 113, 121
trijunction points 12
Troubadour field xi, 13
Truman, President 5
Truth and Friendship Commission 145
Twomey, Margaret 192, 195–6, 226, 234, 239

UDT party (*União Democrática de Timor*) xi, 21
UN Commission of Inquiry 252, 253
UN Convention on the Law of the Sea (UNCLOS) 61, 63, 66, 103, 126, 196, 208
UN Human Rights Unit 77
UN Security Council 256–7, 258, 165
UN Transitional Administration East Timor (UNTAET) xiii, 50, 51, 52, 53, 55–6, 59, 70, 89–90
United Nations Development Programme 148
United States Department of Energy 42
Uniting Church 111, 172
USAID 54

Vieira de Mello, Sergio 53, 59, 62, 90, 99
Voelte, Don 95–6

Wall Street Journal, The 128–9, 192
Wemans, Carlos Empis 1, 8
Westpac Bank 90–1
Wheatley, Mervin 216

Whitlam, Gough 13, 19–20, 24, 32
Wilcock, Greg 203–5
Wilkie, Kim 84, 265
Willesee, Don 20
Willheim, Ernst 36, 37, 39
Willox, Innes 150
Wilson, Nigel 113
Wong, Kee Jin 77
Wood, Dr Ian 111
Woodside Petroleum xi, 6, 49, 93–7, 105, 111, 113, 135, 150, 156, 168, 183, 184–5, 188, 194, 201, 207, 227–8, 261–2, 264
Woolcott, Peter 19, 20–2, 23, 24, 25–6, 27, 32
Woolcott, Richard 15, 18–19, 32–3, 82, 165, 267
World Bank 3, 66, 78, 245

Xavier do Amaral, Francisco 68, 69, 115

Ytreland, Geir 9, 184
Yudhoyono, Susilo Bambang 253

Zephyr-1 2, 9, 238, 260
Zone of Cooperation xii, xiv, 38, 39, 64